W9-AJO-243

PRO/CON VOLUME 14

INTERNATIONAL DEVELOPMENT

Published 2004 by Grolier,
an imprint of Scholastic Library Publishing
Old Sherman Turnpike
Danbury, Connecticut 06816

Library of Congress Cataloging-in-Publication Data
Pro/con
  p. cm
  Includes bibliographical references and index.
  Contents: v. 13. U.S. History – v. 14. International Development – v. 15. Human
Rights – v.16. Education – v. 17. New Science – v. 18. Commerce and Trade.
  ISBN 0-7172-5927-7 (set : alk. paper) – ISBN 0-7172-5930-7 (vol. 13 : alk. paper) –
ISBN 0-7172-5929-3 (vol. 14 : alk. paper) – ISBN 0-7172-5931-5 (vol. 15 : alk. paper)
– ISBN 0-7172-5928-5 (vol. 16 : alk. paper) – ISBN 0-7172-5932-3 (vol. 17 : alk.
paper) – ISBN 0-7172-5933-1 (vol. 18 : alk. paper)
  1. Social problems. I. Scholastic Publishing Ltd Grolier (Firm)

HN17.5 P756 2002
361.1–dc21

                                                            2001053234

Printed and bound in Singapore

SET ISBN 0-7172-5927-7
VOLUME ISBN 0-7172-5929-3

For The Brown Reference Group plc
Project Editor: Aruna Vasudevan
Editors: Rachel Bean, Mark Fletcher, Chris Marshall, Lesley
Henderson, Jonathan Dore
Consultant Editor: Timothy M. Shaw, Professor of Commonwealth
Governance and Development, and Director, Institute of Commonwealth
Studies, School of Advanced Study, University of London
Designer: Sarah Williams
Picture Researchers: Clare Newman, Susy Forbes
Set Index: Kay Ollerenshaw

Managing Editor: Tim Cooke
Art Director: Dave Goodman
Production Director: Alastair Gourlay

GENERAL PREFACE

Decisions

Life is full of choices and decisions. Some are more important than others. Some affect only your daily life—the route you take to school, for example, or what you prefer to eat for supper—while others are more abstract and concern questions of right and wrong rather than practicality. That does not mean that your choice of presidential candidate or your views on abortion are necessarily more important than your answers to purely personal questions. But it is likely that those wider questions are more complex and subtle and that you therefore will need to know more information about the subject before you can try to answer them. They are also likely to be questions where you might have to justify your views to other people. In order to do that you need to be able to make informed decisions, be able to analyze every fact at your disposal, and evaluate them in an unbiased manner.

What is *Pro/Con*?

Pro/Con is a collection of debates that presents conflicting views on some of the more complex and general issues facing Americans today. By bringing together extracts from a wide range of sources—mainstream newspapers and magazines, books, famous speeches, legal judgments, religious tracts, government surveys—the set reflects current informed attitudes toward dilemmas that range from the best way to feed the world's growing population to gay rights, from the connection between political freedom and capitalism to the fate of Napster.

The people whose arguments make up the set are for the most part acknowledged experts in their fields, making the vast difference in their points of view even more remarkable. The arguments are presented in the form of debates for and against various propositions, such as "Should Americans Celebrate Columbus Day?" or "Are human rights women's rights?" This question format reflects the way in which ideas often occur in daily life: in the classroom, on TV shows, in business meetings, or even in state or federal politics.

The contents

The subjects of the six volumes of *Pro/Con 3*—*U.S. History, International Development, Human Rights, Education, New Science,* and *Commerce and Trade*—are issues on which it is preferable that people's opinions are based on information rather than personal bias.

Special boxes throughout *Pro/Con* comment on the debates as you are reading them, pointing out facts, explaining terms, or analyzing arguments to help you think about what is being said.

Introductions and summaries also provide background information that might help you reach your own conclusions. There are also tips about how to structure an argument that you can apply on an everyday basis to any debate or conversation, learning how to present your point of view as effectively and persuasively as possible.

VOLUME PREFACE
International Development

Since people first began to gather in communities, some of those communities have been stronger or weaker, richer or poorer. Resources, population, climate, fertile land, technological innovation, strong leadership: Numerous factors have traditionally given certain societies advantages over others. With the coming of the Industrial Revolution from the end of the 18th century, such inequity was reflected on a global scale. By the late 19th century the world was split into industrialized and nonindustrialized nations.

Commentators today characterize this division in various ways—the western world versus the rest of the world, the First World versus the Third World, the developed world versus the developing or nondeveloped world—but at its heart the division is economic. Those nations that underwent industrialization and adopted a market economy from the end of the 18th century onward included most of western and northern Europe and North America. Later, significant industrialization also brought economic growth to Japan and many of the countries of the Pacific Rim, particularly in Southeast Asia.

Much of the world, particularly in parts of Africa and Asia, remains largely excluded from the economic growth brought by industrialization and involvement in international trade. A central debate in international affairs concerns the relationship between richer and poorer nations. There is a consensus among richer nations that they have a moral obligation to help less fortunate nations on humanitarian grounds. Many people also argue that there is a practical impulse to contribute aid: Global economic growth depends on the growth of undeveloped economies, not just on those that are already established. Numerous international organizations, from the United Nations to charitable institutions, now play an active part in international aid. The United States, as the world's richest nation, also has an important role to play.

However, any development brings with it a range of dilemmas. The relationship between rich and poor countries has often been characterized by exploitation. This reached its height with colonialism, when richer states took over poorer nations, or by the dominance of western values and practices over those of other parts of the world. Many observers are dubious that the developed world can help poor nations without re-creating such exploitation. There are also questions about priorities: Education, for example, is seen by developed countries as key to economic growth. In poor countries, however, health and the reduction of poverty often seem more immediate problems.

Pro/Con
To form a balanced judgment about the issues facing humanity requires accurate information about the debates that are taking place. *International Development* features for and against arguments about 16 key topics that will help you reach informed conclusions about relations between developed countries and poor countries.

HOW TO USE THIS BOOK

Each volume of *Pro/Con* is divided into sections, each of which has an introduction that examines its theme. Within each section are a series of debates that present arguments for and against a proposition, such as whether or not the death penalty should be abolished. An introduction to each debate puts it into its wider context, and a summary and key map (see below) highlight the main points of the debate clearly and concisely. Each debate has marginal boxes that focus on particular points, give tips on how to present an argument, or help question the writer's case. The summary page to the debates contains supplementary material to help you do further research.

Boxes and other materials provide additional background information. There are also special spreads on how to improve your debating and writing skills. At the end of each book is a glossary and an index. The glossary provides explanations of key words in the volume. The index covers all 18 books, so it will help you trace topics in this set and the previous ones.

marginal boxes
Marginal boxes highlight key points of the argument, give extra information, or help you question the author's meaning.

summary boxes
Summary boxes are useful reminders of both sides of the argument.

further information
Further Reading lists for each debate direct you to related books, articles, and websites so you can do your own research.

other articles in the *Pro/Con* series
This box lists related debates throughout the *Pro/Con* series.

background information
Frequent text boxes provide background information on important concepts and key individuals or events.

key map
Key maps provide a graphic representation of the central points of the debate.

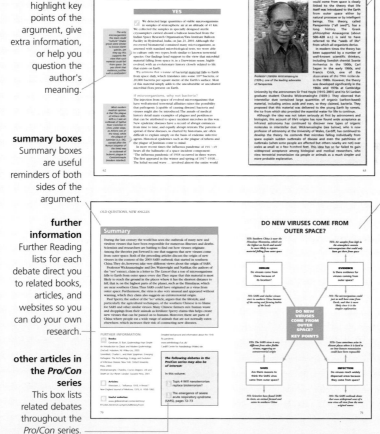

CONTENTS

PART 1
ISSUES IN INTERNATIONAL DEVELOPMENT

INTRODUCTION

In 1998 the World Bank reported that, "Across the world, 1.3 billion people live on less than one dollar a day; 3 billion live on under two dollars a day; 1.3 billion have no access to clean water; 3 billion have no access to sanitation; [and] 2 billion have no access to electricity."

Many people, however, believe that economic security, water availability, and decent sanitation, among other things, are basic rights; they claim that all humankind should have the right to live economically, politically, and socially viable lives in environmentally safe conditions. They assert that the only way to achieve these standards for the more than 6 billion people who inhabit the planet is through international development.

What is development?

"Development" is broadly a positive process of transforming a society to achieve three main objectives: to increase the availability and distribution of essentials such as food, clean water, shelter, and health care; to improve living standards by increasing employment opportunities, access to education, strengthening cultural values, and building individual and national pride; and finally, to expand the range of choices to individuals and nations.

There are several ways by which to judge development. The World Bank, for example, divides the 133 countries with populations of greater than one million into four groups according to income per person: Low (under $785), middle ($786–$3,125), upper middle ($3,126–$9,655), and high-income economies ($9,656 and over). There are 24 industrialized countries in the last group located mainly in Europe and North America, plus the oil-rich but developing countries of Kuwait and the United Arab Emirates. But are purely economic indicators, such as a rise in income per person, an adequate measurement of development?

There are other issues, critics argue, that are of equal or greater importance, such as greater equity in income distribution, access to clean water, health care and education, participation in the political process, gender equality, and environmental issues. They claim that the Human Development Index, for example, developed by the United Nations Development Program (UNDP) is a much better system since it takes into account noneconomic factors, such as life expectancy at birth and educational attainment.

Causes

While defining and measuring development is important, some people argue that they are secondary to the actual problems that prevent a nation from developing. Critics, for example, argue that colonialism is to blame and that rich nations are obligated to help their former colonies achieve acceptable standards of development. This issue is explored in Topic 1.

Other economists and politicians, among others, believe that this

whose nations have high corruption ratings and blacklist any international companies caught paying bribes. Others argue that these measures just hit the poor hardest and are not an effective way of achieving a working civil society.

The questions of whether corruption hinders economic growth or whether good governance is key

---

"Being poor means making hard choices, such as whether to work more or to eat less."
—STEVEN E. LANDSBURG WALL, UNIVERSITY OF ROCHESTER, NEW YORK

---

explanation is too simplistic and that poor nations are prevented from developing because of issues such as political instability, corruption, or bad governance. But if this is the case, what can be done to solve these problems?

The Transparency International Corruption Perceptions Index (CPI) 2003 charted levels of corruption in 133 countries. It found that 7 out of 10 countries scored less than 5 out of a clean score of 10, and 5 out of 10 developing countries scored less than 3 out of 10. Peter Eigan, the chairman of the CPI, has argued that countries with the highest rate of corruption need the support rather than the condemnation of rich nations. He has stated that the governments of developing nations need to "implement results-oriented programs to fight corruption," but that they also require "help tailored to the needs of their national anticorruption strategies."

Some commentators suggest that rich nations should threaten to withhold financial support from governments

to poverty reduction are examined in Topics 2 and 3.

For some people, however, many of the problems associated with bad governance, such as terrorism and national security issues, stem from the influence of religion. Others counter that religion has historically helped countries develop. The Catholic church, for example, funded many schools around the world, and provided skills training in poor nations. The question of whether religion has helped or hindered development is examined in Topic 4.

Sustainable development
Other commentators claim that one of the most important issues in modern international development is ensuring that it is sustainable. Some argue that the cost of industries like tourism on local economies have outweighed any benefits. They assert that international regulation and codes of conduct are essential. Topic 5 considers the issue of tourism and sustainable development.

Topic 1
DO RICH COUNTRIES HAVE A DUTY TO GIVE FINANCIAL HELP TO FORMER COLONIES?

YES
"REMEMBRANCE OF THINGS PAST"
THE GUARDIAN, SEPTEMBER 7, 2001
LIZ MCGREGOR

NO
FROM "THE IRRATIONALITY OF 'COLONIAL GUILT': A HOMAGE TO LORD BAUER"
HTTP://WWW.CWRL.UTEXAS.EDU/~BENJAMIN/316KFALL/316KUNIT3/
STUDENTPROJECTSSPRING/BRENT/GUILT.HTML
MICHAEL NEWLAND

INTRODUCTION

The term "colonialism" refers to a country's imposition of its rule over a foreign territory and its people. Former colonies around the world have largely become independent and self-governing. The lasting effects of historical colonialism, however, and the question of who should take responsibility for former colonies continue to be hotly debated. Do the former colonial powers have a continuing financial responsibility for their ex-colonies?

Groups of people have colonized other areas since the dawn of civilization. When the European sea powers began to explore across the oceans from the late 15th century onward, they founded trading colonies in many of the places in which they landed. Often these colonies were small enclaves of merchants dependent on local rulers for their protection. In time, though, the power and influence of the home countries grew to the extent that these enclaves began to dominate the surrounding territory, and eventually they established political and military control over large areas and even whole continents.

The new colonies gave their home countries great economic advantage through new trade routes and the control of lucrative resources. Some theorists also claim that the colonized areas themselves made long-term gains through the development of infrastructure, industry and the introduction of new technology, all of which helped their economies develop. Colonial expansion reached its peak in the 19th century, when European nations controlled much of Asia and carved up Africa into spheres of influence. The United States replaced Spain as the colonial power in the Philippines as late as 1898.

During the 20th century, however, the expense of administering large overseas territories, coupled with the promotion of democracy and self-determination, made colonialism less attractive. In the three decades after World War II (1939–1945) the European colonial powers, weakened by the financial and economic demands of war, dismantled their empires.

"It is far easier for the proverbial camel to pass through the needle's eye ... than for an erstwhile colonial administration to give sound ... counsel of a political nature to its liberated territory."

—KWAME NKRUMAH

(1900–1972),

PRESIDENT OF GHANA

Although some commentators believe that the former colonies are better off than before colonial intervention, others see colonialism as a negative force that left behind damaged economies dependent on resource extraction. These critics argue that former colonizers have a duty to give financial help to their one-time colonies. They claim that decades after decolonization, the comparative wealth of the former colonizers and the ex-colonies has hardly changed. The Organization for Economic Cooperation and Development (OECD) showed this disparity when it reported that the average income per person in Britain in 2002 was equivalent to $69 a day, while in Kenya, a British colony from 1920 to 1963, it was less than $1 a day.

Observers also urge action on the debt crisis, which began with large-scale borrowing by the developing nations during the 1970s. Many commentators believe these debts should be canceled, allowing developing nations to progress, and some regard the debt crisis as another form of colonialism. Instead of being able to invest in basic infrastructures such as public transportation, education facilities, or water resources, critics argue that former colonies have to concentrate on repaying debts.

But should the colonial powers be responsible for helping rectify the situation in their former colonies? Are leaders in former colonies right to blame the old colonial powers for their countries' problems, or are they, as some critics argue, simply using the perceived shortcomings of the former colonizers as a way of deflecting criticism of their own misrule?

In the first of the following articles journalist Liz McGregor argues that the colonial powers exploited Africa and its people. She believes that the former colonizers have a duty to keep their promises of "debt relief, aid, foreign investment and fairer trade." Michael Newland, press officer of the right-wing Freedom Party, however, focuses on the arguments of economist Peter Bauer, who argued that former colonial powers should not be blamed for the problems of their ex-colonies.

REMEMBRANCE OF THINGS PAST
Liz McGregor

YES

The slave trade was at its height a very long time ago so why should we pay for the centuries-old sins of our forefathers? This has been a constant response to demands for reparations from the United Nations conference on racism in Durban that ends today. European governments—particularly the UK—express this reluctance in legalistic terms: an apology might have financial implications, they say.

But what did not happen such a long time ago was colonialism, the successor to slavery in Europe's long and inglorious relationship with Africa. It mostly happened in the last century, well within living memory. Colonialism allowed Europe direct access to Africa's mineral wealth and provided cheap labour to extract it. This may not have been slavery—although the labour was sometimes forced—but many Africans were turned into servants in their own countries.

Land inequality in Zimbabwe

It was, for example, the British who handed Rhodesia over to the white settlers by granting them self-government in 1923; the 1930 Land Apportionment Act drew the faultlines in contemporary Zimbabwe by allocating 50% of the best land to whites. Some 48m acres of the land went to 50,000 whites and 28m acres of inferior land to 1m black people. Today, the ratio is 70% of land for whites—who comprise less than 1% of the population. Robbed of their own land, Africans were forced to work for the whites; 65% of black people in Zimbabwe are still employed by whites.

Apartheid in South Africa

And in South Africa, it was under British colonial rule that the institutions of apartheid were created. Despite vigorous protest from the South African native convention (later to become the African National Congress), the British gave in to settler demands that the vote should go only to whites, except in the Cape (an omission which the Afrikaner National party later put right) when it conferred self-government on the colony in 1910. In 1913, a land act was passed which, together with another in 1936, gave 87% of the land to the whites (who comprised less than 10% of the

COMMENTARY: The impact of colonization

Opinion on the legacy of colonization ranges from those who think that colonization was largely a force for good to those who believe it had a purely negative effect on the territories and peoples concerned. Some commentators regard colonization as the great modernizer, having enabled progress through exposure to western government, education, industry, and ideas. Others view it as the racist and condescending imposition of unwanted values and systems, and as the central obstacle to progress in developing countries.

A major accusation laid at the door of the colonizers is that they plundered poorer countries for their resources. Minerals, timber, and agricultural products such as cotton were removed for the benefit of the colonizers' industries back home, often by the forced labor of the indigenous populations. Local people were robbed of their lands, and the reorganization—and violence—required to put the colonizers' plans into effect destroyed traditional ways of life and societies. Furthermore, the resources removed were then shipped back to the colonies in the form of manufactured goods that people had little choice but to buy because they were allowed to trade only with their colonizers. Critics of colonialism assert that the dependency on the home country that developed left colonies ill-equipped to survive economically when the powers finally left. Indeed, critics contend that a situation of "neocolonialism" exists whereby former colonies have "flag" or technical independence but are still tied economically to their former masters. From a political point of view decolonization resulted in the creation of numerous artificial states, since the new countries, based on the former colonies, were often made up of disparate populations that struggled to coexist peacefully.

A different view

If the situation is viewed from a different angle, it is possible to argue that colonization was not a one-way street, and that the process brought some benefits. For example, the home countries' quest for resources led to the creation of new industries in the colonies. Extraction of minerals such as gold, copper, and diamonds required the development of large-scale mining enterprises, and the intensive cultivation of agricultural products led to the creation of plantation-style farming and in some cases the introduction of new crops—rubber, a native of South America, to Malaya, for example. These industries remained in place when decolonization took place. In addition, colonization led to the creation of roads and especially railroads to enable the movement of resources and goods, and to the development of towns and ports, not to mention the establishment of schools and hospitals—all of which also remained when the colonizers departed.

population). In South Africa today, the gulf between rich (mostly white) and poor (mostly black) is rivalled only by Brazil and is a major source of tension.

But the UK was sophisticated and benign in comparison with other European colonialists. King Leopold II of Belgium murdered and mutilated thousands of Congolese who failed to meet quotas for rubber extraction. His long, brutal kleptocracy softened up the Congolese for their next ruler, Mobutu Sese Seko.

Merriam-Webster's Collegiate Dictionary defines "kleptocracy" as "a government by those who seek chiefly status and personal gain at the expense of the governed."

And here is another European—or western—injury to Africa, which might well merit a little contrition: the extent to which it became a playground for rival superpowers in the cold war. When Congo won independence from the Belgians in 1960, an era of hope beckoned with the election of their first prime minister, Patrice Lumumba. But Lumumba, feeling let down by the west after promises of help failed to materialise, appealed to the Soviet Union for help. This fatally offended the United States and shortly afterwards he was murdered and the western-approved Mobutu came to power.

War and greed in Angola

Congo is an ongoing tragedy—some 2.5m people have died there in the past three years as rival armies compete for its cobalt, diamonds and gold. These feed western markets. Angola, also still at war, has a similar history. It lost almost half its population to the slave trade, mostly to Brazil, a Portuguese colony. Portugal only granted independence to Angola in 1975 and the subsequent battle for power between the Popular Movement for the Liberation of Angola (MPLA) and the National Union for the Total Independence of Angola (Unita) was intensified by the intervention of the superpowers. Some 26 years later, the war limps on but ideology has given way to greed; with the multinationals and the MPLA and Unita elites the only winners and ordinary Angolans seeing nothing of the billions from the offshore oilfields, which rival Kuwait in quantity and quality. BP recently announced it was pumping $7bn into Angola. Whether this translates into food, healthcare or education for its war-weary people remains to be seen.

This article was written in 2001. On April 5, 2002, representatives of the Angolan government and UNITA signed a peace accord, bringing the civil war to an end.

The rationalisation for all this is "context". Many Victorians believed they had a mission to civilise Africa: black people, like the Irish, were child-like, excitable, superstitious, excessively sexual and had no concept of property. White Europeans were a superior breed who had a duty to save Africans from savagery. The Americans and their allies were saving Africans from the evils of communism.

Those excuses no longer work because Africans are saying who they are and what they want: they are no longer a blank canvas on to which Europeans can project their ambitions and their fantasies.

There is a quietly insistent message underlying the babel of voices at the UN conference: Africa wants to purge itself of the degradations of the past few centuries and enter the 21st on its own terms. To be able to move on, it needs its former oppressors to acknowledge the hurt they have caused and help Africa to fulfil its ambitions for a better future. These are not reparations as such, merely a fulfilment of existing promises of debt relief, aid, foreign investment and fairer trade.

Tony Blair made a second-term commitment to help Africa get back on to its feet: a good start would be to listen to Africans and find the grace and generosity to say sorry.

The author is critical of the European colonizers. Do you agree with her, or do you think we should be wary of judging the past on the basis of modern views and ideas?

In 2001 the leader of the British Labour Party, Tony Blair, was elected for a second term as prime minister of Britain.

THE IRRATIONALITY OF "COLONIAL GUILT": A HOMAGE TO LORD BAUER
Michael Newland

The author is the treasurer and press officer of the Freedom Party, a minor British right-wing political party whose objects are "to defend and restore the freedoms, traditions, unity, identity and independence of the British people." He was former treasurer of the right-wing British National Party (BNP).

NO

Among the official myths propagated upon the British people during the post-war period, one of the most effective has been the supposed requirement for a sense of white guilt about colonial rule and its aftermath.

As with so many political manoeuvres, the effectiveness of the 'colonial guilt' swindle has emanated from its support by a curious alliance of forces.

A guilty nation?

The mainstream establishment no longer identifies itself with the interests of the British people, but with larger international economic interests. 'Colonial guilt' offers a ready weapon with which to attack those who wish Britain to continue to exist as a nation. The British supposedly make up a 'guilty nation', on account of their past record as masters of the British Empire, and have therefore renounced the right to existence—or at the least are obligated to pay unlimited reparations for the depredations they have inflicted on the world.

Banging the anti-colonial drum

The Soviet block found colonialism to be a popular stick with which to beat the West for decades, as a part of the larger strategy ... of undermining Western morale—as an alternative to military conquest. In the case of Britain, the United States, for most of this century, saw the British Empire as a rival to be destroyed. The banging of the anti-colonial drum could serve yet another interest.

Allied to the establishment, within Britain, is a broad swathe of left-wing interests. The spectrum runs from Hampstead sentimentalists, with largely neurotic notions of angst about their comfortable lives, to more calculating forces of the left, who perceive that anything which undermines the sense of self of the British might pave the way for their traditional route to power—a collapse in society.

One of the few to speak out openly against the mythology of colonial guilt has been Lord Bauer.

Hampstead is a wealthy district of North London, UK.

Peter Bauer is Professor of Economics at the London School of Economics, and specialises in development economics. He is a person whose views can hardly therefore be dismissed as ill-informed.

In 1981 he published *Equality, the Third World and Economic Delusion*—a book which should be on the reading list of everyone who wishes to be well-informed on the political forces at large in the post-war world. 1981? Just early enough to escape the beginnings of 'The Terror' of 'political correctness' which took off in earnest later in that decade.

"The Terror" is a reference to the period of the French Revolution from 1793 to 1794 during which the regime executed anyone it considered an enemy of the revolution. This period is also called the "Reign of Terror."

A case of too much reality?

Sadly, but unsurprisingly, the book is at the moment out of print. T.S Eliot's well-known remark that 'humankind cannot bear very much reality' appears close to the title page. 'The West has never had it so good, and has never felt so bad about it' says Bauer. We in the West are supposedly to blame for Third World poverty and backwardness.

'We took the rubber from Malaya, the tea from India, raw materials from all over the world and gave almost nothing in return'. A Cambridge student group included those words in a pamphlet on Western obligations during the 1970s. Could any reasonable person disagree?

Peter Bauer amusingly points out that the reverse is in fact the case. Rubber plants are not native to Malaya, and were introduced there from South America by the British a century ago. Tea plants were brought to India, from China, by the British during the eighteenth century.

The title of Connolly's article is an ironic reference to the procolonial poem "The White Man's Burden," written in 1899 by the British poet and author Rudyard Kipling (1865–1936). Kipling's poem presents the colonization and civilization of other races as a noble cause that it is the duty of the "white man" to pursue.

Black man's burden?

During the 1960s, Cyril Connolly wrote an article in *The Sunday Times* called 'Black man's burden'. 'It is a wonder that the white man is not more thoroughly detested than he is' wrote Connolly. The behaviour of white people in their colonies could be summed up in one word—exploitation.

The question is then begged, says Bauer, as to why Third World countries are generally much better off than before they came under Western influence. The most advanced areas of the Third World, following colonial rule, were those which had the greatest input from the West.

Most of the basics of modern life were introduced into Africa by white people. Slavery had almost disappeared from West Africa by 1914—and on the initiative of white nations. It is now returning.

Ghana, until the rule of Dr. Nkrumah, prospered from cocoa exports to the West. The cocoa farmers were the most

COMMENTARY: Peter Bauer

Peter Thomas Bauer (1915–2002) was born in Budapest, Hungary, the son of a bookmaker. Financed by one of his father's clients, Bauer studied at Cambridge University, England, during the 1930s and went on to teach economics both there and at the University of London, UK. In 1960 he became professor of economics at the London School of Economics and Political Science (LSE), part of the University of London.

An opponent of foreign aid
Bauer specialized in the economics of the developing world and was a critic of the view that poor countries needed foreign aid in order to progress. Advocates of aid believed that developing countries could not generate the reserves of money necessary to establish industries and thus would always remain poor. These economists were in favor of providing money to the governments of developing countries, which would in turn build industries and put import tariffs (taxes) in place to protect them from cheap foreign competition. Bauer rejected this government planning idea, characterizing foreign aid as "an excellent method for transferring money from poor people in rich countries to rich people in poor countries." He believed in the free market—private trade without government interference or protectionist barriers—and that the people of the developing world were as capable as anyone else of operating successfully within it.

Later life
In 1982, during her first term as prime minister, Margaret Thatcher (1925–) appointed Bauer to the House of Lords, the unelected upper house of Britain's legislature. In 2002, shortly before his death, Bauer was awarded the inaugural Milton Friedman Prize for Advancing Liberty.

This article was written before Hong Kong reverted from British to Chinese rule on July 1, 1997. Along with, in particular, Singapore, South Korea, and Taiwan, Hong Kong was said to have a "tiger economy," a reference to the country's dynamic economic growth from the 1980s.

prosperous group. This did not prevent Dr. Nkrumah from claiming 'enslavement and oppression', by the West, while himself dragging the country into a morass of corruption.

Some of [the] least developed countries in the world were never colonies. Examples are Afghanistan, Liberia, and to all intents and purposes Ethiopia, which only came under colonial rule for six years during the Mussolini era. Hong Kong, on the other hand, is still a European colony, yet enjoys a 'tiger economy'.

European countries which acquired colonies, Bauer says, were already far ahead economically at the time, and their comparative prosperity is not the result of colonialism. Some of the richest Western nations, Switzerland, and the Scandinavian countries, never had any colonies.

Since the end of colonial rule, a new terminology has developed to maintain the theme of a 'guilty West'. 'Economic colonialism' or 'neo-colonialism' is now supposedly the cause of continuing Third World poverty. The behaviour of so many recent Third World leaders, who have wrecked their countries, particularly those within Africa, is excused as in some way the responsibility of the West.

The essence of the economic case against the West is that international trade has been, for the Third World, a zero-sum game. The enrichment of the West has been at the expense of the Third World. In reality, most [of] the exported goods would never have existed in the first place without a Western input of technology—witness rubber and tea.

Migration of the skilled to the West is one accusation on which the neo-colonialist argument is on safer ground. Bauer points to much of the training of the immigrant skilled being paid for by the West as a defence to this complaint. This is both an exaggeration, and misleading, since there exists a moral obligation among the skilled emigrants to return and build their own countries.

Two criticisms accepted

Bauer accepts two criticisms of the West, both of which are very different from the usual accusations.

Firstly, Western medicine has allowed massive and very rapid population growth in the underdeveloped world, with the problems that brings.

Secondly, he says that the late colonial policy of increasing politicisation of Third World economies has been carried over into recent times, with damaging effects in the form of state-controlled or totalitarian regimes—albeit imposed by local leaders, but not without encouragement in the form of demands by the West for particular allocations of aid funds.

The overall effect of Western influence in the Third World has been beneficial—the caveats to this view are minor. 'Western guilt' exists to serve very different interests than those of the welfare of the peoples of the Third World....

> Most commentators no longer use the term Third World, preferring to use Developing World. Does Newland's use of the term tell you anything about his viewpoint?

> Why would emigrants have a duty to return to their own countries? Would anyone ever advance such an argument in the United States?

> How can the advances in medicine be termed a problem?

Summary

The preceding articles take opposing views on the impact of colonialism. Liz McGregor, writing in 2001 against the background of the World Conference against Racism, argues that colonialism was "the successor to slavery" and "allowed Europe direct access to Africa's mineral wealth and provided cheap labour to extract it." She goes on to describe the activities of colonizers in Zimbabwe, South Africa, and the Congo, and how Africa, with specific reference to the Congo and Angola, later became "a playground for rival superpowers in the cold war." The explanations that they were being liberated from savagery or from the threat of communism no longer impress Africans, according to McGregor. "To be able to move on," she says, Africa "needs its former oppressors to acknowledge the hurt they have caused and help Africa to fulfil its ambitions for a better future."

Michael Newland, by contrast, claims that a feeling is abroad in Britain, supported by the establishment and political left-wingers, that people should feel ashamed of the colonial past of their country. Newland cites the late Lord Peter Bauer as one of the few people to be openly critical of this "mythology of colonial guilt." He explains that Bauer's view was that "Third World countries are generally much better off than before they came under Western influence." Referring to the notion of "neocolonialism," Newland scoffs that "The behaviour of so many recent Third World leaders, who have wrecked their countries … is excused as in some way the responsibility of the West." He concludes that "The overall effect of Western influence in the Third World has been beneficial—the caveats to this view are minor."

FURTHER INFORMATION:

 Books:

Fieldhouse, D.K., *The West and the Third World: Trade, Colonialism, Dependence, and Development.* Malden, MA: Blackwell Publishers, 1999.

Herbert, Eugenia W., *Twilight on the Zambezi: Late Colonialism in Central Africa.* New York: Palgrave Macmillan, 2002.

Keay, John, *Empire's End: A History of the Far East from High Colonialism to Hong Kong.* New York: Scribner, 1997.

Useful websites:

http://african-american-reparation.com
Resource site on slavery reparations for African Americans.
http://africanhistory.about.com/cs/eracolonialism
about.com page on colonialism in Africa, with links.

The following debates in the Pro/Con series may also be of interest:

In this volume:
 Part 1: Issues in international development, pages 8–9

 Topic 6 Should rich countries donate a set percentage of their GNP to aid?

In *Economics*:
Topic 12 Should rich countries cancel "Third World Debt"?

DO RICH COUNTRIES HAVE A DUTY TO GIVE FINANCIAL HELP TO FORMER COLONIES?

YES: Economics and trading relationships with the home countries left the colonies dependent on their ex-masters

YES: The powers plundered resources, stole land, imposed forced labor, and used violence if resisted

DEPENDENCE
Did the powers leave the colonies unprepared for independence?

EXPLOITATION
Did the ex-colonial powers take but give nothing in return?

NO: The struggles of many former colonies can be attributed to misrule and corruption within their governments

NO: The former colonizers left working infrastructure such as railroads and introduced new industries to the colonies

DO RICH COUNTRIES HAVE A DUTY TO GIVE FINANCIAL HELP TO FORMER COLONIES?
KEY POINTS

YES: A large proportion of the income of poor countries is spent on paying off debts. Relief from this would aid progress.

YES: The powers introduced western government, education, medicine, and ideas to the colonies and helped them modernize

DEBT RELIEF
Would debt cancelation help solve the ex-colonies' problems?

HUMANITARIANISM
Did the powers improve life for the populations of the colonies?

NO: Borrowers should repay their debts. It is not fair to others if certain countries have their obligations waived.

NO: The colonizers operated from a racist viewpoint, underpinned by the belief that their ideas and way of life were superior

Topic 2

IS CORRUPTION A MAJOR ISSUE IN PREVENTING ECONOMIC GROWTH?

YES

FROM "CORRUPTION: A PERSISTENT DEVELOPMENT CHALLENGE"
ECONOMIC PERSPECTIVES (USIA ELECTRONIC JOURNAL), VOL. 3, NO. 5, NOVEMBER 1998
J. BRIAN ATWOOD

NO

"DR. HANKE PRESENTED A MARKET ECONOMY MANIFESTO FOR BULGARIA"
HTTP://WWW.BIFORUM.ORG/20066, 2002
BULGARIAN ECONOMIC FORUM

INTRODUCTION

Economists attempt to judge to what degree negative factors, such as corruption, will affect the performance of an economy. Many people associate poor economies with corruption—small or large—and many economists believe that corruption harms economic growth. Other economists believe that corruption does not have a significant effect on an economy.

Economics is an inexact science; the judgment of what an "ideal" model for economic growth might be is largely a matter of economic opinion. Because there is no one set of universally accepted conditions under which economic growth is always going to flourish, it is difficult to judge the effects of corruption on a country's economy. Some economists would argue that corruption has a major influence on economic growth, and that countries have achieved better growth rates without corrupt practices. Other economists believe that there are

far more important influences at work, such as the principles under which the economy is run—free market, socialist, or a mix of the two.

Generally, corruption is accepted to be a willingness "to act dishonestly in return for money or personal gain." However, there is a wide spectrum of possible acts that might be classified as being corrupt. At one end of the spectrum are the small sums of money many overseas travelers and tourists find that they have to pay government officials in some parts of the world in order to secure, for example, a seat on a train. At the other end are the vast sums of public money that some political leaders and dictators are known to have siphoned off into personal bank accounts for their own personal use. For example, Uganda's military dictator from 1971 to 1979, Idi Amin, and the dictator of the Philippines from 1965 to 1986, Ferdinand Marcos, both stole billions of dollars from their countries.

Corruption in many countries has a historical, even a cultural, basis. In India jobs are often handed out by politicians, bureaucrats, and employers on the basis of religion, family influence, or the payment of bribes. But corruption is not just present in developing and transitional countries.

In 2002 the billion-dollar corporation Enron collapsed because of hidden debts. The Enron saga showed that corruption and inadequate auditing procedures were also common in the United States. Italy, another major western economy, is constantly beset by accusations of bribery and corruption, both in government and in business. Yet both the United States and Italy have maintained good rates of growth.

> *"Growing crime and corruption threaten not only Russia, but the entire world."*
> —ARIEL COHEN, HERITAGE FOUNDATION, 2001

So how might corruption have a negative effect on economic growth? Clearly, if a country's political elite is using its power to secure vast sums of public money for its own personal use, then that will affect people directly. Public services, such as health and education, will suffer as a result.

Favors being paid by government officials to particular business interests—to family members or in return for bribes, say—will also have a negative effect on the economy. Awarding contracts on the basis of nepotism rather than competitiveness is

likely to promote inefficient industries. Such corruption will also act as a deterrent to foreign investors, if they must first hand over large amounts of money before a contract is awarded.

However, it can also be argued that corruption, while certainly a negative factor, is actually quite a trivial issue in terms of what governs economic growth. Some economists, such as Irwin Stelzer, columnist for *The Times* of London, argue that a little corruption is "not altogether a bad thing." In India, a country renowned for its bureaucracy and regulations, a small bribe can provide a more efficient route around many of the regulations that prevent businesses from working properly.

Other economists see corruption as a symptom of a disease, not the disease itself. They believe that agencies and governments should look first to improving the openness of government. Governments should review systems of taxation, reduce barriers to trade and investment, improve business auditing, or strengthen their public institutions— the police and judiciary. For some commentators such factors are not only more important than corruption but, where they are dealt with adequately, will in themselves make corrupt practices a thing of the past.

In the first article J. Brian Atwood, dean of the Humphrey Institute of Public Affairs, University of Minnesota, argues that corruption in the developing world has a serious negative effect on rates of economic growth. In the second article Steve Hanke, professor of applied economics at Johns Hopkins University, Baltimore, stresses that other changes to a country's economic system must take priority, and that corruption has only a minor effect on economic growth.

CORRUPTION: A PERSISTENT DEVELOPMENT CHALLENGE
J. Brian Atwood

✓ Worldwide economic conditions in 1998 show that the path to sustained economic growth has taken some unexpected detours. Even the largest and most powerful nations are not sheltered from the economic and political meltdowns happening elsewhere. The economies of virtually all nations are closely linked through electronic commerce, the Internet, and the free flow of international capital. However, the freedoms of the global economy also have an ominous downside if misused.

The recent turmoil in global markets, with its widespread economic and social fallout, will test the commitment of developing countries to free market economies and democratic government. Many of these countries are experiencing severe economic downturns and social disruptions. One contributing factor, perhaps, is the lack of institutional safeguards to protect their economies. Lacking the framework for good governance and the rule of law, and troubled with inadequate regulation of banks, unsound investment decisions, questionable evaluation of risks, nontransparent accounting procedures, and limited openness in government, opportunities for crony capitalism and corruption often surface in developing countries. While economies were booming, these seemed to be ancillary issues. However, they deter economic growth and social progress.

> The author is referring to the economic recession in Asia in 1997 and the collapse of the Russian economy in 1998. How convincing do you find his argument that this economic turmoil was partly caused by corruption?

The fallout from corruption

In recent years, corruption has had devastating impacts in such countries as Nigeria, Indonesia, and Russia by corroding their economic and political systems. Not surprisingly, these countries fall at the bottom (most corrupt) of Transparency International's 1998 Corruption Perceptions Index, with ranks of 81, 80, and 76, respectively, out of 85 countries.

> In 2002 the United States was ranked 16th on the Transparency International Corruption Perceptions Index. Finland came in first (least corrupt), while Bangladesh was the most corrupt, in 102nd place. See page 30 for further information.

In Nigeria, the late General Sani Abacha and his cronies siphoned billions of dollars out of the oil industry, which is the country's primary source of wealth and accounts for 80 percent of government revenue. Diversion of funds from state coffers led to a marked deterioration in infrastructure and social services and a near-collapse of state-owned oil refineries. The country's per capita income, which was as high as $800 in the 1980s, has now dropped below $300. As this oil-rich country faced a fuel shortage and depression, the government resorted to ever greater repression to stay ensconced in its position of advantage. ...

Another well-known example of government corruption that undermined the national economy is in Indonesia, where state banks channeled money to projects involving former President Suharto's family and friends. In the 1990s, banks allowed arrears on loan repayments to mount unchecked and circumvented rules to prevent excessive foreign-currency borrowing. Consequently, when the value of the rupiah fell in 1997, the whole financial system began to collapse. Bankruptcies and massive layoffs have returned as many as half of Indonesia's 200 million people to poverty.

Russia provides a third notable example of corruption damaging political and economic development. In Russia, corruption linking an oligarchy of financial-industrial groups with government officials has distorted privatization, undermined economic reform, deterred trade and investment, and eroded public confidence in state institutions. The weak state of the economy, combined with the recent financial crisis, has given a substantial political boost to former communists and other opponents of reform.

Some positive steps

Despite this sobering picture, many countries are attacking the underlying problems that give rise to corruption. In Africa, for example, major anti-corruption conferences have been held within the last 18 months in Ethiopia, Mozambique, and Ghana. These conferences provided a forum for African leaders to develop innovative strategies to fight corruption, to exchange information with other countries from around the world, and to inform the international community about the steps they need to take to reduce corruption.

Parallel to these Africa-wide initiatives, several African countries have moved from rhetoric to action in addressing corruption. In Botswana, the Directorate on Corruption and Economic Crime is a model for anti-corruption institutions, with more than 4,200 corruption cases handled since 1994. In Uganda, the constitution established an Office of the Inspector General, which has a broad mandate and specific powers to address corruption and which is required to submit periodic reports to parliament.

Suharto (1921–) was president of Indonesia from 1967 until 1998, when he resigned. He ruled Indonesia as a virtual dictator for most of that time. In the late 1990s he was ranked as the world's sixth-richest person, with an estimated worth of $16 billion.

Merriam-Webster's Collegiate Dictionary defines oligarchy as "a government in which a small group exercises control especially for corrupt and selfish purposes."

According to the 2002 Transparency International 2002 Corruption Perceptions Index, Botswana is ranked 24th, one place above France. See page 30 for further information.

25

There is a growing consensus among the developed and developing countries alike that the fight against corruption advances their national and economic interests. At recent summits of the G-7 leaders and at meetings of development ministers, communiques unambiguously condemn corruption for weakening the global trading system, impeding sustainable economic development, and stifling the functioning of democratic institutions. Combating corruption is now one of the highest priorities on the agenda....

The United States... is committed to combating corrupt business practices and improving the poor functioning of institutions that allow corruption to flourish. Bribery is a barrier to trade that hurts U.S. commercial interests and undermines the U.S. objective of promoting democracy and economic development in developing countries. In addition, the prevalence of corruption inhibits our ability to foster the reconstruction of economies where there are important foreign policy interests.

USAID'S response

As a development agency, USAID has a major interest in seeing that bribery does not become commonplace. Consequently, USAID has identified anti-corruption—which is a key element in the Clinton administration's strategy to fight international crime—as a priority in its development agenda. To borrow a phrase, "all international crime is local." Thus, any long-term solution to the problem of international crime, including corruption, must rely ultimately on strengthening government institutions, engaging civil society, and establishing the rule of law in individual countries. ...

Some of the major USAID activities include:

Raising awareness about the costs of corruption. Efforts to raise awareness about the costs of corruption and to mobilize the political will for fighting it are central components of USAID's program activities. USAID supports efforts to publicize procedures and rights, conduct corruption perception surveys, sponsor integrity workshops, foster anti-corruption nongovernmental organizations, promote civic monitoring, provide training in investigative journalism, promote private sector efforts to prevent corruption, and advocate international cooperation and conventions.

Promoting good governance. USAID works to improve transparency and oversight in government through activities such as integrated financial management systems and training and technical assistance for audit institutions and anti-corruption agencies. USAID also seeks to realign incentives to government officials through ethics codes and financial disclosure requirements.

Strengthening the justice sector. Corruption flourishes where institutions in the justice sector—including the judiciary, prosecutors, police investigators, and the private bar —are weak and incapable of investigating and prosecuting criminal activity. To strengthen these systems, USAID programs support drafting new criminal and anti-corruption laws, training prosecutors and judges, and improving court administration to prevent tampering with records and reduce delays in hearing cases.

Reducing the government's control over the economy. Governments exert significant control over the economy through state-owned enterprises, licenses, tariffs, quotas, exchange rate restrictions, subsidies, public procurement, and provision of government services. Often such controls create opportunities for abuse and impede economic growth. USAID works to reduce these opportunities through deregulation, delicensing, privatization, and competitive procurement....

This article argues that the way to combat corruption is to strengthen government institutions. Yet some countries, such as Italy, are corrupt but also have strong democratic institutions. Could corruption ever be justified as a way around inefficient government?

The development challenge

Corruption is a global problem. The industrialized countries are certainly not immune from corrupt practices, and all have a responsibility to be part of the solution. However, corruption appears to exact a higher toll in developing countries and transition economies because they can least afford the consequences. Corruption prevents many countries from addressing their most serious development challenges, deters foreign and domestic investment, undermines confidence in public institutions, and exacerbates budgetary problems by depriving governments of significant customs and tax revenues.

...USAID programming to further sustainable development and foreign policy objectives supports a wide array of activities to combat the root causes of corruption.

By supporting such efforts, countries become better trading partners with the United States and can attract foreign investment. Also, one of the United States' key foreign policy interests is the promotion of democratic development around the world; by supporting programs to combat corruption, developing country governments gain greater legitimacy and are better able to promote political stability and economic development. And they become better development partners as well as countries in which long-term sustainable development can be achieved.

Can you think of reasons why it is in the United States' interest to promote democratic development around the world? Or are homeland security and the prevention of foreign terrorism more important than helping foreign nations develop democratically?

DR. HANKE PRESENTED A MARKET ECONOMY MANIFESTO FOR BULGARIA
Bulgarian Economic Forum

Bulgaria was a communist state and part of the Soviet bloc from 1946 until the lifting of the Iron Curtain in 1990.

NO

"Bulgaria is a classic 'good news'—'bad news' story. First the good news: Bulgaria adopted a modified currency board system (MCBS) in 1997. And as I documented in a recent essay, Bulgaria's MCBS has confounded its critics. This good news has not surprised me. Indeed, it represents the result I anticipated in 1991, when I first proposed that Bulgaria adopt an orthodox currency board system." With these words Dr. Steve Hanke began his speech, named "A Market Economy Manifesto for Bulgaria" at the Investment Forum 2002.

"The bad news part of the story is that Bulgaria is still not a market economy. The Economic Freedom of the World Annual Report 2001 published by the Cato Institute in Washington makes that perfectly clear. Of the 116 countries surveyed, Bulgaria ranks 95th, along with Burundi. Based on work I conducted for the Joint Economic Committee of the U.S. Congress, this is unfortunate. Economic freedom, which accompanies a market economy, is the engine of economic prosperity. If Bulgaria is to prosper, it needs a market economy, now.", Dr. Hanke added.

A free-market, or capitalist, economy is one in which market forces are dominant. All resources, including labor, factories, and natural resources, as well as goods and services, are allocated according to the market's demand.

Four-point manifesto

Mr. Hanke presented a four-point manifesto, which would deliver a major confidence shock and put Bulgaria on the road to a market economy. The four points follow:

Fiscal order and transparency must be established. Bulgaria lacks the fiscal institutions to guarantee that budget deficits and government spending can be controlled. To put its fiscal house in order, Bulgaria's government should begin to publish a national set of accounts which includes a balance sheet of its assets and liabilities and an accrual-based annual operating statement of income and expenses. These financial statements should meet International Accounting Standards and should be subject to an independent audit.

A supermajority is a majority greater than a simple majority, such as two-thirds or three-fifths.

Supermajority voting must be established for important fiscal decisions. Many countries require supermajority voting for important decisions. Such a voting rule protects the

Black-market traders on the streets of Moscow, Russia. Illegal trading, when buyers and sellers avoid paying taxes, continues to be common practice in Eastern European countries.

COMMENTARY: Transparency International

Established in 1993 at the instigation of Peter Eigen, a World Bank official, Transparency International (TI) is a nongovernmental organization devoted to combating corruption. Its main office is in Berlin, with national chapters in over 90 countries globally. The organization is nonpolitical and does not expose corrupt individuals, businesses, or governments; that, it believes, is the role of journalists. Instead, it aims to act as a positive influence— encouraging transparency and accountability, raising awareness of corruption, advocating policy reforms, implementing conventions, and monitoring the performance of governments and institutions. Since its founding TI has become one of the main sources of information on corruption. Its statistics and tables are regularly referred to by leading newspapers and magazines, such as *The Economist*, and are used by national government departments.

TI argues that corruption is something that not only affects the officials and businessmen who take part but also the poorer people of the country, because good projects are forced out by bad ones. It monitors all types of corruption, from international business corruption to small-scale domestic incidents, such as the paying of bribes to corrupt police, customs officers, or politicians.

Corruption indexes

One of the most important innovations of Transparency International has been the establishment of the Bribe Payers Index (BPI) and the annual Corruption Perceptions Index (CPI). The BPI measures the likelihood of companies from leading export countries to pay or offer bribes in emerging countries, such as Brazil, India, Mexico, Nigeria, Poland, and Thailand. In 2002 the data suggested that Australia, Sweden, Switzerland, Austria, and Canada were least likely to pay or offer bribes, while Italy, South Korea, Taiwan, China, and Russia were most likely.

The CPI measures the perceptions of business people and country analysts, both resident and nonresident. In 2002 Finland was perceived as the least corrupt country and Bangladesh as the most corrupt. The index has highlighted the fact that corruption is not something that only developing countries suffer. Research by TI has done much to challenge stereotypes about corruption on different continents. For example, Italy— one of the world's leading industrial nations—was ranked as being more corrupt than Namibia, Taiwan, and Estonia in 2002. While Singapore is ranked as having a clean government, its neighbor Thailand has consistently been ranked toward the bottom of the table. In Africa Nigeria and Angola rank toward the bottom of the league, while Botswana is toward the top. In this way it has become possible to compare corruption in countries from specific regions.

"minority" from the potential tyranny of a simple "majority." A supermajority voting rule is particularly important for the protection of minorities in countries, like Bulgaria, where the democratic process is not circumscribed by a firm rule of law.

Reforming the tax system

The tax system must be simplified and tax rates must be lowered. Bulgaria's tax system is too complicated and tax rates are too high. In consequence, economic incentives are distorted and the formal economy is unnecessarily burdened. Not surprisingly, corruption is widespread and the gray economy flourishes. To reform the tax system, Bulgaria should follow the Russian example. Russia's President Putin has it right. Putin has largely ignored the IMF and has developed his own Russian economic strategy. His first step to reforming the Russian tax system was to introduce a 13% flat tax in which that single rate applies to all personal income. The second step was to reduce the corporate tax rate from 35% to a 24% flat rate. The third step is to grant small businesses the choice between a 20% flat tax on profits or an 8% flat tax on revenues, beginning January 1, 2003. In three short years, Russia will have completely overhauled its tax system. And not surprisingly, these tax changes have resulted in a significant increase in government revenues and a reduction in the gray economy.

> The gray, or black, economy is one in which companies avoid doing business in the open in order to escape taxes and avoid laws.

Changes to the legal system

Commercial law must be privatized. At present, Bulgaria's legal and judicial systems are unreliable and do not meet market-economy standards. They explain why corruption is widespread, why private property and contract rights are not properly protected and why foreign direct investments are much lower than they could be. This is unacceptable. After all, the enforcement of the rule of law, which encompasses the sanctity of private property and contracts, is the foundation of all private morality and the foundation of every sane social order. To reform the current legal system, which is a state monopoly, would take years, if not decades.

> The sanctity of private property is enshrined in most western democracies. However, owning private property in communist Bulgaria was illegal. Therefore, how realistic do you think it is to expect Bulgaria to change its laws and public institutions quickly?

Summary

In the first of the two articles J. Brian Atwood argues that corruption is indeed a major obstacle to economic growth for many of the world's poorer countries. In his overview of the U.S. Agency for International Development's (USAID) anticorruption policies and programs Atwood assumes that development can only take place in a country that is committed to both a free-market economy and democratic government. Anything that stands in the way of these two principles—and corruption is one such obstacle—is also standing in the way of economic growth.

The second of the two articles outlines some of the main points made by economist Dr. Steve Hanke in a speech at the Bulgarian Investment Forum in 2002. Dr. Hanke acknowledges that corruption is a problem in Bulgaria, but he believes that corruption is a symptom of important weaknesses in Bulgaria's economic system, and that it is those weaknesses that are the major obstacles to economic growth, not corruption itself. Thus corruption is not a "major issue" preventing economic growth; rather, there are other more important obstacles that must be addressed first, such as a lack of a transparent system of fiscal control, an overcomplex tax system, high rates of taxation, and unreliable legal and judicial systems. Hanke argues that once measures to address these obstacles have been put in place, secondary problems, such as corruption, will be addressed automatically.

FURTHER INFORMATION:

Books:

Brzezinski, Matthew, *Casino Moscow: A Tale of Greed and Adventure on Capitalism's Wildest Frontier.* New York: Free Press, 2001.

Palast, Greg, *The Best Democracy Money Can Buy: The Truth about Corporate Cons, Globalization and High-Finance Fraudsters.* New York: Plume, 2003.

Rose-Ackerman, Susan. *Corruption and Government: Causes, Consequences, and Reform.* Cambridge, UK: Cambridge University Press, 1999.

Useful websites:

www.transparency.org
Official site for Transparency International, including corruption and bribery indexes.
www.usaid.gov/democracy/anticorruption/
USAID's anticorruption resources site.
www1.worldbank.org/publicsector/anticorrupt/
The World Bank's anticorruption site, with information about harmful effects of corruption.

The following debates in the Pro/Con series may also be of interest:

In this volume:
Part 1: Issues in international development, pages 8–9.

Topic 1 Do rich countries have a duty to give financial help to their former colonies?

Topic 3 Is good governance key to poverty reduction?

In *Economics*:
Topic 1 Is the free market the best form of economic organization?

IS CORRUPTION A MAJOR ISSUE IN PREVENTING ECONOMIC GROWTH?

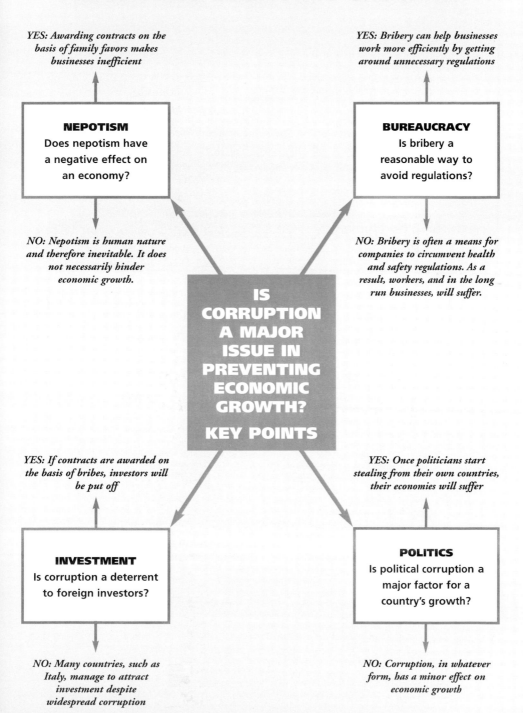

YES: Awarding contracts on the basis of family favors makes businesses inefficient

YES: Bribery can help businesses work more efficiently by getting around unnecessary regulations

NEPOTISM
Does nepotism have a negative effect on an economy?

BUREAUCRACY
Is bribery a reasonable way to avoid regulations?

NO: Nepotism is human nature and therefore inevitable. It does not necessarily hinder economic growth.

NO: Bribery is often a means for companies to circumvent health and safety regulations. As a result, workers, and in the long run businesses, will suffer.

IS CORRUPTION A MAJOR ISSUE IN PREVENTING ECONOMIC GROWTH?

KEY POINTS

YES: If contracts are awarded on the basis of bribes, investors will be put off

YES: Once politicians start stealing from their own countries, their economies will suffer

INVESTMENT
Is corruption a deterrent to foreign investors?

POLITICS
Is political corruption a major factor for a country's growth?

NO: Many countries, such as Italy, manage to attract investment despite widespread corruption

NO: Corruption, in whatever form, has a minor effect on economic growth

Topic 3
IS GOOD GOVERNANCE KEY TO POVERTY REDUCTION?

YES
"GOOD GOVERNANCE: THE KEY TO POVERTY REDUCTION & PROSPERITY IN BANGLADESH"
JOINT WORLD BANK/ERD SEMINAR ON LOAN ADMINISTRATION CHANGE INITIATIVE
(LACI) & FINANCIAL ACCOUNTABILITY, DHAKA, DECEMBER 1, 1999
FREDERICK T. TEMPLE

NO
"GOOD GOVERNANCE: ISSUES FOR ACP-EU POLITICAL DIALOGUE"
PRESENTED TO THE 28TH SESSION OF THE ACP–EU COUNCIL OF MINISTERS, MAY 16, 2003
NANCY KACHINGWE

INTRODUCTION

In recent years the term "good governance" has become central to any discussion on poverty reduction in the international community. For many people good governance—or the process of decision-making by which plans are successfully implemented— is the motivating factor behind economic development. In contrast, "bad governance" is seen to be the cause of many ills existing in society.

Developing countries are often accused of bad governance and criticized for being undemocratic, corrupt, and unaccountable When international aid fails to bring about positive change for a struggling nation, the shortcomings in that country's governance are sometimes blamed. International financial and development organizations are increasingly basing aid on the condition that reforms are put in place to ensure good governance for nations that require help.

According to the United Nations Economic and Social Commission for Asia and the Pacific (ESCAP), good governance consists of eight factors: it is based on participation; rule of law; transparency; responsiveness; consensus; equity and inclusiveness; effectiveness and efficiency; and accountability. But what do these factors mean in practice?

Any nation that has good governance requires the participation of its people to help it work. The protection of civil and human rights impartially and fairly depends on the rule of law. Transparency means that any decisions made or enforced happen openly. Good governance also depends on the presence of institutions and processes serving the people, and it must also exist with the consensus of the people. This entails mediation, discussion, and understanding of what is in the best interests of every person in society, including those from minority groups. This ensures that everyone feels included and has a stake in working toward what is deemed best for their community. Good governance also requires that resources are used efficiently and effectively for the benefit of the society as a whole. Finally, accountability is also key to good governance; this means that every sector of society, as well as government, is held responsible for its actions.

Although most countries, including those with representative democracies, strive to achieve good governance, ESCAP argues that it is "an ideal that it is difficult to achieve in its totality." However, like most advocates of good governance, ESCAP believes that actions must be taken to try to make the "ideal" a reality so that poverty can be erased.

"The impact of poor standards of governance in fact usually falls most heavily on the poor."
—FROM *ENSURING GOOD GOVERNANCE FOR POVERTY*, POVERTY TASK FORCE, JUNE 2002

Some critics, however, claim that the current emphasis on the creation of good governance is short-sighted. They believe that governments and theorists promote the idea simply because it is more easily achievable in the short term than a proper policy of sustained development in a secure environment, which would take more time and more resources. Advocates, however, counter

that the two factors are linked and that sustainable development can only occur if some—if not all—of the principles of good governance are in place.

Some critics also claim that good governance is not possible because it is impossible to take into account all of the often competing needs, interests, and ideals of different groups in society. At some point one group or another will have to give up some of its rights in order for a consensus to be reached.

Advocates, however, claim that good governance can only exist if there is enough understanding between different groups for them to reach consensus regarding acceptable rules, regulations, and standards of behavior. In a badly governed state the poor are more likely to suffer since they are excluded from any decision-making processes and have little economic, social, or political power. Good governance allows them to have a say in resource allocation, development, and other important issues.

Most developing nations have adopted good governance among their achievement goals. Nepal, for example, in 2003 publicly recognized its importance in helping achieve poverty-reduction goals in its five-year plan, which included improving transparency and accountability of the civil service, and adopting anticorruption measures.

The first article, by Frederick T. Temple of the World Bank, argues that good governance is necessary because without it the poor will not receive any benefits. In the second article NGO (nongovernmental organization) worker Nancy Kachingwe argues that the lack of good governance is not the real cause of poverty—rich nations are responsible for poverty in developing countries by burdening them with debt.

GOOD GOVERNANCE: THE KEY TO POVERTY REDUCTION AND PROSPERITY IN BANGLADESH
Frederick T. Temple

When this speech was made in 1999, Frederick T. Temple was the World Bank country director for Bangladesh. A small coastal country east of India, Bangladesh is one of the world's poorest nations.

By repeating the phrase "without good governance," Temple stresses his point in the same way that a preacher might in a religious sermon. This technique is highly effective in a speech. Do you think it works as well when written down?

YES

☑ During the last few years it has been increasingly recognized that good governance is essential to reducing poverty and increasing prosperity, in Bangladesh as well as elsewhere. By good governance, I mean that public institutions function transparently, accountably and responsively to citizens. Without good governance, the benefits of public programs will not reach their target recipients, especially the poor. Without good governance, there is a real danger that domestically raised financial resources as well as donor funds will be not be used effectively. Without good governance, corruption will flourish. Without good governance, citizens will become increasingly disillusioned with their governments and politicians. I believe all of these statements are particularly applicable to Bangladesh.

A growing body of comparative international research has demonstrated that good governance and good social outcomes that reduce poverty are mutually reinforcing—as are poor governance and poor social outcomes. That is, good governance—especially strong rule of law—leads to increases in income and improvements in social indicators such as literacy and infant mortality. Good social outcomes in turn support good governance. Low levels of education and health and high levels of inequality and unemployment contribute to lawlessness and poor governance. This mutual causality between governance and social justice gives rise to both virtuous and vicious circles. In virtuous circles, progress on social outcomes contributes to good governance, which in turn helps create a conducive environment for households and firms to save and invest, leading to further social gains. In vicious circles, poor social outcomes contribute to weak rule of law and governance more generally, creating a poor environment for savings and investment, and hence stagnation or backtracking on incomes and social progress.

World Bank support

The World Bank is endeavoring to help you improve governance in your country in essentially three ways— through public information efforts with both government and civic society; through studies, dialogue and projects in our country work program; and through the arrangements and requirements for the implementation of IDA-financed projects. I'd like to comment briefly on each.

The International Development Association (IDA) is part of the World Bank. It provides long-term loans at zero interest to the poorest developing nations as part of its aim to reduce wealth differences between countries.

Public awareness

First, our public information efforts with government and civic society are primarily intended to raise awareness, disseminate information about the linkages between good governance and economic and social outcomes, identify and support champions for reform both within and outside government, and help increase the demand for good governance. Strengthening the "voice" of the people— especially the voice of the poor—can go a long way in improving public performance. These are vitally important activities, because only Bangladeshis can solve Bangladesh's governance problems. Development partners such as the World Bank can help, but experience has shown that reforms must be homegrown, built on a solid base of broad social support, and supported and driven at the highest levels of government to be effective.

Governance concerns

Second, efforts to improve governance are an aspect of virtually all of the studies, dialogue and projects included in the World Bank's country assistance program in Bangladesh. For example, our support for banking reform has focused heavily on improvements in regulation and bank governance, primarily to deal with the massive backlog of default and to prevent new bad loans. Our dialogue in the power system has emphasized that the main problem is unacceptably high system loss due to the theft of power. We have therefore urged the Government to give priority to fixing the distribution system rather than focusing mainly on new generation projects to overcome supply constraints, which in fact would be much less severe if distribution were managed on a commercial basis. We have been working closely with the NBR to help it modernize customs and tax administration. Many of the reforms being adopted by NBR essentially reduce the scope for corruption. We are particularly pleased to be cooperating closely with the Law Ministry, the Supreme Court and other legal bodies to help

The Washington-based National Bureau of Asian Research (NBR) is a nonprofit, nonpartisan institution that undertakes research on policy in Asia. It promotes and informs U.S. policy toward the region. Go to www.nbr.org/ for further information.

> *Bangladeshi people often do not have enough food to eat since their country is one of the world's poorest. How do you think this affects the way development programs are implemented there?*

them prepare a major legal reform program which we look forward to supporting through an IDA credit. We believe strongly that without the effective, even-handed protection of human and property rights, equitable development isn't possible. Poor governance also affects human development programs. If teachers and doctors are absent from their jobs in public schools and medical facilities, and medical supplies are diverted, educational and health outcomes will not improve as rapidly as they need to. Therefore attention to management and governance issues, especially greater local oversight, is an important element of our assistance in human development activities.

The report, *Government That Works*, received considerable public attention a few years ago, but we have been disappointed at the lack of political will to take on vested interests and implement its recommendations. We are now engaged in a second round of governance-oriented studies intended both to assess why there has been so little progress and to address governance issues more directly. An Institutional Review will employ a broad socio-cultural framework which, hopefully, will improve our understanding of the context of reforms—and therefore the underlying forces which often undermine them—as well as assess the institution-building efforts we've supported in Bangladesh.

> *Do you think it is realistic to expect a very poor, undeveloped country to be able to reform its government institutions and procedures quickly?*

A Financial Accountability assessment will build on a previous country profile and examine accounting, financial reporting, audit and financial accountability in the public sector. The Government's procedures for purchasing civil works, goods and equipment and hiring services are extremely important, because they set the framework within which most corruption occurs. Bangladesh loses the equivalent of hundreds of millions of dollars a year through poor procurement policies, and its citizens are paying for this through higher costs and inferior goods and services. We have already prepared a draft Procurement Assessment which makes recommendations to tighten and streamline procurement processes for all public purchases, not just under IDA-financed projects. Finally, we will be drawing on several case studies and various surveys to prepare an Anti-Corruption Study early next year.

> *Bangladesh is perceived to be the most corrupt country in the world. According to the 2002 Transparency International Corruption Perceptions Index, Bangladesh was ranked last—in 102nd place.*

These studies will be a critical input to the up-date of our Bangladesh Country Assistance Strategy—our CAS—which we will prepare next year. Although we have only recently begun to think about our next CAS, I'm sure that building effective and accountable institutions to address development issues and reduce poverty will continue to play a central role in our strategy. We will begin to monitor developments in various aspects of governance in Bangladesh more closely and rigorously in the future and use improvements in governance as one of the key factors to determine how much financial assistance IDA will make available to Bangladesh. This mainstreaming of governance concerns should lead to greater selectivity in our lending to Bangladesh. The Bank cannot justify lending in situations in which we are not confident the funds will be used effectively.

In 1999 the Bangladeshi government bought eight new MIG-29 fighter planes from Russia at a cost of $120 million. Do you think such spending on military hardware affects the World Bank's decisions about whether to lend money to developing nations?

Governance issues

The third dimension of World Bank support for governance improvement in Bangladesh concerns the arrangements and requirements for the implementation of IDA-financed projects. The World Bank Group has a responsibility to its owners, including Bangladesh, to insure that the projects which we finance are implemented economically and efficiently, without fraud or corruption. We also owe it to the citizens of our client countries to do everything we can to insure that the benefits of projects financed by Bank loans or IDA credits are not diminished through mismanagement. We take this responsibility very seriously, and we are taking a number of steps, in Bangladesh and elsewhere, to improve the way we discharge it.... Corrupt procurement is very difficult to verify, but let me assure you that we are intensifying our efforts to identify such cases and will exercise the remedies available to us every time we have a sufficient basis for doing so.

See Topic 2 Is corruption a major issue in preventing economic growth?

Conclusion

I'd like to conclude by recognizing that improving governance is challenging because there are powerful vested interests which benefit from the status quo and resist change. Courageous political leadership and vigilant citizens who demand change are essential. But the rewards are worth the effort, because without improved governance, Bangladesh will not rise out of poverty and create prosperity for its people. The World Bank—and other donors, I'm sure—would be more than willing and proud to be your partner in such an essential endeavor.

What vested interests do you think might most benefit from a corrupt and inefficient country?

GOOD GOVERNANCE: ISSUES FOR ACP–EU DIALOGUE
Nancy Kachingwe

Nancy Kachingwe is program officer at MWENGO, a Zimbabwe-based reflection and development center for NGOs (nongovernmental organizations) in eastern and southern Africa. She is referring to the joint parliamentary assemblies in Africa held between the African, Caribbean, and Pacific Group of States (ACP) and the European Union (EU). The purpose of these assemblies is to try and work out ways of promoting development and eliminating poverty in Africa.

The author argues that rich nations' behavior is marked by "double standards" because, on the one hand, they preach freedom, democracy, and justice, and on the other hand, they pursue political and economic goals through military means. Do you agree?

NO

X Within the ACP–EU cooperation framework, good governance is said to be one of the fundamental principles of the partnership. This is a welcome development. But it has been unfortunate that the focus of the discussion has been disproportionately on the ACP side. It is in fact of little use to tackle the issue of governance in ACP countries without situating these problems in a more global analytical framework. In other words, we cannot isolate one set of governance problems—even if they are commonly associated with a particular region—from the rest. All states are players on the same world stage. There may be different plots and sub-plots running simultaneously, but all these are inter-woven into one script. For the purpose of this discussion, we are defining governance as the actions and conduct of states in our "global village", and the different interests that they choose to defend, promote or undermine in the exercise of the power that is vested in them.

A viable situation?

The current global context is not a very good place for good governance to begin to take root and flourish in those countries which are "badly governed". We would like to imagine a community of nations that are peace-loving, responsible, accountable and enlightened guardians of humanity and the planet. This is far from the case. Despite the noble rhetoric on freedom, democracy and justice, the global arena is characterized by well marked double standards there is one set of rules for the rich and mighty and a different set of rules for the poor and weak. Superpower status allows for a state and its allies to be able to violate the principles of international law and multilateralism upon which our "modern" world is founded, and pursue political and economic goals through military means.

The US–Iraq war [2003]—use of force, violations of rule of law, double standards, disregard for human life, impunity—is simply a larger scale of a pattern that replicates itself again and again in the way that power relations play themselves out everywhere: between North and South, between states and their people and even between husbands and their wives. If anything, the global context is generating more governance problems in developing countries than it is resolving.

On June 23, 2000, in Cotonou, Benin, a partnership agreement was signed between the members of the African, Caribbean, and Pacific Group of States (ACP) and the European Community and its member states (EU).

The introduction of political dialogue in the Cotonou Agreement was sold as one of new pillars of the partnership. As ACP citizens, this innovation will lose credibility and legitimacy unless it takes as a point of reference the global geo-political context, and allows for the space to discuss all issues. This political dialogue can not single out what happens within a particular state in isolation from the global dynamics and expect that lasting solutions will be found.

Social and economic agenda

It is important to link the issue of good governance very closely with the social and economic justice agenda. We live in a world characterized first and foremost by inequality and inequity. In the Cotonou framework, the EU is providing aid to ACP countries, but that is nothing in comparison to the drain of resources from South to North through various ways. For over 20 years, ACP countries have called upon the EU to work with them to try to reverse these flows, particularly through addressing the very central problem of the debt burden. Regardless of the responsibility creditors share for creating the debt crisis, year after year, people starve and die because of a refusal to find sustainable solutions. Entire societies are disintegrating because of the lack of resources to guarantee adequate income for the most basic human needs. The magnitude of the debt crisis can only lead to tensions, conflict and violence. The best response so far has piecemeal measures in policy packages that exacerbate the problem. In fact the debt could be written off with the stroke of a pen. It is that simple.

What evidence does the author use to support her assertion? Do you agree that the world is inequitable?

It is estimated that the world's poorest 50 nations spend more than twice as much on debt repayments as they receive in aid.

If solving the problem of debt is that simple, why has it not already happened?

Again, it is important to state that the perpetuation of the crisis is not simply an issue of economics and finance … on the one hand, a major factor in this crisis has been the overwhelming balance of power in favour of the creditor countries and the misuse of that power. On the other hand, the debt crisis also demonstrates the weakness—if not the complicity—of our own governments when they fail to mobilize themselves into a bloc to present a consolidated front to deal with this injustice.

ACP governments are continually compromised because they have failed to follow their own prescriptions to redress power imbalances and dependency in the global order. One of the reasons why we as citizens clamour for good governance, is so that as people we can live in dignity. There is no dignity in the poverty and vulnerability we experience when we cannot cover even our most basic needs with our own resources.

This phrase is taken from a speech by British Prime Minister Tony Blair. In October 2001 he said, "The state of Africa is a scar on the conscience of the world. But if the world as a community focused on it, we could heal it. And if we don't, it will become deeper and angrier."

A scar on the conscience of the world?

While certain leaders in the West rightly lament that Africa is a scar on the conscience of the world, the dust gathers on reams of resolutions containing international commitments to tackle pressing social, economic, political and environmental problems. Some people might say we should acknowledge progress where it has happened. Indeed, we celebrate the few minor victories and advances, including in the Cotonou Agreement. We appreciate progress, but how is it that with all this progress, things are getting worse?

When it comes to spending relatively small sums for social programmes that would do good for very large numbers of poor people, responses are slow and wallets have to be prised open. In contrast, when it comes to helping rich corporations make more money, somehow we are seeing states mobilize themselves and with missionary zeal, preach the gospel of the free market. Here again in the Cotonou Agreement, it takes years to establish procedures that will ensure that money can be disbursed rapidly to fund much needed development programmes. But somehow it is not unrealistic to expect to finish negotiations for free trade areas (ie. 8 years) in less time than it takes to spend one EDF (13 years).

The EDF, or Economic Development Facility, is a form of loan from the World Bank to poor countries.

Good governance and poverty: myths and reality

Ghandi said "poverty is the worst form of violence." In that case, today all states stand accused. In the current context and given the challenges that humanity faces, what is this "good governance" supposed to deliver? If it is true that we have better governance in ACP countries, why is there more poverty? How is it that we have more democracy, and yet somehow, we have less choice?

The governance question will not be solved by a few consultations with civil society here and there, or even by staging democratic elections every five years. Good governance might in part mean allowing civil society, the media and business to operate more freely and autonomously, but it does not mean that the state is supposed to abdicate its economic, social and welfare responsibilities as has happened

Mahatma Ghandi (1869–1948) was a political and social reformer. He used nonviolent means to fight injustices and bring about change in both India and South Africa. His principles have been adopted by other great social reformers like Dr. Martin Luther King, Jr.

in the past 20 years. The governance problems and challenges that we face call for a much deeper kind of transformation in our social, political and economic orders. It calls for a rethink of how we have come to interpret the role of the State beyond the market, and look towards reconstituting the developmental state. Trends such as privatization of public services and many other proposals for the new multilateral trade regime, to which there are growing protests in the ACP and EU, are not compatible with good governance. This is simply because they put profits before people. Our world is not for sale and governments must stop those who believe that they can buy, own and try to sell it back to us—damaged and with a hefty mark-up.

Developing the private sector was one of the objectives of the Cotonou Agreement. Privatization has been successfully introduced in many western countries, but how appropriate do you think this economic policy is for the developing world?

Good governance means that at the global level, states must take their international commitments and obligations seriously. Within the Cotonou Agreement, morally it is Europe, not the ACP, on whom the obligations fall most heavily to respect commitments. Yes, the ACP governments and peoples must take first responsibility for securing a prosperous and peaceful future for themselves, and time is running out for excuses. But where our relationship with the EU is concerned the basis of the "partnership" remains, in our view, a historical debt accumulated over the past 400 years which must be repaid honestly and unconditionally.

Why should the current generation of Europeans feel a "historical debt" for their forefathers actions? Do developing countries have a right to expert aid for development?

It is necessary to say these things this bluntly because as women, our backs are broken from having to bear the burden of the fallout from decades of exploitation, bungled development, predatory partnerships and unfulfilled promises. We do not have access to power structures where we can speak, be heard and orchestrate change. We are excluded from the mainstream economy where national resources are turned into profits for the benefit of small groups of wealthy elites and even foreign corporations. We are expected to be able to feed, clothe and educate our children with no public support, and yet we contribute over 50% of the nations wealth. For centuries we have held together communities and families, kept social breakdown at bay and provided a free social welfare system to the nation and yet we are consistently denied the enjoyment of universal social, political and civic rights. We are ridiculed, castigated or threatened when we try to come forward to make change happen. Our exclusion [is] the ultimate proof that whatever states have done, it is not good enough. It is proof that yesterday is not too soon for a deep change in the values and priorities driving our political, social and economic systems. ...

Are the grievances Kachingwe lists the concern of international bodies or of the people of Zimbabwe?

Summary

The concept of good governance is believed by many people to be central to poverty reduction in the world. However, some critics claim it is an unrealistic ideal that can never be attained.

In the first extract World Bank country director for Bangladesh Frederick T. Temple claims that "good governance is essential to reducing poverty and increasing prosperity in Bangladesh as well as elsewhere." He defines good governance as meaning that public organizations behave transparently, responsively, and accountably to members of society. He claims that recent evidence supports the idea that the existence of the rule of law increases prosperity and improves literacy, among other things. He argues that poor social outcomes contribute to economic stagnation and decline since the environment is conducive neither to saving nor investment, and corruption may flourish. He concludes by stating that without "improved governance Bangladesh will not rise out of poverty."

The second article, by Nancy Kachingwe, a development worker in Africa, argues that good governance on a national level is not enough to reduce poverty. She suggests alternatively that changes in the way the world is governed are necessary. The richest nations have to take their share of responsibility for the situation in the poorest nations and do their utmost to help reduce the burden on poorer countries by canceling debts.

FURTHER INFORMATION:

Books:

Deng, Francis M., and Terrence Lyons (eds.), *African Reckoning: A Quest for Good Governance*. Washington, D.C.: The Brookings Institution, 1998.
Pincus, Jonathan R., and Jeffrey A. Winters (eds.), *Reinventing the World Bank*. NY: Cornell University Press, 2002.
Bangladesh: Financial Accountability for Good Governance (World Bank Country Study). Washington, D.C.: World Bank, 2002.

Useful websites:

www.unescap.org/huset/gg/governance.htm
A United Nations site explaining the meaning of good governance.
www1.oecd.org/dac/htm/pov.htm
Organization for Economic Cooperation and Development page that features a policy statement on reducing poverty.
www.iss.co.za/Pubs/ASR/6No4/Editorial.htm
Article in *African Security Review* on governance debate.

The following debates in the Pro/Con series may also be of interest:

In this volume:

Topic 1 Do rich countries have a duty to give financial help to former colonies?

Topic 2 Is corruption a major issue in preventing economic growth?

Topic 10 Are protectionist policies essential to economic growth in developing nations?

IS GOOD GOVERNANCE KEY
TO POVERTY REDUCTION?

YES: Good governance is achievable. Countries such as the United States prove this.

YES: Most countries that have strengthened the rule of law, for example, have reduced corruption

REALITY
Is good governance achievable?

CORRUPTION
Does good governance reduce corruption?

NO: Good governance is an ideal that in reality is very difficult to achieve in its totality

NO: Corruption exists in every economy regardless of the rule of law, accountability, and other good governance principles

IS GOOD GOVERNANCE KEY TO POVERTY REDUCTION?
KEY POINTS

YES: Aid fails to reach those who need it most in badly governed states. By promoting good governance, aid agencies ensure that international aid reaches the needy and poor.

YES: Well-governed nations usually experience better growth and investment than badly governed nations

FAIR
Is it fair to link aid and loan decisions to the enforcement of good governance?

SUSTAINABLE DEVELOPMENT
Will good governance lead to sustainable development?

NO: Rich countries have a responsibility to help anyone in need without strings attached

NO: Sustainable development in a secure environment requires more than just good governance. It needs time and resources.

INTERVIEW SKILLS

"Discretion of speech is more than eloquence, and to speak agreeably to him with whom we deal is more than to speak in good words, or in good order."

—FRANCIS BACON (1561–1626), ENGLISH PHILOSOPHER

At some point in your life you are likely to experience a formal interview. When you apply for a place in college or for a job or internship, you will probably be invited for an interview; or you may have to conduct an interview for a student body or a research project. Interviews can be held on the telephone, online, or in person. The skills you need for the interview process, from the perspective of both the interviewer and the interviewee, can be put to good use in almost any career. Special questioning and listening skills will be particularly useful in journalism, political debate, counseling, teaching, the law, and the police.

Interviews

Interviews can be a daunting experience. No matter how eager you are for the job or placement, it is important to remember that you must also "interview" the college, institution, or company to ascertain whether the situation meets your needs. Always remember that interviews are a two-way process.

Preparation

Preparation is essential for an interview. Read the college prospectus or company profile, and research using the Internet. In the interview use your knowledge of the institution to show your commitment. Understand the job specification, and ensure that you can match the expected criteria (job description, qualifications, and individual qualities). Make a note of relevant experience to prove that you can fulfill the demands of the post. You may not have had work experience, but try to communicate your knowledge and skills by giving examples of your abilities in other areas of your life. Ask friends, teachers, and family to help you practice interview questions. Use positive phrases such as "I am" and "I would" rather than "I think" or "I suppose." Avoid using slang or nonwords such as "uh" or "er." Be confident in yourself and your abilities. The better prepared you are, the more confident you will be.

Presentation

It is important to create a good first impression. The interviewer has a short time in which to assess your skills and ability. The way you look and act during the interview is crucial. Wear appropriate clothes, and try to find out the company or college dress code before the interview. Be polite but positive, and greet your interviewer with a firm handshake. Remember that an interview is an exchange: Be yourself, maintain eye contact, smile, and ask questions.

BEING INTERVIEWED

An interview is a chance to promote yourself. Remember that you have done well to reach the interview stage, and that the interviewers have chosen to meet you. Your aim is to convince the interviewers that you are the best person for the post.

Interview techniques

You may be interviewed in different ways. Be prepared for the following:
- An informal interview is conversational in manner. The interviewer will try to get an idea of your personality. Use this situation to your advantage by emphasizing your knowledge, skills, and abilities.
- A formal interview consists of prepared questions that all the candidates are asked. It is useful to think about such questions in advance and rehearse your answers so you can reply promptly. Your answers should be concise.
- A psychometric test assesses your character and suitability for the position. Be honest—there is no point in being appointed to a post that does not suit you.

Questions

The best way to make sure you can answer the questions is to prepare some possible answers. All interviewers are after the same basic information. You may, for example, be asked to explain how you would act in a certain situation, or how you have handled a difficult person in the past. You could recount a situation that did not work out well to explain how you learned from your mistakes. Use common sense, and show a willingness to ask questions. If during the interview you do not understand a question, politely ask for it to be explained. Never be tempted to lie—you may find yourself in a very difficult situation. Talking from experience is much more convincing.

CONDUCTING AN INTERVIEW

Besides selecting people for a course or a job, conducting an interview can be a good way to gather information for a project and to find out about a subject. The following may help you when you are interviewing:
- Be prepared: Learn something in advance about the person you are to interview. Know what you want to get out of the interview, and make a list of questions. Organize all the items you might need—pen, paper, tape recorder, etc.
- During the interview: Ask your questions clearly, and do not be tempted to interrupt or to correct the interviewee. Avoid asking questions that can be answered with "yes" or "no," and ask thought-provoking questions where possible. Listen carefully—the person you are interviewing may say something that leads you to a question you had not planned. It is important to take notes and ensure that you get all the information you need before the interview ends.

Topic 4
DOES RELIGION HINDER DEVELOPMENT?

YES

INTERVIEW WITH REV. MANCHALA DEENABANDHU ON THE SUBJECT OF CASTEISM
ECHOES, ISSUE 17/2000
WORLD COUNCIL OF CHURCHES

NO

FROM "RETHINKING BUDDHISM AND DEVELOPMENT:
THE EMERGENCE OF ENVIRONMENTALIST MONKS IN THAILAND"
JOURNAL OF BUDDHIST ETHICS 7 (2000)
SUSAN M. DARLINGTON

INTRODUCTION

Religion is a vital and pervasive force in many developing countries: Islam, Christianity, and traditional beliefs in sub-Sharan Africa, for example, Buddhism and Hinduism in South Asia, and Roman Catholicism in Latin America. In such countries religion helps define the ethical and moral frameworks of life and the institutions of society, such as education and justice systems. It thus has the potential to play an influential role in development—in reducing poverty and hunger, improving education and health, and promoting equality and justice.

All of the world's major faiths stress compassion, charity, and peace. These are the same values that underlie the aims of virtually every agency involved in international development. Charities affiliated to all of the major faiths play an important role in the delivery of aid and services—especially education and health care—in developing countries.

However, the relationship between religion and development is highly complex—on faith, philosophical, and practical levels. While Catholic charities, agencies, and individuals work hard to assist development in Latin America, for example, the church's continued opposition to contraception does nothing to promote the population control that many argue is essential to guaranteeing development. In sub-Saharan Africa, meanwhile, where HIV/AIDS is the single biggest obstacle to development, religious objections to the use of condoms undermine the safe-sex message promoted by campaigners. For critics the church is being short-sighted in refusing to adjust its traditional beliefs to the realities of modern life. For the Catholic authorities, however, not using contraceptives is a fundamental tenet of their faith. They believe that using contraceptives goes against the biblical injunction "Thou shalt not kill."

The relationship between religion and development can also become complicated for philosophical and practical, rather than religious, reasons. Charity, for example, is a fundamental value of Islam, the religion practiced by Muslims. Yet much of the Islamic world, particularly in the Middle East, North Africa, and parts of South and Southeast Asia, has developed a great suspicion of the west and its values, as was demonstrated by the aftermath of the 2003 U.S.-led war in Iraq. Muslim clerics, who under the secular regime of the dictator Saddam Hussein had little freedom to express their views, used their new-found freedom to attack the Americans and their allies who had enabled them to achieve that freedom.

"The goal ... should be to bring [the] core morality of all religions to the global stage in a unified effort to reduce poverty and deal with conflicts wisely."
—WORLD LEADERS ON FAITH AND DEVELOPMENT, REPORT ON OCTOBER 2002 MEETING

To some western observers such a response seems contradictory and short-sighted. To the clerics and their followers, however, it is necessary to protect their society from what they see as the permissive values of western society. They argue, for example, that Islam has somewhat different definitions of individual freedoms from those of the Christian world, and thus that some of the human rights that are a fundamental aim of development

agencies—and a fundamental yardstick for measuring development itself—are inappropriate to an Islamic society. A well-known example of the clash between Islamic tradition and the developed world is the adoption by some Islamic states of Sharia, or traditional Islamic law. Sharia includes punishments—such as execution by beheading or stoning—that western observers, and many Muslims, perceive as barbaric. It also restricts women's rights and status in society. Its supporters argue, however, that Sharia reflects many centuries of tradition, that it is based on the tenets of Islam, that it allows great tolerance, and that it is as valid as any legal code advanced by the developed nations.

Despite such apparent obstacles to their work, development organizations also stress the practical role that religions often play. Religious organizations and institutions— mosques, temples, and churches—often form the focal point of communities, and their members are highly respected. As such, they are aware of the needs of their local community and are well placed to disseminate information and deliver development, especially in remote, often marginalized areas far from centralized government.

The articles that follow illustrate different sides of the debate. In the first Manchala Deenabandhu, of the World Council of Churches, argues that casteism, the division of Hindu society into strict hierarchical divisions, or castes, has impeded development in India. In the second article U.S. academic Susan Darlington discusses how Buddhist monks in Thailand have responded to the needs of local communities and the environment, and thereby promoted development.

INTERVIEW WITH REV. MANCHALA DEENABANDHU ON THE SUBJECT OF CASTEISM
World Council of Churches

Manchala Deenabandhu is executive secretary for peace concerns in the World Council of Churches. He comes from Andhra Pradesh, India, and is a member of the Evangelical Lutheran Church. In 1994 he became assistant professor in the Department of Dalit Theology in Gurukul, Madras. The World Council of Churches is an international fellowship of Christian churches. Go to http://www. wcc-coe.org/ to find out more.

The use of the term untouchable and the prejudice associated with it were made illegal in the constitution adopted by the Constituent Assembly of India in 1949.

YES

ECHOES: One does not hear the word "racism" in India. Of course you hear of casteism. Tell me about it.

DEENABANDHU: There is racism in India although not the way it is experienced elsewhere in the world. Casteism is the synonym for racism in India. Caste is a system of hierarchy by which people are put into rigid social categories. These categories are not based on physical features but on the religious ideology of Brahminical Hinduism (Hindutva) which holds that people are born with certain qualities (varnas) and therefore some are born superior and others inferior. Thus it advocates that one's social status is determined by birth and that one cannot simply get out of it. Caste, therefore, is a culture that ensures powers and privileges to the dominant through the subjugation and exploitation of the lower castes.

This pervasive culture has a decisive hold on Indian social behaviour and relationships. Community is always conceived as caste community, resulting in social distance and the discrimination and subjugation of the lower castes in all spheres of life. The prevalence of the practice of untouchability even today in the Indian villages, despite several laws restricting it, makes casteism more dehumanising than racism. The Dalits (Untouchables) live outside the village, are not allowed entry into temples, are served food and beverages in separate cups at teashops, and even have separate burial grounds. They are told that they are not only inferior but despicable and untouchable. This is the most inhuman expression of … casteism.

E: We talk about racism being a combination of power and privilege. Does that apply to casteism?

D: Absolutely. Because of this deep-rooted religio-cultural legitimisation, the dominant caste communities have monopolised power, privileges and assets to themselves, and are able to ensure loyalty and obedience from the lower castes. Even today, a large number of the victims of the caste system believe that it is divinely ordained that they should thus live and be treated. The practice of caste by its victims has been its strength.

E: Would you say that racism and casteism are the same?

D: Yes. These two cultures of domination and exclusion penalise people for no fault of their own and deny them a dignified human identity. But there are some differences.

As I said earlier, caste is based on a religio-cultural ideology, and that makes the task of combating caste and dealing with caste discrimination very difficult. Secondly, in situations where racism is practised, you are able to identify the victim straight away. By making certain political decisions, you can also ensure relative justice to the victims. But caste has a different operating principle. The Indian government swears by an egalitarian constitution that prohibits any form of discrimination in public life. But the fact is that it is everywhere. Caste loyalties play a decisive role in all social, political and economic formations, decisions and dynamics.

E: Racism can be described as the assumptions people make about other people that they put into practice because they have the power to do so. They act on those assumptions, using their power to discriminate. It seems to me that in casteism there are no assumptions but definite demarcations.

D: There are assumptions. But these are used as instruments of exclusion to justify and perpetuate the hegemony of those who have managed to grab positions of power and privilege. The upper castes' behaviour is glorified and the lower castes' limitations are derided. One's social behaviour, skills, abilities, etc. are seen along caste lines.

These assumptions have dehumanised and continue to dehumanise the Dalits. They suffer multiple forms of disabilities, and the prominent among these is the assumption that their touch is polluting, that they are not capable of learning, not worthy enough to think and decide, but are made only for hard physical labour and for the service of others. Even if many of them do not do any polluting jobs any longer, their polluted identity remains. Is this not a form of racism?

Do you think that religious sanction of a belief, practice, or hierarchy, such as casteism, gives it more authority than if it is based on social or economic criteria alone?

The Indian government has a policy of positive discrimination to involve people from the lower castes and tribes in education and government, at both state and local levels. This often takes the form of allocating quotas of certain jobs for the formerly disadvantaged members of society. This policy itself is unpopular with many people in India. Do you think that positive discrimination is better than the inequalities it seeks to redress?

By "polluting jobs," Deenabandhu is referring to occupations that higher castes traditionally made Dalits perform because they were considered unholy, or unclean. They included jobs associated with the taking of life (such as fishermen) or those entailing contact with emissions of the human body (like cleaners).

By using the word "poison," the interviewer and interviewee stress their view of the all-pervasive and destructive nature of casteism.

E: Racism exists in other parts of Asia. In India it is casteism. It is said that racism is like a poison in a society, and that no society can live with that poison. Is that true for casteism?

D: Yes. But Indian society has lived with this poison for nearly 3,500 years and continues to do so. However, I hasten to assert that it has been a poison for millions of people who have been its victims, who have been denied the right to live as human beings. Furthermore, since caste has such a pervasive hold on every sphere of life including our political life, it has virtually prevented the emergence of any just, progressive and inclusive ideological rallying points to help us march into the future as one strong nation. Caste has become a tool of grabbing and wielding power. Each caste group tries to assert its prominence and hegemony over the rest. Some fields of public life are monopolised by certain caste communities. It is certainly a kind of poison that divides people, destroys creativity and makes people insensitive to the dehumanisation it causes.

In 1997 Kocheril Raman Narayanan (1920–) was elected president—the first to come from the group traditionally considered to be untouchable. Go to http://www. geocities.com/ sheela_arji/Ind President.html. to find out more.

E: What does it mean to be a Dalit in the current political situation in India, with the rise of Hindutva and Hindu nationalism?

Hindutva, or Hindu Nationalism, is the concept of Indian society embraced by the Bharatiya Janata Party (BJP), which came to power in India in 1998. While the BJP is one of India's largest parties, it is also one of its most controversial—its concept of Hindutva is contrary to the tolerance expressed in the country's constitution. Go to http://www.bjp.org/ philo.htm to find out more about the BJP and Hindutva.

D: Firstly, as I said earlier, the current political situation is marked by the fragmentation of political power. Narrow ideologies, local issues and local parties dominate the national political scene. These narrow political interests lack ideological bases capable of guiding the life and future course of a nation as large and diverse as India. These local powers exploit caste, ethnic, religious, linguistic, and other, sentiments to consolidate their hold over the masses. The Dalits gain nothing from these powers except unfulfilled promises and continued bondage.

Secondly, the protagonists of Hindutva are the wealthy upper castes who have monopolised the country's business and industry and, using the pretext of India's economic growth, are striving hard to see that their interests are met in the market world. This version of cultural nationalism, as preached and practised by those who have benefitted from the caste system, can only be destructive to the majority of Indians—nearly four-fifths of the population. And the Dalits are its worst victims.

Thirdly, during the past two decades there has been a significant trend of growing awareness and solidarity among the marginalised sections of the Indian society. The rural and urban poor—who are mostly the Dalits, tribals, backward castes, women, agricultural labourers—are getting organised and are threatening to shake the unjust foundations on which Indian society stands. Hindutva forces want to deal with this growing solidarity among the oppressed by sowing seeds of hatred along communal lines, and thus ensure their continued hold over the politics and economy of the country. The recent atrocities against Christians in Gujarat and Orissa illustrate this point. These hitherto oppressed and exploited tribal communities, with the moral strength and dignity their new faith has given them, began to raise their voices against unjust wages and unfair treatment. So right-wing political leaders want a debate on conversions, not on the evil practice of caste. They hope thereby to arouse Hindu sentiments and cover up some of the gross injustices.

E: Do you think the caste system will be overthrown?

D: As a Dalit and as a part of the Dalit movement, I am committed to the vision of a casteless Indian society. But it has always been and is a very arduous struggle. Caste is changing its manifestations and dynamics. Today it has become a political weapon. Caste identities are an important feature in the political games. Political adjustments, alignments and compromises take place along caste lines. Within this ethos, the Dalits are also getting organised politically, but without a well-marked ideological focus. Unfortunately, instead of fighting caste by submerging their given caste identities, some Dalits have begun to fight with each other in some places. So, it seems to me that caste will be with us for some time.

The silver lining is that Dalits and Bahujans (backward castes) are struggling hard to overcome these internal divisions and to fight together to overthrow the shameful practice of caste. These movements of the despised are the only hope for a united and progressive India. What is needed is a coordinated effort to develop a strong and pragmatic Dalit ideology that would inspire the victims of caste to shed their given identities and to work together for a society free of discrimination and oppression.

Christians account for less than 3 percent of the Indian population. The interviewee here refers to religiously motivated attacks—linked by some commentators to the ruling BJP party—on Christian communities in Orissa (which began with the killing of a Christian missionary and his sons in January 1999) and in villages in Gujarat. In 2002 Gujarat was also the center of violent clashes between Hindus and Muslims, in which over a thousand people died. Bills designed to discourage people from converting from Hinduism to other religions have been passed in several Indian states, including Orissa and Gujarat. The authorities want to prevent the poorest members of society adopting new religions in return for food and aid; critics believe that their real intention is to prevent the least-advantaged members of society from attaining greater freedoms. Go to http://news.bbc.co.uk/1/hi/world/south_asia/2967196.stm to read about the issues.

RETHINKING BUDDHISM AND DEVELOPMENT...
Susan M. Darlington

Susan M. Darlington is associate professor of anthropology and Asian studies at Hampshire College, MA. The Journal of Buddhist Ethics is an online academic journal. Go to http://jbe.gold.ac.uk/about journal.html to find out more.

Siam was renamed Thailand in 1939 by the military dictator Phibun Songkhram. The renaming reflected a wave of nationalism— Phibun reasoned that Siam was a name bestowed by foreign powers rather than the Thai people.

The Sangha is the Buddhist monkhood. In Thailand today it comprises two sects: the Thammayut, which emphasizes scholarship and meditation, and the older and larger Mahanikai, which encourages monks to pursue activities within the community.

NO

In 1991, the Thai Buddhist monk Phrakhru Pitak Nanthakhun sponsored a tree ordination in Nan Province. The ritual—conducted by twenty northern Thai monks and attended by close to 200 villagers, district officials, and journalists—formally established and sanctified a protected community forest for ten adjoining villages.... This ritual was one of numerous tree ordinations conducted by Buddhist monks in the 1990s in an effort to preserve the nation's rapidly depleting forest and protect people's livelihoods within it.

"Environmentalist monks" ... form a small percentage of the total number of monks in Thailand. Nevertheless, their actions are visible in Thai society. They tackle urgent and controversial issues, such as deforestation and the construction of large dams, using modified Buddhist rituals and an ecological interpretation of Buddhist teachings....

Development in Thailand

Siam, as Thailand was formerly known, remained a small, relatively isolated kingdom until 1855 when the Bowring Treaty with Great Britain formally brought it into the emerging global economy. Even as the Siamese attempted to limit foreign access to their markets, the colonial economies being developed in neighboring countries forced them to rethink their relations with the international community and begin to modernize. Initiated by King Mongkut (Rama IV, reigned 1851-1868), Siam introduced modern scientific concepts, economic practices, and education.

Mongkut also instituted religious reform in the 1830s and 1840s, and established the Thammayut Order of the Sangha.... he rationalized the religion, aiming to eliminate practices that he felt were too ritualistic, metaphysical, or overly influenced by local or regional culture.

Mongkut attempted to develop an interpretation of Buddhism consistent with Western science and learning[,] and this attempt marked the beginning of a fundamental epistemological shift in doctrinal Thai Buddhism. The theoretical shift, which continues to have significant religious implications today, involved the rejection of the layered or hierarchical notion of truth which underlay traditional Buddhist teachings and its replacement with the notion of a single, universal, and all-encompassing truth.

Mongkut linked the Sangha hierarchy with the absolute monarchy based in Bangkok, using it to legitimize the central government and weaken the influence of regional forms of religion and the power of regional political leaders. The legitimizing role that the Sangha played toward the state was strengthened as Bangkok expanded its control to the peripheral regions, using wandering forest monks to forge relations with remote rural peoples....

Buddhism and the state in the 20th century

Three Sangha Acts enacted by the Thai government in 1902, 1941 and 1962 brought the Sangha formally under the government's control.... Underlying the Acts, especially that of 1962, was an effort to garner support not only for the current government, but to legitimize its development policies as well. The 1962 Act, in particular, aimed to use the Sangha to foster Prime Minister Sarit Thanarat's development agenda.

After coming to power through a coup in 1958, Sarit aggressively pushed Thailand into an intensive development policy. Based on a Western model, Sarit promoted agricultural intensification and expansion toward an export-oriented, industrial economy. He encouraged a shift toward cash-cropping, bringing more forest land under cultivation....

Using the concept of a single, absolute truth and a centralized Sangha organization, Sarit incorporated Buddhism into his development campaign through community development and missionary programs involving monks....

Governments following Sarit's have continued his aggressive industrial and export-oriented development and agricultural intensification policies. The results have been mixed: Thailand's growth until the economic crisis of 1997 was phenomenal, but the rate of environmental degradation, especially forest loss and pollution levels, was among the highest in Asia. The gap between rich and poor widened, and consumerism spread ... Rural people's quality of life deteriorated as they moved from subsistence to market farming or left the countryside to seek work in urban factories. Through the use of a national, centralized concept of Buddhism, local culture and regional diversity were devalued.

The United States is founded on the separation of church and state. What advantages might there be in linking government more closely with religion?

Over 90 percent of the Thai population is Buddhist. As the most respected members of any community, monks are influential in the dissemination of ideas and information.

Go to http://www.thaibuddhism.net/page6.htm to find out more about the Sangha acts.

The author discusses two strands of the Buddhist monkhood. Do you think that the existence of different values and traditions within a religion is beneficial? Should all its followers believe the same things?

"Development monks"

Not all members of the Sangha agreed with either the government's development agenda or the involvement of monks in it. Beginning in the early 1970s, a handful of monks began independent rural development projects based on their interpretations of Buddhist teachings and in opposition to the capitalism promoted by the government. Of particular concern was the impact of the government's rapid development program on rural people's lives, and because of the government's emphasis on Buddhism as a form of nationalism, the erosion of traditional local Buddhist values. These monks feared the effects of growing consumerism and the dependence of farmers on outside markets. Working in specific villages and addressing localized concerns and problems, these self-proclaimed "development monks" ... began conducting alternative development projects.

One of the first development monks, Phra Dhammadilok ... formed his own NGO, the Foundation for Education and Development of Rural Areas (FEDRA), in 1974 just outside of Chiang Mai city in Northern Thailand. He realized that if people are hungry, cold, and sick, they will not and cannot devote their energy toward religious ends. Similarly, without spiritual development and commitment, they cannot overcome material suffering. FEDRA was established with the goal of developing spirituality and economics simultaneously. The organization has four major objectives: 1) to support agriculture; 2) to encourage education (specifically that which is appropriate for the rural occupation of the farmers); 3) to promote religion; and 4) to develop local areas....

Do you think that centralized and localized structures of development are necessarily opposed to each other? The United Nations Development Program is working with the Thai government to reconcile the two approaches. Go to http://www.undp.or.th/UNV/index_unv.html to find out more.

Local development

Unlike most government programs, the projects of Phra Dhammadilok and other development monks are aimed at local, rather than national or regional, development. They respond to immediate needs identified by the rural peoples themselves. Most of the development monks are from the areas in which they work, making them aware of the problems that rapid economic change has brought to rural people. They initiate projects designed for a specific location and problem using local cultural concepts and beliefs rather than pulling people into a national agenda that often ignores their needs and wants.

The emergence and growth of development monks paralleled and accompanied the rise of NGOs engaged in alternative development. NGOs since the 1970s have become a major social opposition movement within Thai society.

Both secular NGOs and development monks emerged because of concern over the negative impacts of government development policies toward Thai society, culture, and environment. Together they have fostered the rise of a national environmental movement.

Rise of the environmental movement

While development monks worked on a local level, the environmental movement grew on a national level in response to the government's economic development agenda. Many of the NGOs that were engaged in a search for alternative forms of development moved into environmental activism because of their concerns about the rate of environmental destruction and degradation caused by the policies of the central government....

Environmentalist monks cannot be described as forming a coherent social movement, although the potential for effecting social change clearly exists within their actions. Many of the monks engaged in environmental projects participate in an informal network that periodically brings them together to share their activities, concerns, obstacles, and successes and generate new ideas. It is through these Buddhist environmental seminars, sponsored by NGOs ... that a new concept of human relations with nature and human responsibility toward nature is being constructed.

Despite the importance of the dialogue and exchange of ideas that take place at these seminars, the real construction of knowledge occurs through the interaction between monks and villagers as they implement their ecological projects ... The new social relations forged between monks and villagers, local officials and businessmen are as important as the localized ecological conservation efforts enacted....

Conclusion

[The] emergence [of development monks] within a particular historical, political, economic, and environmental context enables them to reassess Buddhism to fit that context and engage in debates over modernity and one of its primary institutions: development. They demonstrate a willingness to confront the traditional mutual support of the Sangha hierarchy and the state—a relationship that was itself a product of modernization. The impact of their individual projects may be impossible to assess, but the potential of their activism to challenge Thai Buddhists to rethink their religion, their society, and their place in both the political and the natural world cannot be denied.

Nongovernment organizations (NGOs) devoted to protecting the environment in Thailand include the Thailand Environment Institute, founded in 1993. Go to http://www.tei.or.th/main.htm to find out more.

Summary

The question of whether religion hinders development is a complex one, affected among other things by the nature of different religions and their relationship to the societies and states in which they are practiced. The preceding articles discuss the situations in two different countries.

In the first Reverend Manchu Deenabhandu argues that casteism in India restricts development. He explains how the caste system, which has its basis in Brahminical Hinduism, has produced a rigid society and culture of inequality, prejudice, and exclusion. He argues that the discrimination suffered by the Dalits, or Untouchables, the lowest order of the social hierarchy—of which he himself is a member—is a form of racism. However, he believes that it is worse than racism because casteism is so deeply ingrained in society, and because it is sanctioned by religion. He believes that it is a dehumanizing and self-perpetuating system, which has divided society and prevented personal and national development.

In the second article Susan M. Darlington reports how some Buddhist monks in Thailand are working to promote conservation and to develop small rural communities. She discusses their work in the context of the close relationship that the Thai state has created between itself and the Sangha, or Buddhist monkhood, as part of the modernization and centralization polices that it has pursued from the mid-19th century. She explains that from the mid-1970s a small number of monks began to question the efficacy of government policies on rural communities and created organizations to address issues of poverty and deforestation. She views their work as a positive example of Buddhism providing a moving force in the promotion of personal, communal, and social development.

FURTHER INFORMATION:

 Books:

Harper, Sharon (ed.). *The Lab, the Market, and the Temple: Reflections at the Intersection of Science, Religion, and Development.* Bloomfield, CT: Kumarian Press, 2000.

 Useful websites:

http://www.wfdd.org.uk/index.html
Site of the World Faith Development Dialogue, containing articles on religion and development, and comprehensive links to related websites.
http://www.wcrp.org/RforP/MISSION_MAIN.html
Site of World Conference of Religions for Peace.
http://www.millenniumpeacesummit.com/
Site of the World Council of Religious Leaders.

http://www.wits.ac.za/economics/Journal/religion.htm
Paper on the relationship between religion and economics.

> **The following debates in the Pro/Con series may also be of interest:**
>
> In this volume:
> Topic 7 Will the Millennium Challenge Account foster sustainable development?
>
> Topic 13 Is population control essential in poor countries?

DOES RELIGION HINDER DEVELOPMENT?

YES: Many religions foster inequality in society, for example, the caste system, which developed in close association with Hinduism in India, and in the treatment of women in some Islamic nations

YES: If development organizations are associated with a particular religion, they should bring the values of their faith to help improve the societies in which they are active

INEQUALITY
Does religion foster inequality?

DOMINANCE
Should faith-based agencies impose their beliefs on recipient countries?

NO: Most faiths stress equality; casteism was a social and cultural institution as well as a religious one, and today India's legislation stresses equality; Muslim fundamentalists do not reflect wider Islamic teachings in their treatment of women

NO: Development organizations should not impose systems of religious belief on developing countries because that is a form of cultural imperialism. They should concentrate on economic and social programs with no religious agenda.

DOES RELIGION HINDER DEVELOPMENT?
KEY POINTS

YES: Religions are ancient systems of belief that often conflict with the realities of the modern world, for example, the Catholic Church's opposition to the use of contraception and condoms as a means of controlling population growth and the spread of HIV/AIDs

YES: Local religious institutions and individuals have good knowledge of local needs and can assist in development programs, particularly in outlying communities remote from central government control

PROGRESS
Is religion antithetical to progress and modernization?

LOCAL KNOWLEDGE
Can religious institutions in developing countries promote development?

NO: Religions provide important ethical frameworks for modern societies; history shows their moral values to be correct

NO: Local religious leaders and institutions lack the overview necessary for successful social and economic development

Topic 5
IS TOURISM CONSISTENT WITH SUSTAINABLE DEVELOPMENT?

YES
"HOW TOURISM CAN CONTRIBUTE TO ENVIRONMENTAL CONSERVATION"
HTTP://WWW.UNEPTIE.ORG/PC/TOURISM/SUST-TOURISM/ENV-CONSERVATION.HTM
UNITED NATIONS ENVIRONMENT PROGRAM (UNEP)

NO
"TOURISM'S THREE MAIN IMPACT AREAS"
HTTP://WWW.UNEPTIE.ORG/PC/TOURISM/SUST-TOURISM/ENV-3MAIN.HTM
UNITED NATIONS ENVIRONMENTAL PROGRAM (UNEP)

INTRODUCTION

Tourism is a billion-dollar business, supplying many economies with vitally needed income. In 2000 there were 698 million international tourists worldwide, nearly 50 million more arrivals than in 1999, and international tourist receipts totaled $478 billion. The fastest developing regions were East Asia and the Pacific.

While the desire to travel and see new and exotic locations is increasing, many commentators are questioning what impact tourism has on the environment. Some critics ask if tourism is compatible with sustainable development. If not, they ask, what can the international community do to make it more so?

During the 20th century changes and innovations in transportation—the availability of cheap sea and train travel and the introduction of commercial airlines—made it possible for many people to visit new and exotic locations cheaply and quickly. But as tourism

grew, so did the desire to have abroad the kind of accommodation, food, and lifestyle Europeans and North Americans are accustomed to at home. Initially developers were concerned to supply what their market wanted as quickly, and with as little cost to themselves, as possible. This often involved building large resorts in rural places with little regard for the local environment, culture, or economy.

Most countries did not object, since tourism brought much-needed wealth to their economies. Indeed, all countries need tourism, and often it is the poorest countries that need it the most. Supporters of tourism argue that tourism can have positive effects, such as supporting small domestic industries, fostering respect and pride in local traditions and cultures, and generating new jobs.

However, as tourism grew, critics claimed that the sociocultural cost to local culture and the environment was too high. Today they point out that large numbers of tourists destroy the very things they were traveling to see—the wilderness and the natural world. Tourism results in new buildings and roads being built, and in increased pollution and water use, which in turn cause irreversible damage to the environment. They argue that tourism uses up all the local resources and is, therefore, nonsustainable. For example, new golf courses require water, swimmers often destroy coral, and hotels can erode beaches.

> *"Tourism has a tendency to become ... a steamroller wherever it goes. It can completely destroy natural places. Ecotourism is about trying to stop that."*
>
> —MEGAN EPLER WOOD, PRESIDENT, THE INTERNATIONAL ECOTOURISM SOCIETY (TIES)

Critics also believe the host country or community often suffers through its interaction with tourists, and its value systems, behavior, and moral standards change as a result. For example, in countries like Thailand the increase in child prostitution is often blamed on the influx of western tourists.

Critics and supporters both agree that many developing countries facing debt burdens and worsening trade terms have promoted tourism in the hope that it will bring foreign exchange and investment. In response to rising global tourist numbers and a predicted 4–4.5 percent annual growth in tourism over the coming years the World Tourism Organization (WTO) proposed that there be a set of international environmental standards. In the last 10 to 20 years there has been increasing support for making tourism compatible with sustainable development. Organizations like The International Ecotourism Society (TIES) and International Center for Sustainable Development (ICSD) were established to promote ecotourism (responsible travel to natural areas, which conserves the environment and sustains the well-being of local people).

The United Nations (UN) declared 2002 the International Year of Ecotourism, and the World Ecotourism Summit took place in Quebec from May 19 to 22, 2002. This shows, advocates claim, that interest in ecotourism has grown, and that people are interested in conserving the environment. However, while members of the tourist industry are enthusiastic about ecotourism, many nongovernmental organizations (NGOs) remain skeptical about it. They argue that the problems caused by unsustainable tourism cannot be solved by ecotourism alone, since in itself ecotourism is a small niche market that needs a tourist infrastructure in areas that require protection.

The following two articles are both produced by the United Nations Environment Program (UNEP). The first examines the contributions tourism makes to the environment in countries like Indonesia. The second discusses the negative effects the tourism industry has on the environment.

HOW TOURISM CAN CONTRIBUTE TO ENVIRONMENTAL CONSERVATION
United Nations Environmental Program

YES

 The tourism industry can contribute to conservation through:

Discovery Initiatives works in partnership with local wildlife agencies to offer travel programs around the world. Go to DiscoveryInitiatives. com to see the programs on offer.

Direct financial contributions
Tourism can contribute directly to the conservation of sensitive areas and habitats. Revenue from park-entrance fees and similar sources can be allocated specifically to pay for the protection and management of environmentally sensitive areas....

The Tanjing Putting National Park is in Indonesia.

The tour operator Discovery Initiatives, which is a member of the Tour Operators Initiative [TOI] for Sustainable Tourism Development, makes an annual financial contribution to the Orangutan Foundation of some U.S.$45,000. The money is earned from only 5 tour groups of 10 people each visiting the Tanjing Putting National Park in Central Kalimantan. The park is under huge pressures from deforestation and river pollution from unrestricted gold mining. This money directly funds park staff and rangers, rehabilitation efforts for young orangutans, and the care center. It provides almost the only economic support for saving this park, where the park fees are officially only the equivalent of 12 pence a day.

Contributions to government revenues
Some governments collect money in more far-reaching and indirect ways that are not linked to specific parks or conservation areas. User fees, income taxes, taxes on sales or rental of recreation equipment, and license fees for activities such as hunting and fishing can provide governments with the funds needed to manage natural resources. Such funds can be used for overall conservation programs and activities, such as park ranger salaries and park maintenance.

What methods can you think of to raise funds for conservation programs? At www.nrcs.usda. gov/programs/ you can find further information on planning for conservation.

In Belize, a U.S.$3.75 departure tax goes directly to the Protected Area Conservation Trust [PACT], a Belizean fund dedicated to the conservation of the barrier reef and rainforest.

For Costa Rica, for example, tourism represents 72 percent of national monetary reserves, generates 140,000 jobs and produces 8.4 percent of the gross domestic product [GDP]. The country has 25 percent of its territory classified under some category of conservation management. In 1999, protected areas welcomed 866,083 national and foreign tourists, who generated about U.S.$2.5 million in admission fees and payment of services.

Improved environmental management and planning

Sound environmental management of tourism facilities and especially hotels can increase the benefits to natural areas. But this requires careful planning for controlled development, based on analysis of the environmental resources of the area.... By planning early for tourism development, damaging and expensive mistakes can be prevented, avoiding the gradual deterioration of environmental assets significant to tourism.

Cleaner production techniques can be important tools for planning and operating tourism facilities in a way that minimizes their environmental impacts. For example, green building (using energy-efficient and non-polluting construction materials, sewage systems and energy sources) is an increasingly important way for the tourism industry to decrease its impact on the environment. And because waste treatment and disposal are often major, long-term environmental problems in the tourism industry, pollution prevention and waste minimization techniques are especially important for the tourism industry.

Raising environmental awareness

Tourism has the potential to increase public appreciation of the environment and to spread awareness of environmental problems when it brings people into closer contact with nature and the environment. This confrontation may heighten awareness of the value of nature and lead to environmentally conscious behavior and activities to preserve the environment. For instance, Honduran school children from the capital city of Tegucigalpa are routinely taken to visit La Tigra cloud forest visitor center, funded in part by eco-tourist dollars, to learn about the intricacies of the rainforest.

If it is to be sustainable in the long run, tourism must incorporate the principles and practices of sustainable consumption. Sustainable consumption includes building

Costa Rica has in place a National System of Conservation Areas (SINAC). The country is divided into 11 territorial conservation areas, each with the responsibility of managing and sustaining Costa Rica's natural resources. Ecologists have proposed SINAC as a model for other countries, such as the United States.

Construction of tourist development sites on Egypt's Red Sea coast is devastating the nearby marine environment. Coastal alteration, such as the excavation of artificial lagoons, has led to deposits of waste materials along the coast. This has caused damage to the coral reefs, mangroves, and marine life that initially attract the tourists. If tourists knew the role they had in the destruction of the coastal environment, do you think they would try to act more responsibly?

The cloud forest is part of La Tigra National Park. The park is home to over 200 species of bird and restricts trail access to 70 people per day.

consumer demand for products that have been made using cleaner production techniques, and for services—including tourism services—that are provided in a way that minimizes environmental impacts. The tourism industry can play a key role in providing environmental information and raising awareness among tourists of the environmental consequences of their actions. Tourists and tourism-related businesses consume an enormous quantity of goods and services; moving them toward using those that are produced and provided in an environmentally sustainable way, from cradle to grave, could have an enormous positive impact on the planet's environment.

Do you think most tourists are concerned about the environment when they go away?

Protection and preservation

Tourism can significantly contribute to environmental protection, conservation and restoration of biological diversity and sustainable use of natural resources....

Should a conservation area be exclusive to wealthy people? At www.sustdev.org/ issues about conservation funding and the people who benefit from conservation are debated.

Grupo Punta Cana, a resort in the Dominican Republic, offers an example of how luxury tourism development and conservation can be combined. The high-end resort was established with the goal of catering to luxury-class tourists while respecting the natural habitat of Punta Cana. The developers have set aside 10,000 hectares (24,700 acres) of land as a nature reserve and native fruit tree garden. The Punta Cana Nature Reserve includes 11 fresh water springs surrounded by a subtropical forest where many species of unusual Caribbean flora and fauna live in their natural state. Guests can explore a "nature path" leading from the beach through mangroves, lagoons of fresh water springs and dozens of species of Caribbean bird and plant life. The Punta Cana Ecological Foundation has begun reforesting some parts of the reserve that had been stripped of their native mahogany and other trees in the past. Other environmentally protective policies have been put into effect at the resort, such as programs to protect the offshore barrier reefs and the recycling of wastewater for use in irrigating the grounds. The fairways of the resort's new golf course were planted with a hybrid grass that can be irrigated with sea water. The grass also requires less than half the usual amounts of fertilizer and pesticides. The resort has also established a biodiversity laboratory run by Cornell University.

Tourism has had a positive effect on wildlife preservation and protection efforts, notably in Africa but also in South America, Asia, Australia, and the South Pacific. Numerous animal and plant species have already become extinct or may become extinct soon. Many countries have therefore established wildlife reserves and enacted strict laws protecting the animals that draw nature-loving tourists....

In the Great Lakes region of Africa, mountain gorillas, one of the world's most endangered great apes, play a critical ecological, economic and political role. Their habitat lies on the borders of northwestern Rwanda, eastern Democratic Republic of Congo and southwestern Uganda. Despite 10 years of political crisis and civil war in the region, the need for revenue from ape-related tourism has led all sides in the conflict to cooperate in protecting the apes and their habitat.

Establishment of a gorilla tracking permit, which costs U.S.$250 plus park fees, means that just three habituated gorilla groups of about 38 individuals in total can generate over U.S.$3 million in revenue per year, making each individual worth nearly U.S.$90,000 a year to Uganda. Tourism funds have contributed to development at the local, national and regional level. The presence of such a valuable tourism revenue source in the fragile afromontane forests ensures that these critical habitats are protected, thus fulfilling their valuable ecological function including local climate regulation, water catchment, and natural resources for local communities.

Alternative employment

Tourism can provide an alternative to development scenarios that may have greater environmental impacts. The Eco-escuela de Español, a Spanish language school created in 1996 as part of a Conservation International [CI] project in the Guatemalan village of San Andres, is an example. The community-owned school, located in the Maya Biosphere Reserve, combines individual language courses with home stay opportunities and community-led eco-tours. It receives around 1,800 tourists yearly, mostly from the U.S. and Europe, and employs almost 100 residents, of whom around 60 percent were previously engaged in mostly illegal timber extraction, hunting and milpas, or slash-and-burn agriculture.

Careful monitoring in 2000 has shown that, among the families benefiting from the business, the majority has significantly reduced hunting practices, and the number and extension of "slash-and-burn" agricultural plots. Furthermore, as most families in the village benefit directly or indirectly from the school, community-managed private reserves have been established, and social pressure against hunting has increased....

Go to www.wwfus.org/ to find out more about mountain gorillas and other endangered species.

"Afromontane forests" are indigenous to Africa and are most common in southern Africa. Because of their isolation most Afromontane forests are well conserved. Among other factors, pine tree plantations pose a threat to these ecosystems, since they contend for water supply.

"Slash-and-burn" agriculture involves clearing land of large vegetation by cutting it down, then burning the low-lying vegetation. Burning produces carbon and nutrients, which over time, fertilize the ground.

65

TOURISM'S THREE MAIN IMPACT AREAS
United Nations Environmental Program

Beginning an extract with a definition or clear explanation ensures that the audience understands an argument from the outset.

NO

Negative impacts from tourism occur when the level of visitor use is greater than the environment's ability to cope with this use within the acceptable limits of change. Uncontrolled conventional tourism poses potential threats to many natural areas around the world. It can put enormous pressure on an area and lead to impacts such as soil erosion, increased pollution, discharges into the sea, natural habitat loss, increased pressure on endangered species and heightened vulnerability to forest fires. It often puts a strain on water resources, and it can force local populations to compete for the use of critical resources.

DEPLETION OF NATURAL RESOURCES
Tourism development can put pressure on natural resources when it increases consumption in areas where resources are already scarce.

Water resources
Water, and especially fresh water, is one of the most critical natural resources. The tourism industry generally overuses water resources for hotels, swimming pools, golf courses and personal use of water by tourists. This can result in water shortages and degradation of water supplies, as well as generating a greater volume of waste water. In dryer regions like the Mediterranean, the issue of water scarcity is of particular concern. Because of the hot climate and the tendency of tourists to consume more water when on holiday than they do at home, the amount used can run up to 440 liters a day. This is almost double what the inhabitants of an average Spanish city use.

Is tourist entertainment a justifiable reason for taking water away from the local population? Go to www.unesco.org/water/ for further discussion about sustaining water resources.

Golf course maintenance can also deplete fresh water resources. In recent years golf tourism has increased in popularity and the number of golf courses has grown rapidly. Golf courses require an enormous amount of water every day and, as with other causes of excessive extraction of water, this can result in water scarcity.... An average golf course in a tropical country such as Thailand needs 1500kg of chemical fertilizers, pesticides and herbicides per year and uses as much water as 60,000 rural villagers.

Local resources

Tourism can create great pressure on local resources like energy, food, and other raw materials that may already be in short supply. Greater extraction and transport of these resources exacerbates the physical impacts associated with their exploitation. Because of the seasonal character of the industry, many destinations have ten times more inhabitants in the high season as in the low season. A high demand is placed upon these resources to meet the high expectations tourists often have (proper heating, hot water, etc.).

Land degradation

Important land resources include minerals, fossil fuels, fertile soil, forests, wetland and wildlife. Increased construction of tourism and recreational facilities has increased the pressure on these resources and on scenic landscapes. Direct impact on natural resources, both renewable and nonrenewable, in the provision of tourist facilities can be caused by the use of land for accommodation and other infrastructure provision, and the use of building materials....

> At www. afdc.doe.gov/altfuels. html alternative sources of energy are compared. Are there more environmentally friendly ways to develop and maintain tourist sites?

Air pollution and noise

Transport by air, road, and rail is continuously increasing in response to the rising number of tourists and their greater mobility. To give an indication, the International Civil Aviation Organization [ICAO] reported that the number of international air passengers worldwide rose from 88 million in 1972 to 344 million in 1994. One consequence of this increase in air transport is that tourism now accounts for more than 60 percent of air travel and is therefore responsible for an important share of air emissions. One study estimated that a single transatlantic return flight emits almost half the CO_2 emissions produced by all other sources, such as lighting, heating, car use, consumed by an average person yearly.

Transport emissions and emissions from energy production and use are linked to acid rain, global warming and photochemical pollution. Air pollution from tourist transportation has impacts on the global level, especially from carbon dioxide (CO_2) emissions related to transportation energy use. And it can contribute to severe local air pollution. Some of these impacts are quite specific to tourist activities. For example, especially in very hot or cold countries, tour buses often leave their motors running for hours while the tourists go out for an excursion because they want to return to a comfortably air-conditioned bus.

> Economists suggest a way of controlling emissions is to trade the right to emit waste gas. In this case, polluting companies would compete for licenses permitting them to emit waste gasses not exceeding a government-set level. At www. economist.com you can find more information about solving emission problems.

The U.S. National Park Service has banned snowmobiles from 25 national parks in the United States. At www.parkalert.org/ snowmobiles and other forms of polluting transportation are discussed.

In 1999 Royal Caribbean cruise line, a tourist cruise company based in Miami, agreed to pay a record $18 million fine for dumping waste such as dry-cleaning chemicals overboard from 1994 to 1995. Go to www.justice.gov/ to read about this and other similar cases.

Noise pollution from airplanes, cars, and buses, as well as recreational vehicles such as snowmobiles and jet skis, is an ever-growing problem of modern life. In addition to causing annoyance, stress, and even hearing loss for humans, it causes distress to wildlife, especially in sensitive areas. For instance, noise generated by snowmobiles can cause animals to alter their natural activity patterns....

Solid waste and littering

In areas with high concentrations of tourist activities and appealing natural attractions, waste disposal is a serious problem and improper disposal can be a major despoiler of the natural environment—rivers, scenic areas, and roadsides. For example, cruise ships in the Caribbean are estimated to produce more than 70,000 tons of waste each year. Today some cruise lines are actively working to reduce waste-related impacts. Solid waste and littering can degrade the physical appearance of the water and shoreline and cause the death of marine animals.

In mountain areas, trekking tourists generate a great deal of waste. Tourists on expedition leave behind their garbage, oxygen cylinders and even camping equipment. Such practices degrade the environment with all the detritus typical of the developed world, in remote areas that have few garbage collection or disposal facilities. Some trails in the Peruvian Andes and in Nepal frequently visited by tourists have been nicknamed "Coca-Cola trail" and "Toilet paper trail"....

Sewage

Construction of hotels, recreation and other facilities often leads to increased sewage pollution. Wastewater has polluted seas and lakes surrounding tourist attractions, damaging the flora and fauna. Sewage runoff causes serious damage to coral reefs because it stimulates the growth of algae, which cover the filter-feeding corals, hindering their ability to survive. Changes in salinity and siltation can have wide-ranging impacts on coastal environments. And sewage pollution can threaten the health of humans and animals.

Aesthetic pollution

Often tourism fails to integrate its structures with the natural features and indigenous architecture of the destination. Large, dominating resorts of disparate design can look out of place in any natural environment and may clash with the indigenous structural design. A lack of land-use planning and building regulations in many destinations has facilitated sprawling developments along coastlines, valleys and scenic routes. The sprawl includes tourism facilities themselves and supporting infrastructure such as roads, employee housing, parking, service areas, and waste disposal.

Physical impacts

Attractive landscape sites, such as sandy beaches, lakes, riversides, and mountain tops and slopes, are often transitional zones, characterized by species-rich ecosystems. Typical physical impacts include the degradation of such ecosystems. An ecosystem is a geographic area including all the living organisms (people, plants, animals, and microorganisms), their physical surroundings (such as soil, water, and air), and the natural cycles that sustain them.... The threats to and pressures on these ecosystems are often severe because such places are very attractive to both tourists and developers. ...

In industrial countries, mass tourism and recreation are now fast overtaking the extractive industries as the largest threat to mountain communities and environments. Since 1945, visits to the 10 most popular mountainous national parks in the United States have increased twelve-fold. In the European Alps, tourism now exceeds 100 million visitor-days. Every year in the Indian Himalaya, more than 250,000 Hindu pilgrims, 25,000 trekkers, and 75 mountaineering expeditions climb to the sacred source of the Ganges River, the Gangotri Glacier. They deplete local forests for firewood, trample riparian vegetation, and strew litter. Even worse, this tourism frequently induces poorly planned, land-intensive development....

Xcacel, a beach south of Cancun, Mexico, is a nesting ground for endangered loggerhead turtles. In 1998 part of the beach was bought by Sol Melia, a Spanish hotel developer. Protesters argued that development would endanger the turtles. In 2001 Sol Melia accepted the Mexican Environment Ministry's decision to revoke its planning permit and proposed a land exchange instead.

Extractive Industries (EIs) involve mining and the extraction of natural resources such as oil, gas, metals, and minerals.

Summary

The tourist industry generates income for many developing countries, but critics question whether tourism is compatible with sustainable development. The preceding articles, both published by the United Nations Environmental Program (UNEP), further examine the main issues in the debate.

In the article "How tourism can contribute to environmental conservation" the UNEP examines different ways in which tourism can be beneficial. Not only does tourism contribute much-needed economic resources to local economies, but it can also be useful in promoting environmental issues, maintaining attractive, revenue-raising locations, and funding conservation programs. Tour operators such as Discovery Initiatives provide a model to emulate when it comes to integrating tourism and sustainable development. Examples of countries that have managed to make tourism work alongside conservation are also discussed, such as Costa Rica.

The second extract considers the more negative aspects of tourism. The argument is that negative factors occur when tourist use of an area is greater than the ability of the area to deal with it. This may result in depletion of water and other resources, air and environmental pollution, land degradation, and littering, all of which destroy the local environment and make sustainable development difficult to achieve. Cruise liners are presented as one of the major sources of tourist pollution, responsible for water pollution on a vast scale. The most pressing problems highlighted are the sprawling development that pursues tourists wherever they go and the lack of control over these development sites. Taxing tourists is being adopted around the world as a sure way to fund conservation and maintain the industry.

FURTHER INFORMATION:

Books:

Gunn, Clare A., and Targut Var, *Tourism Planning: Basics, Concepts, Cases*. New York: Routledge, 2002.
Bosselman, Fred P., Craig Peterson, and Claire McCarthy, *Managing Tourism Growth: Issues and Applications*. Washington, D.C.: Island Press, 1999.
Waring, Stephen, and John Neil, *Ecotourism: Impacts, Potentials and Possibilities*. Oxford, Boston: Butterworth-Heinemann, 1999.

Useful websites:

www.unep.org/
Homepage of United Nations Environment Program.
www.sustdev.org
Homepage of Sustainable Development International, an internet publication working in connection with international environmental agencies.

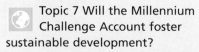

The following debates in the Pro/Con series may also be of interest:

In this volume:

Topic 7 Will the Millennium Challenge Account foster sustainable development?

Topic 16 Does water scarcity prevent economic development?

IS TOURISM CONSISTENT WITH SUSTAINABLE DEVELOPMENT?

YES: Most tourists want to experience countries as they really are and are willing to pay for that privilege

YES: If everyone is aware of the effects of their behavior on local economies and the global environment in general, they will behave properly

ECOTOURISM

Is ecotourism viable?

RESPONSIBILITY

Is the key feature of sustainable tourism responsibility?

NO: People do not want to pay higher prices to go to beautiful locations. They want home comforts in an exotic setting.

NO: It is much more than that. It is about respect for the environment, the local communities, and for the world in general.

IS TOURISM CONSISTENT WITH SUSTAINABLE DEVELOPMENT?

KEY POINTS

YES: 2002 was the international year of ecotourism, and the United Nations and various member countries did a lot to raise public awareness of this issue

YES: The "get-rich-quick" tourist operators are often the worst sinners when it comes to abusing the environment. They need further education.

INTERNATIONAL COMMUNITY

Is it doing enough to support sustainable tourism?

EDUCATION

Does the tourist industry need educating about sustainable development?

NO: Developing countries in particular are still having their resources depleted and exploited by tourists and foreign tourist agencies. Something has to change.

NO: Education is not enough. Fines for abuses would be far more effective.

PART 2
AID, INVESTMENT, AND GROWTH

INTRODUCTION

According to the United Nations Development Report 2002, among the 73 countries with data (and 80 percent of the world's people), 48 have seen inequality increase since the 1950s, 16 have experienced no change, and only 9—with just 4 percent of the world's people—have seen a fall.

Some experts view income distribution as critical to a country's development. Where growth is inequitable, they argue, there is a greater chance of political instability. In addition those marginalized and excluded from the new economic growth will be less productive. They see the real challenge as creating conditions in which poor people can work their way out of poverty, contributing to national wealth in the process.

Some commentators believe that the only way for this to occur is through foreign aid and investment. But critics question how effective aid is. Do rich countries, they ask, really have a responsibility to help poor nations? Or does aid result in the permanent dependence of the recipients on donor nations, as some economists believe?

The politics of aid

Historically there have always been examples of rich benefactors giving money or help to poorer individuals or countries, but it was during the 20th century that the international community created a more formal system of giving financial or other necessary assistance to countries in need, through organizations like the World Bank and the World Trade Organization (WTO).

The question of whether aid is a good or bad thing has caused much heated discussion. Among the criticisms are that it often benefits the donor country more than the recipient country. For example, some countries give a share of their aid in the form of technical cooperation, which is sometimes spent on well-paid advisers from rich countries, and is, critics argue, rarely demand driven. Similarly, aid is often "tied" in that it has to be spent on purchasing products and services from the donor country, rather than from the cheapest available source. Some economists also argue that aid discourages savings and investment in the recipient country, creating a climate of dependency.

But advocates claim that even if foreign aid comes with conditions, it is still much needed. Some commentators even argue that there should be more regulation of the amount of aid donated and that rich countries should be forced to give a set percentage of their Gross

National Product (GNP) to poor nations. This issue is discussed in Topic 6.

Many politicians believe that aid can be used for the good of the international community. Sanctions can, for example, be used to stop human rights abuses as seen, for example, in the case of the Apartheid system in

education, will naturally improve. But others argue that although this was historically the way development occurred in Europe and North America, the developing world has often followed a different pattern. This has led many people to focus on investment in education, for example, as a way of helping development in poorer nations.

"When a person is down in the world, an ounce of help is better than a pound of preaching."
—EDWARD G. BULWER-LYTTON (1803–1873), BRITISH AUTHOR

South Africa. Similarly, some people argue that loans should only be given to nations that adhere to internationally acceptable standards.

In 2002 President George W. Bush (2001–) announced a dramatic increase in U.S. development assistance to poor countries that demonstrated a commitment to good governance, investment in people, and sound economic policies. The increased aid was put into a Millennium Challenge Account (MCA) which received $5 billion of federal money over FY 2004–2006. Although many people have welcomed the introduction of the MCA, others have questioned the stringent criteria that recipient nations have to meet in order to qualify for aid. Topic 7 discusses whether the MCA can foster sustainable development.

Helping others help themselves

Many development experts consider economic growth as crucial to development. Once an economy has reached a certain rate of growth, other areas, such as health care and

Many educationalists and aid agencies argue that by investing in education and training the international community is helping developing nations to help themselves. By giving everyone an accepted standard of education, some argue, that the cycle of poverty that often prevents growth in poor nations can be broken. This also helps reduce dependency between recipient and donor nations. The importance of investment in education in poor nations is examined in Topic 8.

Others argue that education can also help improve conditions in other areas. Through learning some people are exposed to different moral and ethical codes. They can become aware that child labor or the death penalty, for example, are not globally accepted practices. Education can also help reduce prejudice and intolerance based on race, minority status, or gender. Some critics argue that gender inequality especially has contributed to poor growth in developing nations. Topic 9 looks at this issue in relation to Latin America.

Topic 6
SHOULD RICH COUNTRIES DONATE A SET PERCENTAGE OF THEIR GNP TO AID?

YES
"BOOST U.S. FOREIGN AID, BIG-TIME"
THE CHRISTIAN SCIENCE MONITOR, DECEMBER 13, 2001
HELENA COBBAN

NO
FROM "DOES AID MATTER?"
NEW INTERNATIONALIST, ISSUE 285, NOVEMBER 1996
DAVID RANSOM INTERVIEWING ALEX DE WAAL, HOPE CHIGUDU, AND NAILA KABEER

INTRODUCTION

Foreign aid is given by richer states to poorer nations. It takes many forms, from direct shipments of foodstuffs and clothing to the cancelation of debts. It can be private, such as that provided by charities and nongovernmental organizations (NGOs) like Oxfam, or it can be public—so-called official development assistance (ODA). ODA may be bilateral—that is, one country assisting another. In the United States bilateral projects are funded through the U.S. Agency for International Aid (USAID). ODA may also be multilateral, with countries contributing by funding international agencies such as the International Monetary Fund (IMF), which in turn produce aid packages.

There are no international rules governing which countries should donate aid, nor how much they should give. Neither are there any regulations concerning which states should receive assistance. While some politicians argue that aid is not the answer to promoting sustainable development in poor nations, some critics of this viewpoint, including some development economists and aid agencies, believe that all rich countries should donate a set percentage of their gross national product (GNP) to helping poor countries. A country's GNP is the total value of goods it produces and services it provides, plus the income it earns from foreign investments.

In 1969 the Commission on International Development, sponsored by the World Bank and chaired by Lester B. Pearson (1897–1972), a former prime minister of Canada, recommended that the richer countries should aim to contribute 0.7 percent of their GNP in official development assistance by 1975. By 2001 only a handful of countries had managed to reach or exceed this figure: Denmark, the Netherlands, Sweden, Norway, and Luxembourg. The U.S. foreign aid contribution for 2001 was 0.11 percent.

This was the lowest in terms of proportion of GNP among the 22 members of the Development Assistance Committee (DAC) of the Organisation for Economic Cooperation and Development—the world's richest countries—although the United States never signed up to the 0.7 percent target. In terms of its absolute contribution the United States actually came out on top: 0.11 percent of GNP translated into $10.9 billion in actual terms. In 2001 the total contribution of the DAC's 22 members amounted to 0.22 percent of their combined GNP.

"[G]overnment-to-government transfers ... are an excellent method for transferring money from poor people in rich countries to rich people in poor countries."

—PETER BAUER (1915–2002),

BRITISH ECONOMIST

There are two principal reasons for earmarking a substantial proportion of a nation's wealth for aid. First, there is the humanitarian motive—the belief that the "haves" should help out the "have-nots." The second motive is more pragmatic—the belief that the giving of aid can benefit the donor nation and its citizens. In the early days of foreign aid, during the Cold War of the 1950s to 1980s, western governments granted assistance to countries that were perceived to be vulnerable to the spread of communism in order to keep them aligned with the west. In the post-Cold War era, particularly after 9/11, people tend to view international terrorism as the chief threat to national security. Supporters argue that aid can help prevent developing nations from becoming centers of terrorism fueled by alienation and poverty.

Some commentators disagree with the principle of giving aid to poorer nations. They believe that it creates dependency in the receiving nations, making them less competitive and perpetuating the rich–poor, master–servant relationship that originated in colonialism. They further question the motives of donor nations and claim that there is no such thing as a "free ticket," and that it is not in the interest of a donor nation to give aid without expecting some kind of return—usually in the form of favorable trade terms. However, advocates argue that aid can help valuable income-earning industries develop in regions that previously could not sustain themselves.

Critics also argue that often aid has to be paid for by taxes, and it is the poorest people who pay. Others paint a bleak picture of the effectiveness of aid; they argue that much of it never reaches the people who need it most. Corruption within recipient governments as well as inefficiency on the part of aid agencies are blamed for the inability of aid to make more of an impact in poor regions. But advocates argue that aid can be used to promote good governance in these areas.

Helena Cobban, a specialist in international affairs, in the first of the following articles calls on the United States to raise its aid contributions. The second shows three aid workers' views on why aid lets down poor nations.

BOOST U.S. FOREIGN AID, BIG-TIME
Helena Cobban

YES

In 1999 the United States' 0.1 percent was the lowest level of foreign aid spending among rich countries as a proportion of GNP. However, its $9.1 billion contribution put it second in absolute terms behind Japan. Denmark gave the most relatively, its $1.7 billion contribution equating to 1.01 percent of GNP. In 2001 the United States gave $10.9 billion (0.11 percent) and Denmark $1.6 billion (1.01 percent).

☑ The United States spends 0.1 percent of its GNP on foreign aid. To be able to fight terrorism and work for peace and development the US must make a U-turn on aid. A quick quiz for this holiday season: What portion of our country's gross national product might it be appropriate for Americans to devote to helping poor countries develop? One percent? Maybe a third or a half of that?

Aid in decline

Here's the actual portion for 1999: one-tenth of 1 percent.

This is tiny, but not anything new. It's the end point of a decades-long process of congressional cutbacks—with successive administrations going along. In 1970, aid was three-tenths of 1 percent. In 1990, two-tenths.

Now, as an urgent part of our antiterror campaign, Congress and the executive must work quickly to jack aid up considerably. The United Nations is asking rich countries to allocate 0.7 percent of their GNP to overseas development aid. We should aim at getting close to that goal—fast!

Alienation and terrorism

The article was written in December 2001, two months after the September 11 terrorist action in New York and Washington, D.C. Do you agree with the author that low aid levels may have helped terrorism to flourish in poor nations? Is poverty a justification for terrorism?

Our aid's 30-year decline has not served American interests well. The shockingly low level of aid throughout the 1990s prepared the ground for the kind of chaos and social despair in which the Taliban, Al Qaeda, and their ilk have flourished. This is not to excuse those groups' actions. But their operatives were able to organize their hate-filled acts undisturbed while living in communities that didn't feel like they had much stake in a world system that seemed to treat them so poorly.

President Bush is right to pledge that the United States will not "walk away" from the needs of Afghanistan's people, as it seemed to in the early '90s. But the problem is far broader than Afghanistan. Hundreds of millions of people live in failed and failing states around the world. Many feel they have little stake in the stability of the world system. If we want to prevent those countries from continuing to incubate desperation and cruelty, we need to think soberly about how to give those people such a stake.

That will take, among other things, a sustained investment in overseas development aid. The needs seem most pressing in Afghanistan, which could fall back into warlordism, opium production, and terrorism if we and other donors turn our backs again. But it is also urgent in 15 to 20 other countries. Many are in Africa; some are already accused of having links to Al Qaeda.

Regarding Afghanistan, UN development chief Mark Malloch Brown has stressed that aid donors need to prepare for a long-term commitment to national rebuilding—as well as "instant" donations to meet urgent needs. After a recent visit to Afghanistan, he said, "I have a sense of a great national U-turn at the grassroots level; of ordinary Afghans rejecting the cycle of war and decline, and wanting to seize this moment to make a nation where their kids—girls and boys— can go to school; where mothers and fathers can go to work in the mornings and expect to come home in the evening ... without threat of violence."

Mr. Malloch Brown listed four priorities in Afghan rebuilding: security, agriculture, community-based programs, and the return of displaced persons. He said the UN would present a five-year recovery plan to a donors' conference in Tokyo in January—and he noted that the latter years of that program would be the more expensive ones. Development experts warn that the US and other donors must be ready to stay the course in Afghanistan—and that the funds for this must not come out of those already earmarked for Africa.

A British former journalist, Mark Malloch Brown has been administrator of the United Nations Development Program (UNDP) since July 1999.

Mozambique and the case for aid

Can the UN "deliver" on organizing rebuilding programs in failed and failing states? Treasury Secretary Paul O'Neill has cast doubt on the effectiveness of development aid. I wonder if he's ever been to a country like, say, Mozambique, a very poor country that is still recovering from a long and brutal civil war that ended in 1992. That war killed a million of Mozambique's 16 million people, displaced 5 or 6 million more, and caused massive infrastructure degradation that led to long years of drought and famine.

Paul H. O'Neill (1935–) was the first secretary of the treasury in the administration of President George W. Bush (2001–). O'Neill held office from January 20, 2001, to December 31, 2002, and was succeeded by John W. Snow.

I was in Mozambique last August. Eight years into a UN-led rebuilding effort, it's still poor. But I saw how much its people have already benefited from programs similar to what Malloch Brown is proposing for Afghanistan. In addition, the UN ran special programs to reclaim roads and arable land from land mines, and to support the demobilization and reintegration into civilian life of former combatants. (Afghanistan could benefit from programs like that, too.)

COMMENTARY: American foreign assistance

The modern idea of foreign aid dates from the 1940s, and the United States was at the forefront from the beginning. The United States hosted the 1944 UN Monetary and Financial Conference at Bretton Woods, New Hampshire, at which representatives from more than 40 countries met to discuss how they would cooperate economically when World War II (1939–1945) was over. Among the results of the conference was the establishment of the International Bank for Reconstruction and Development (IBRD, or World Bank) and the International Monetary Fund (IMF) to provide funds to nations in difficulty. These two United Nations agencies, both of which are headquartered in Washington, D.C., are today among the world's principal multilateral aid organizations, disbursing billions of dollars in loans each year. However, critics accuse both of tying loans to economic conditions—for example, the removal of trade tariffs (taxes) and reductions in government spending—that hurt the poor of the borrowing country.

The Marshall Plan

Also in the 1940s President Harry S. Truman (1884–1972) warned of the threat to American values posed by communism in the harsh postwar world and proposed raising U.S. economic aid to bolster floundering economies in Europe and elsewhere. This strategy, he argued, was the best way to preserve democracy. In April 1948 Truman signed the Economic Cooperation Act, which brought into effect the European Recovery Program, or Marshall Plan. Formulated by General George C. Marshall (1880–1959), formerly chief of staff of the army and at the time secretary of state, the project called for European countries to get together and produce a plan for the continent's reconstruction. The United States would then foot the bill.

The idea was to get Europe functioning again after the ravages of war, and so the plan focused on heavy industry, increasing production and foreign trade, and bringing about economic cooperation between European countries. The Organisation for European Economic Cooperation (OEEC) was set up to administer the aid. The body still exists, in enlarged form, as the international economic forum now named the Organisation for Economic Cooperation and Development (OECD).

The Marshall Plan led to the transfer of some $13 billion in aid to European countries from 1948 to 1952 in the form of grants and loans. It was successful except in its aim of controlling inflation (rising prices and the consequent fall in the value of money). U.S. foreign aid spending was at its peak during this postwar period—in 1949, for example, it stood at 2.75 percent of GNP. That same year, with the Marshall Plan proving effective, President Truman, in Point Four of his inauguration address, proposed an annual foreign aid budget to provide assistance to developing countries.

Is Mozambique a reported haven for global terrorists? No. Do most Mozambicans feel they have a stake, however small, in global stability? Probably so.

I'll admit, there have been failures in UN rebuilding efforts, as well as successes. Turning from war to peace and stability has to be a people's choice. But if we structure the incentives wisely—which we did far too rarely during the "stingy '90s"—most folks around the world will make the right decision. Just as they did in Western Europe, in the late 1940s, when the Marshall Plan invested one-fourth of 1 percent of US GNP, every year for four years, in postwar recovery and reconstruction.

See box on page 78 for further information.

Time for a U-turn

Now we must plan once again to invest seriously in peace.

It's true, our economic prospects look murky. But we're still a rich country. All the world's other rich countries invest a considerably larger portion of their GNP in overseas aid than we do. There are scores of ways our budgeters could find the money to bring our aid figures up—including deferring tax cuts or paring back some of the planned growth in military spending.

If the starving, war-ravaged Afghans can make a U-turn toward peace, can't we Americans support them and the world's other very-low-income folks by making our own U-turn on aid? The time to do that is now.

In late 2001, as a part of the War Against Terrorism, the United States led a military campaign in Afghanistan, toppling the Taliban regime and attacking Osama Bin Laden's Al Qaeda terrorist network. The United States then provided aid to reconstruct the country. The 2003 U.S. budget for the purpose was $900 million, and an announcement that summer suggested the figure might be about to double.

DOES AID MATTER?
Alex de Waal, Hope Chigudu, and Naila Kabeer

NO

ALEX DE WAAL

No, but Aid is essentially a Western, Anglo-Saxon model of charitable endeavour that's being imposed on the rest of the world. It goes back to Elizabethan times when Queen Elizabeth's Privy Councillors—wise, cynical souls that they were—saw the dissolution of the monasteries as creating unrest, even famine. They realized that the best way to keep a lid on unrest is to promote charitable endeavour. The truth of that insight echoes down the centuries, reinforced by the 1961 court judgement on Amnesty International which said: 'Justice is political, justice is not charitable. Amnesty cannot be a charity.'

The reality is that if you look at major problems—such as civil war and famine—around the world, the way they are solved is not through charitable action, it's through political action. The more resources—financial, political and intellectual—that are put into the charitable/technical model, the more the political discourse withers on the vine.

A need for accountability

What's happening is that international law is being rewritten by the UN Security Council to take any element of criminality or moral deviance out of famine and invert it, so that the only moral issue is: Are Médecins sans Frontières or Oxfam allowed to operate? Which of course is completely beside the point. What we need to do is put back culpability and guilt—up to and including criminal guilt—into these situations, which is an act of solidarity with the victims. There are all sorts of public, transparent processes to go through to find out who's guilty, who's innocent, who behaved heroically, what mechanical procedures were at fault. In provincial India, if there's a massive food shortage, Members of Parliament or senior civil servants lose their jobs. If there's a famine in Africa international civil servants get promoted.

Alex de Waal works for African Rights.

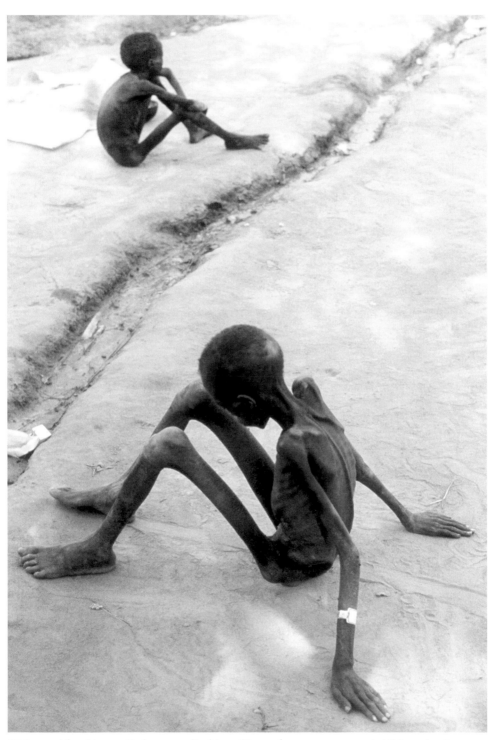

Water and food insecurity have resulted in millions of men, women, and children starving in Africa despite the efforts of international aid agencies to counter the problem.

HOPE CHIGUDU

Not much. Aid is decreasing and perhaps it does not matter, if one considers the way it is used. I don't think it is effective in terms of reaching the poor. All I do know is that very, very few people benefit from it. The poor remain poor.

If aid ended, life would still go on. It would only change for the people who benefit from aid. They are driven in huge cars and without it they would be forced to ride bicycles and would definitely lose weight.

The powerful benefit

Resources benefit those people who are better placed to exploit them. Who, in the first place, negotiates aid? Who defines what are considered the 'development needs' of a country?

People in powerful positions also happen to be men, and it is not always true to say that they represent the poor. Some have lived in positions of power so long that they have forgotten what it means to be poor. There are many people who are getting poorer despite aid, and because of aid. It is as if there is some kind of strategic silence about the fate of the extremely poor: 'Let them pull their socks up! If they do not have any, let them borrow from the non-governmental organizations!'

Aid conditions of limited benefit

Take the example of aid and the conditions that are imposed before it is given, like democracy and human rights in the receiving country. What is meant by democracy? Who defines it? To most people 'democracy' means one man, one vote. The man who casts that one vote is as much a tyrant at home with his family as the one he votes for. Both are in their sixties. Are they going to learn democratic values in the afternoon of their lives? No. Democracy starts at home and in other institutions such as schools and churches. Yet when one raises issues of the family, gender relations, patriarchy, one is told that these are 'cultural' issues. We are talking about power relations here. Where does 'culture' come in?

Poor people should be able to have a say. In fact they have said many times over that they know what their problems are. They want food, schools, hospitals. But beyond that they want to build a strong, democratic society.

Hope Chigudu works for the Zimbabwe Women's Resource Centre and Network, Harare.

The author uses rhetorical questions to illustrate her point. This kind of phrasing carries more emphasis than a simple statement.

The author highlights a complaint that foreign aid often comes on condition that the receiver reforms its political system or its economic system (under so-called structural adjustment programs), or agrees to buy the exports of the donor country. Do you believe that aid should come without strings, or is it reasonable for donors to expect something in return for their help?

NAILA KABEER

Sometimes. A lot of us who were very much for aid as a tool for development have become a bit disillusioned about how effectively it has been used.

Along with the move to private enterprise, it is non-governmental organizations (NGOs) which have been identified as healthy, rather than the state. Everyone is very critical of the Government of India, say, for its failure to deliver effectively to the poorest of the poor, to low-caste people and to women. The reason they are so critical is because it has been documented—it's out there in the public domain, it's published. When we come to NGO evaluation—nothing. Absolutely nothing!

'Gender' has served a lot of these organizations in the same way as 'empowerment' and 'participation', as a trendy label. Women, as long as they suffer from gender subordination, are not going to be a politically volatile category to work with. 'You need people to do free community healthcare for you? Right! We'll get the women. You need people to plant trees for you for free? We'll get the women.'

Some countries, notably India, have a "caste" system in which the population is made up of hereditary groups, or castes, comprising people who typically do similar types of work. The castes form a rank structure in society, with high castes considered socially superior to low castes.

Toward aid as an emergency measure only?

We do not want aid to be an accepted feature of North/South relationships into the indefinite future. We would like a world where aid is limited to humanitarian crisis, conflict situations, rather than an integral aspect of development. Because aid does breed dependency, it is always on the terms of the giver. But if you were to pull aid out of Africa or Bangladesh completely tomorrow, I don't know if anyone on the Left would be prepared to take on the responsibility for what might happen. The Left got it wrong because they forgot that issues around basic needs don't take care of themselves in very poor countries.

Naila Kabeer has written extensively on gender and development and is a Fellow of the Institute of Development Studies, University of Sussex.

Summary

Helena Cobban believes that the United States should increase its overseas development aid contribution—and should do it fast, "as an urgent part of our antiterror campaign." Cobban argues that the 30-year decline in U.S. aid has helped create a climate of despair in poor countries, a climate in which groups such as the Taliban and Al Qaeda "have flourished." She asserts that there are millions of people in these countries who need to feel they have a "stake in the stability of the world system," and that aid is part of the answer. She cites the example of Afghanistan, which could, Cobban believes, once more subside "into warlordism, opium production, and terrorism" without adequate assistance. Cobban points to Mozambique as a country in which aid is showing results and calls on the United States to make a "U-turn on aid."

Alex de Waal, on the other hand, claims that aid "is essentially a Western, Anglo-Saxon model of charitable endeavour that's being imposed on the rest of the world." He argues that the more charitable effort there is, the less political action—and it is through political action that civil wars and famines will be resolved. He also believes that people are responsible for famines, and they should be held to account. Hope Chigudu, meanwhile, maintains that aid rarely reaches the people who need it, those administering it often having only their own best interests at heart. Also, aid is often given with conditions attached. Those conditions are dictated by the donor nations but may not necessarily work to the advantage of those in need. Naila Kabeer admits to some disillusionment about how aid has been used. She looks forward to a world in which aid is a response to crises and not a fact of life in the relationship between rich and developing nations. Aid leads to dependency and "is always on the terms of the giver."

FURTHER INFORMATION:

 Books:

Brainard, Lael, et al., *The Other War: Global Poverty and the Millennium Challenge Account*. Washington, D.C.: Brookings Institution Press, 2003.

Lancaster, Carol, *Transforming Foreign Aid: United States Assistance in the 21st Century*. Washington, D.C.: Institute for International Economics, 2000.

Sogge, David, *Give and Take: What's the Matter with Foreign Aid?* New York: Zed Books, 2002.

 Useful websites:

www.usaid.gov
United States Agency for International Development site.
www.undp.org
United Nations Development Program site.

The following debates in the Pro/Con series may also be of interest:

In this volume:

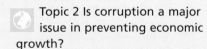 Topic 2 Is corruption a major issue in preventing economic growth?

Topic 3 Is good governance key to poverty reduction?

Topic 7 Will the Millennium Challenge Account foster sustainable development?

SHOULD RICH COUNTRIES DONATE A SET PERCENTAGE OF THEIR GNP TO AID?

YES: The UN recommends 0.7 percent of GNP, and few countries contribute that much

YES: Granting aid may also be in the interests of the donor country's economy or national security

QUANTITY
Should rich countries give more aid to poor countries?

PRAGMATISM
Are there reasons other than moral ones for giving aid?

NO: Because of corruption and inefficiency aid already often does not reach those who need it most

NO: The aim of aid is to eradicate poverty and enable development, not to create alliances and export markets

SHOULD RICH COUNTRIES DONATE A SET PERCENTAGE OF THEIR GNP TO AID?

KEY POINTS

YES: The "haves" have a duty to help the "have nots"

YES: Despite doubts about its effects, aid has brought visible results in some receiving countries

HUMANITARIANISM
Should rich countries contribute aid at all?

NO: Aid leads to dependency in the receiving nations and stifles entrepreneurship

NO: Not if it comes with conditions attached, such as the imposition of western values in the receiving nations

85

Topic 7

WILL THE MILLENNIUM CHALLENGE ACCOUNT FOSTER SUSTAINABLE DEVELOPMENT?

YES

"THE MCA PROMOTES SOUND ECONOMIC POLICIES"
ECONOMIC PERSPECTIVES (ELECTRONIC JOURNAL OF THE U.S. DEPARTMENT OF STATE)
VOL. 8, NO. 2, MARCH 2003
E. ANTHONY WAYNE

NO

"THE MILLENNIUM CHALLENGE ACCOUNT: UNLEARNING HOW TO MAKE AID WORK?"
WORLD HUNGER NOTES, AUGUST 6, 2003
ALDO CALIARI

INTRODUCTION

The Millennium Challenge Account (MCA) is a U.S. initiative to help reduce poverty and raise living standards in developing nations. Under the plan the world's richest economy provides money and other aid to foster democratic government, free trade markets, and investment in health and education in the poorest countries.

To this end the United States committed $5 billion of federal money over the three fiscal years 2004–2006. The MCA is not a straightforward overseas aid package, however. In return for financial assistance the United States expects the nations that receive it to satisfy 16 criteria that show measurable progress toward just government, economic freedom, and social welfare programs for their citizens. Some of the requirements are flexible, but two are compulsory:

For a country to qualify, its annual inflation must be below 20 percent, and any country scoring below average on a corruption index is automatically ineligible for assistance.

The rationale for the conditions is derived from bitter previous experience, in which aid funds were diverted to ends that were illegal, indefensible, or both. A leading case in point was the Iran–Contra affair of the 1980s, in which some of the money raised by secret U.S. arms sales to Iran (in the hope of appeasing that hostile nation) was—also secretly—diverted to help the Nicaraguan "contra" rebels at a time when Congress had expressly prohibited such aid.

One MCA objective is to make emergent nations self-sufficient by enabling them to keep more of the money they generate domestically, thus reducing "capital flight," which occurs when nationals of one country transfer their money into a foreign currency in order to avoid an anticipated devaluation of their own. Research has shown that the citizens of many poor countries have substantial financial resources that they are unwilling to plow back into their domestic economies because they have no confidence in their unstable governments: The MCA seeks to revive this "dead capital" by creating confidence in the local rule of law.

"If our assistance is not making a difference, or if we cannot measure our results to know what difference we have made, then we have to change our approach. We owe that to the people of Africa."

—PAUL O'NEILL,

U.S. TREASURY SECRETARY (2002)

The MCA also reflects the economic doctrine prevalent in the United States, that unrestricted markets expand trade, thus encouraging investment and accelerating growth. Each country's openness in trade is measured on an index compiled by the Heritage Foundation, a Washington, d.c.-based conservative think-tank.

To become eligible for MCA funding, countries must receive a clean bill of macroeconomic health from the International Monetary Fund (IMF). In addition to the inflation requirement

they should have a three-year budget deficit that is less than that of other comparable economies. The World Bank Institute's Indicator of Regulatory Quality is used to determine whether each country has a fair and transparent business regulatory system.

Supporters of President George W. Bush, who introduced the MCA in March 2002, regard the initiative as a significant step toward greater global prosperity and security. Yet critics point out that the criteria that need to be satisfied for a nation to receive MCA funding are entirely determined by the United States and argue that the chosen yardsticks for eligibility may be wrong.

For example, the strict rule that a nation may be considered for the MCA only if its inflation is below a certain rate is, they say, arbitrary and ignores the fact that in some cases, the inflation target may be met only by denial of civil liberties and other forms of repression. Inflexible MCA criteria also fail to account for individual differences between economies—an inflation rate that will cripple one country may be sustainable by another. Similarly, some nations will fail the MCA requirement that a certain percentage (determined by the World Bank) of their children complete primary school because their governments will have had to cut their education budgets in order to achieve the stipulated inflation rate. The MCA is also based on the premise that trade liberalization is necessarily conducive to growth. This is not universally accepted as true—numerous recent studies have concluded that adequate export markets are also essential, and that a country's domestic industry must be able to withstand competition.

The following articles look at the issues raised by the MCA.

THE MCA PROMOTES SOUND ECONOMIC POLICIES
E. Anthony Wayne

In 2003 E. Anthony Wayne was assistant secretary of state for economic and business affairs in the administration of President George W. Bush.

YES

✓ In announcing the Millennium Challenge Account (MCA) initiative last March, President Bush reconfirmed the commitment of the United States to bring hope and opportunity to the world's poorest people and called for a new compact for development defined by greater accountability for rich and poor nations alike. To fulfill our part of the compact the United States, with Congressional approval, will increase its core development assistance by $5 billion through the MCA—an increase of 50 percent— over the next three years. The President has submitted this new program to Congress for its authorization and appropriation of funds. These funds, the President said, will be "devoted to projects in nations that govern justly, invest in their people, and encourage economic freedom."

See www. whitehouse.gov/ news/releases/2002/ 03/20020314-7.html for the full text of the president's speech.

Aptly named, this initiative challenges developed and developing countries to work together as real partners to establish a new results-based paradigm for economic development. It aims to tackle one of the most vexing problems of our times—how to support lasting improvements in living standards and reduce poverty in the poorest nations of the developing world.

Providing incentives and seeking results

Why might it benefit the United States to spur development abroad?

Development doesn't just "happen," no matter how much money you throw at it. From over 30 years of experience in attempting to spur development growth abroad, we have learned several simple lessons. Development requires economic growth. Economic growth occurs when people and their governments respond to economic incentives....

We know that aid alone cannot lead to sustainable economic growth. Most of the developing world already possesses substantial assets that could be mobilized to promote their economic development. For a country to build on its wealth, however, that wealth must stay at home. For this to happen, countries must attract capital and put in place economic incentives to discourage capital flight. Estimates of sub-Saharan African country external assets, for example, exceed the stock of their external debt—a sure indication of capital flight. The MCA will promote a sound investment climate that can help pull some of this capital back to Africa.

Trade and investment flows dwarf the MCA's $5 billion and the $50 billion given by all donors in official development assistance each year. Developing countries exported close to $2 trillion in goods and services in 2001. Foreign investment flows to and among developing countries amount to $180–200 billion annually. And, of course, the biggest source of capital are the hardworking people of developing countries themselves, who produce goods and services valued at over $6 trillion dollars each year and savings amounting to over $1 trillion. The MCA will provide incentives and practical support to promote the sound economic policies and build the capacity that developing countries need to tap productively these far greater sources of development finance.

The export performance of developing countries is very unevenly spread. Just three countries—China, South Korea, and Taiwan—account for $656 billion of exports, about a third of this total, whereas 23 countries in sub-Saharan Africa have exports valued at some $40 billion among them.

Encouraging economic freedom

The link between development progress and governments that support freer markets, individual liberties, and effective institutions is robust. Sustainable development also takes hold when good governance is joined with a dynamic private sector. A vibrant private sector gives free rein to human creativity, fostering innovation and improving the living standard of everyday people. The most vital resources a country possesses are the skills and entrepreneurial spirit of its citizens. Unfortunately, domestic economic resources and capital have all too often been squandered, sometimes by conflict, but also by economic policies that do not give individual families and firms the proper incentives to save and invest in their future, and to innovate and engage in productive enterprise.

These are the values that underlie the U.S. economic system. Will they necessarily also work for other nations?

To qualify for the MCA, each MCA candidate will need to encourage economic freedom through good macroeconomic governance, an efficient regulatory system, an open trade regime, and a healthy climate for business investment. The MCA will then help qualifying countries boost their economic growth by providing grants to productivity-enhancing areas such as agricultural development and private enterprise, building trade and investment capacity, and investing in health and education.

"Good macroeconomic governance" includes such things as a transparent tax system, policies that control inflation, and predictably low rates of interest to enable borrowers to take on affordable long-term debt in order to invest.

Good macroeconomic governance

Governments help set the stage for lasting economic development through their macroeconomic policies. The

MCA recognizes this and assesses potential MCA countries on two indicators of macroeconomic health. It will give credit to countries whose inflation rate, based on IMF data, is less than 20 percent and whose three-year budget deficit is less than most other peer countries.

MCA recipient countries provide a supportive economic environment for their private sectors with prudent monetary and fiscal policies. Prudence in these areas reduces currency risk, helps attract foreign investment, and allows domestic enterprises to make long-term investments…. The fundamental elements of good fiscal governance reflect transparency and accountability. They begin with the honest administration of public funds through a transparent budget process—expenditures must be subject to public audit and accountability. Government deficits can lead to higher interest rates, which "crowd out" private sector investment projects. Furthermore, high deficits often lead developing governments to pressure financial institutions to buy government debt, which can erode the stability of the financial system. Government policies are pro-growth when they have limited control of the economy and let the free market flourish in playing its essential role in signaling how to allocate resources….

"Buying government debt" happens when governments issue bonds at a fixed interest rate to raise money. While this enables governments to raise capital for investment, they also have to raise further capital to pay the interest on the bonds.

An open trade regime

Experience shows that opening markets and expanding trade and investment can accelerate growth. Open markets and access to trade unleash creativity and know-how, multiply economic opportunities, and generate self-sustaining growth and investment cycles. Trade has helped nations as diverse as Singapore and Chile create economic opportunities for millions of their citizens. The MCA looks to the Heritage Foundation's Trade Policy Index to measure a country's trade openness….

The fourth Ministerial Conference of the World Trade Organization (WTO) was held in Doha, Qatar, from November 9 to 14, 2001. See www.wto.org/english/thewto_e/minist_e/min01_e/min01_e.htm for reports on the conference.

The Doha Development Round, taking place under the auspices of the World Trade Organization, aims to bring down trade barriers worldwide and will create for developing countries vast new opportunities to trade with each other and with developed economies. A central focus of the Doha Round is to work with the countries of the developing world to ensure that they are able to fully participate in the global trading system to expand their trade in agricultural goods in order to round out their diets and alleviate famine. The United States stands as a strong trade leader, exporting and importing over $450 billion in products from the developing world every year. That is more than eight times the amount these countries receive in aid from all sources. We will work with MCA recipient governments to increase their openness to trade, seize additional trade opportunities, and gain the growth benefits.

A healthy climate for business investment

Productive investment is essential for development. MCA development funds will flow toward countries that create a positive business environment for domestic and foreign investment. Since foreign direct investment not only brings capital but can also bring skilled management, new technology, good environmental practices, and knowledge of foreign markets, it is an especially prized development vehicle. Research evidence shows that where good governance and sound economic policies are in place, each dollar of foreign aid invested attracts two dollars of private investment. For business ventures—whether foreign, domestic or joint venture in origin—to be viable, the regulatory environment established by the host government must be conducive to their profitable operation.

If these conditions are followed, companies operating in MCA-receiving countries will be able to operate profitably for their owners. Does it necessarily follow that the populations of those countries will become better off as a result?

Rule of law

While the rule of law is an essential and measurable MCA indicator of governing justly, it also has a profound influence on a country's economic freedom. Sound, predictable and transparent legal systems must exist to provide the foundation for business confidence and the protection of property rights....

Achieving development

President Bush concluded his announcement of the Millennium Challenge Account initiative with a typical Americanism:"The bottom line for us, and for our developing country partners, is how much development they are achieving." The MCA initiative will only succeed if we select partners that have put in place the policies that allow growth to take place, undertake programs that address the key bottlenecks to development, and hold to the agreed benchmarks that measure progress toward achieving agreed objectives. By requiring these policies in order to qualify for MCA funds and tracking the funds through successful development programs, the Millennium Challenge Account will promote incentives for sound economic policies that will result in economic growth and prosperity in the countries that join us in rising to the challenge.

To meet these conditions, countries must have an effective legislature and institutions to enforce the rule of law and maintain a consistent policy. This would rule out many countries that most desperately need help, such as the Congo, Liberia, or Afghanistan. How do you think the United States should assist those countries?

THE MILLENNIUM CHALLENGE ACCOUNT: UNLEARNING HOW TO MAKE AID WORK?
Aldo Caliari

The author, Aldo Caliari, is a legal research scholar for the Center of Concern, an organization providing information on social justice. He specializes in human rights issues.

The amount of funding on offer has been queried. The president's budget of February 2003 only requested $4 billion for the MCA for the whole period 2004–2006 (40 percent of the expected level). The Congressional Budget Office estimated that the actual amount spent in that period would be just $1.7 billion.

See http://usinfo. state.gov/journals/ ites/0303/ijee/ toc.htm for more detailed information on the MCA criteria.

NO

In March 2002, a few days before the Financing for Development Summit (FFD), President Bush announced his initiative to create the Millennium Challenge Account (MCA). The proposal called for gradually increasing U.S. overseas development assistance over a period of three years, beginning in FY 2004. By FY 2006, the annual amount of U.S. foreign aid would have increased about 50 percent to around $5 billion....[The] Bush Administration announced that the recipients would be those countries that were committed to 1) sound economic policies (economic freedom), 2) ruling justly (good governance), and 3) investing in their people (health and education).

The announcement of the MCA was aimed at appeasing criticism of the obstructionist position that the U.S. had taken throughout the rest of the FFD conference process by showing some willingness to make a concession, even if only in unilateral terms.... The proposal, presenting the most detailed description of the MCA selection criteria available so far, offers reasons to be deeply concerned about its likely impact on the recipient countries.

General concerns

According to the proposal, the MCA recipients will be selected based on a measurement of performance according to 16 criteria grouped into three clusters, each of them covering one of the policy areas originally outlined by the President's March 2002 announcement. To qualify, a country must score above the median on half of the criteria in each policy area. There are two exceptions: for a country to qualify, its inflation must be below a pre-specified rate and a country not scoring above the median in the anti-corruption criterion cannot qualify.

The approach to the selectivity on which the MCA so heavily relies is very troubling. Such selectivity implies that aid is more effective in producing results when directed to countries that have in place "good policies" which is, of course, true.

The question, however, gets tricky as soon as one begins trying to determine what those "good" policies are and who has the right and the knowledge to decide what is "good." For example, there is widespread agreement today that there is no such thing as a universal model of development. Different countries have developed using different policies. Hence, there is [a] need to allow countries the policy space to discern their own mix of policies, tailored to their respective endowments and their social and political circumstances. But the MCA assumes that there is a one-size-fits-all set of policies that is "good" for all countries everywhere and acts as a precondition for growth.

It is also widely accepted that policies can only be successful when they are owned by the government and the society in a country. However, it is clear that under the MCA proposal, a country whose government and society have achieved a democratic consensus on a set of policies that they find suitable might not be eligible for aid unless the policies they "own" reflect the U.S. government's model policies.

An additional problem is that the proposed MCA selectivity does not address the contradictions among the different indicators. For example, many of the economic policies a country needs to implement to qualify under "economic freedom" can only be implemented in a climate of repression and by curtailment of the civil liberties and political freedoms that are essential to approval under the criteria for "good governance," as the experience of several developing countries has shown. As another example, "primary education completion rates," assessed under "investing in people," have declined in many countries due to implementation of budget cuts needed to meet the kind of budget deficit targets that are assessed under "economic freedom." A critical assessment of more specific MCA indicators that would be used to rate countries on each policy area is important from a social justice perspective.

Do you think the United States should accept other countries' decisions about their internal policy even if they conflict with U.S. perceptions of what is good? Should the United States still give aid to such countries? See Volume 8, U.S. Foreign Policy, Topic 9 Should the United States give aid to developing countries irrespective of their politics?

Cuts in health and education spending in Nicaragua in the 1990s are an example of the negative impact of these priorities on the poorest people in aid-receiving countries. See www.jubilee2000uk.org/jubilee2000/features/health0801.html for more information.

Sound economic policies

Some of the indicators under this cluster closely resemble the neoliberal policies that have spread through the developing world via the lending programs of the World Bank and the IMF for the last twenty years. Not only have such policies promoted little in terms of economic growth, but they have also led to disastrous social and environmental impacts. Some specific indicators under this cluster are:

Trade policy: The proposed indicator is an index of economic freedom developed by the Heritage Foundation. Using this indicator amounts to adhering to the view that trade liberalization is always conducive to growth. Yet, this notion has become severely contested even by mainstream economists who have brought to light the serious flaws of the research that underpinned it. New analyses have highlighted that, in order to have a positive impact on the economy, open trade reforms must be well-sequenced and paced, done on a selective basis, and in the context of a national development strategy. The need to consider other factors like the availability of markets for exports, the ability of domestic industry to withstand competition, and the ability of the state to support domestic entrepreneurs and regulate unfair competition has also been highlighted.

The Heritage Foundation is a prominent conservative think-tank, based in Washington, D.C. See www.heritage. org/research/ features/index/ for an online version of its "Index of Economic Freedom."

Inflation rate: Only countries with an inflation rate below 20 percent would be eligible for assistance. Although a low inflation is in general terms healthy for an economy, there is no consensus on how much is too much, particularly given the tradeoffs between level of inflation on the one hand and employment and growth of output on the other.

Country credit rating: Country credit ratings are assessments of the policy environment in a country that are prepared by private agencies to advise investors. A crucial issue with credit rating agencies is that, in spite of the large influence they have on investors' decisions, they remain largely unaccountable. Moreover, the lack of transparency of their assessments has become a major problem for developing countries with large stocks of foreign investment. These countries have seen their attempts to put in place policies enjoying wide support among the population thwarted by negative assessments of risk that threaten to trigger an investors' exit from the country. Using credit ratings as one of the indicators for awarding aid would institutionalize and extend the scope of the damage caused by the practices of these agencies.

An example of that process occurred in March 2002 when the credit rating agency Standard & Poor's announced that it was revising its credit outlook on Venezuela to negative. This was in response to President Hugo Chavez's reforms, which enjoyed wide support among Venezuela's poorest population.

Ruling justly

The indicators under this cluster are also highly controversial. Some studies ... show that today's developed countries became developed when they had weaker institutions than most developing countries have today. They also show that the institutions of today's developed countries have evolved in different ways and taken different shapes. So, even if we agreed that good governance is a necessary precondition for economic development, that does not necessarily imply an Anglo-American model of governance. Leaving aside this debate, a core problem with the measurement of good governance is the potential it offers for subjective and politicized judgments. When the country issuing the judgments has, like the U.S., a history of using aid to reward allies and promote national geopolitical goals, an added dose of skepticism is in order. Measurement of governance thus poses significant challenges. How to discriminate between the institutions that may be legitimate in a particular country's social, cultural and political environment and those that belong to a particular, Anglo-American model of governance? How to ensure that the assessment is objective across countries?... The fact that with two indicators, "civil liberties" and "political freedoms," the proposed indexes are developed by the U.S. conservative organization Freedom House and are based on a paradigm that excludes economic, social, cultural, and communal rights raises serious concerns in this regard.

Do the motives of aid donors matter? Is there such a thing as negative aid?

See www. freedomhouse.org/ research/freeworld/ 2000/methodology. htm for the criteria that Freedom House uses to assess civil liberties and political rights.

Of particular importance under this cluster is the criterion on corruption because, as explained above, it is a pass/fail indicator. Corruption would be measured according to an index developed by the World Bank Institute. This index has been criticized for the unreliability of the data on which it is based, and the World Bank team that prepared it called repeatedly for caution in its application. There has also been note of the fact that it only emphasizes corruption in the public sector, while leaving unmentioned the dubious conduct of the private companies that are on the other end of the bribes reportedly received by public officials....

See www. worldbank.org/ html/schools/issues/ corrupt.htm for a World Bank page of information for schools on its work in monitoring corruption.

A social justice challenge

The Millennium Challenge Account proposal comes at a time of widespread declines in overseas development assistance. Without a doubt, as its implementation advances, it is not only going to raise U.S. aid levels, it is also going to have a strong impact on the way that U.S. development assistance is delivered. And because of the U.S. position in the world, the MCA is also likely to catalyze changes in the way that multilateral development assistance, in general, is delivered. It thus comes as a great tragedy that in such an influential initiative the Bush Administration has chosen to ignore the lessons from the past regarding what works and what does not in terms of promoting sustainable and equitable development....

Summary

In the first article E. Anthony Wayne is clearly of the view that the Millennium Challenge Account (MCA) will foster sustainable development. He states unequivocally that it will bring hope and opportunity to the world's poorest people. He explains that the MCA is a results-based solution to the chronic problem of making the world's least developed nations profitable and self-sustaining. He says that aid alone is not the answer, since money may leave a country as quickly as it arrives unless economic growth and political stability are already in place to encourage and facilitate reinvestment. He outlines the United States' main eligibility criteria for MCA assistance and quotes approvingly President George W. Bush's statement that "the bottom line for us, and for our developing country partners, is how much development they are achieving."

Aldo Caliari, the author of the second article, questions many of the assumptions on which the MCA program is based. He notes that funds will be made available only to nations that can show a track-record of economic freedom, good governance, and adequate investment in health and education, but doubts the validity of the indicators by which they are measured. He concludes that the MCA is based too much on the idea that what works for the United States and other industrialized democracies will also bring prosperity to the nations of the developing world. He says that this contention is flawed, and that there is ample evidence that different economies and political systems can succeed legitimately in quite different ways from the Anglo-American model.

FURTHER INFORMATION:

Books:

Brainard, Lael, Carol Graham, Nigel Purvis, Steven Radelet, and Gayle Smith, *The Other War: Global Poverty and the Millennium Challenge Account*. Washington, D.C.: Brookings Institution, 2003.

Radelet, Steve, *Challenging Foreign Aid: A Policymaker's Guide to the Millennium Challenge Account*. Washington, D.C.: Center for Global Development, 2003.

Sen, Amartya, *Development as Freedom*. New York: Knopf and Oxford University Press, 1999.

Useful websites:

www.wto.org/english/res_e/statis_e/its2002_e/its02_byregion_e.htm
WTO's most recent world trade statistics by region.
www.mca.gov/
Features press releases and background information.

The following debates in the Pro/Con series may also be of interest:

In this volume:

Topic 2 Is corruption a major issue in preventing economic growth?

Topic 3 Is good governance key to poverty reduction?

Topic 6 Should rich countries donate a set percentage of their GNP to aid?

WILL THE MILLENNIUM CHALLENGE ACCOUNT FOSTER SUSTAINABLE DEVELOPMENT?

YES: The MCA will raise the whole economy of target countries, benefiting everybody, not just elites

YES: It is important that any aid recipients are accountable and observe the rule of law

TARGETED AID
Will the MCA help the right people?

FREEDOM AND GOVERNANCE
Does the MCA use the right selection criteria?

WILL THE MILLENNIUM CHALLENGE ACCOUNT FOSTER SUSTAINABLE DEVELOPMENT?

KEY POINTS

NO: The MCA targets countries already doing well, but ignores those most desperately in need of help

NO: MCA criteria are not inclusive enough. Poor countries that meet some and not all criteria should still be eligible to receive aid.

YES: They are independent of both donor and recipient governments, so provide a reliable picture

YES: Criteria are based on universal ideas of human rights, freedoms, and the desire for prosperity

CREDIT RATING
Are credit-rating agencies the best way to assess risk?

ALLOWING DIVERSITY
Do the MCA criteria account for different cultural traditions?

NO: They are only concerned with the narrow interests of western investors, not recipient countries' poorest people

NO: There is no such thing as a universal model of development. MCA criteria are an Anglo-American outlook on good government and ignore diversity in other traditions.

Topic 8

WOULD INCREASED INVESTMENT IN EDUCATION REDUCE POVERTY IN DEVELOPING COUNTRIES?

YES

"CLASS WARS"

NEW INTERNATIONALIST, ISSUE 315, AUGUST 1999

OLIVER ROBERTSON, AMINA KIBRIA, JUANITA ROSENIOR, DUANE O'GARRO, AND KIERRA BOX

NO

"POVERTY REDUCTION IN DEVELOPING COUNTRIES: THE ROLE OF PRIVATE ENTERPRISE"

FINANCE AND DEVELOPMENT (A QUARTERLY MAGAZINE OF THE IMF), JUNE 2001

GUY PFEFFERMANN

INTRODUCTION

During the Global Action week of the Global Campaign for Education (GCE), August 2003, spearheaded by NetAID, Kofi Annan, the UN secretary-general, declared: "The fact that millions are still deprived of [education]—most of them girls—should fill us all with shame."

Many politicians, economists, and educationalists share Annan's opinion; they believe that education leads to employment opportunities, the prospect of an income, security, a sense of well-being, and respect for human rights. An educated workforce transforms the economic prospects of a country by making it able to break out of the trap of relying on exports of raw materials and foodstuffs, and invest instead in high-value industries. An example of this is India, which has become a world leader in the telecom and computer-service industries.

Critics of more investment in education in developing countries argue that too much emphasis has been placed on education's role in poverty reduction and economic growth. They claim that education is a luxury for most people, and having enough to eat is a higher priority. But is that true?

Povertynet, an information agency of the World Bank, defines poverty as being characterized by hunger, lack of shelter, inadequate medical care, insufficient schools, illiteracy, an absence of job opportunities, and a fear for the future. One example of the potential of better educational opportunities in helping to alleviate the effects of poverty in the developing world can be seen in their effect on health. In April 2003 the GCE reported that babies born to mothers without formal education are at least twice as likely to suffer from malnutrition or to die before age five as babies born to mothers who completed primary school. Not only does education reduce infant mortality, but it increases the chances that children of educated parents will be educated too.

"The question is how to distribute most generally and equally the property of the world. As a rule, where education is most general the distribution of property is most general."

—RUTHERFORD B. HAYES,

19TH PRESIDENT (1877–1881)

The inequality in education available in developed and developing countries was acknowledged in 2000 at the World Education Forum. Education campaigners and representatives from around the world gathered in Dakar, Senegal, and drew up a plan called Education For All (EFA). Agreed to by 180 nations, EFA outlined certain Millennium Development Goals (MDGs) to be achieved by 2015. Based around the general intention to have all children everywhere in education, EFA set out to expand early childhood care and education, provide free and compulsory education of good quality, promote the acquisition of life skills by adolescents and youth, increase adult literacy by 50 percent, eliminate gender disparities by 2005, and enhance education quality in general.

Aid in the form of financial investment is one way these objectives are to be achieved. One investor in education and a supporter of EFA is the World Bank. It is the world's largest external funder of education, with 158 education projects in 83 countries. The World Bank's stated belief is that education empowers poor people to take control of their own lives.

Critics disagree, claiming that aid only reaches those who need it when a country pursues sensible economic policies, and that economic growth is more fundamental to development. For financial aid to have a lasting effect, critics argue the recipient country has to be committed to economic reform.

Another aspect is the number of children in developing countries who are forced to work to contribute to their family income—sometimes even helping to keep their families from starving. In these cases eating takes precedence over education. The WHO points out that in developing countries low wages mean children are under pressure to be breadwinners, thus denying them the time to receive any education. Educational organizations are determined to make sure that education is seen as a right, not just a privilege.

The following articles provide two sides of the debate. The first extract is from an article by young participants in Children's Express, a program of learning through journalism. They argue that education is essential for people to lift themselves out of poverty, using examples from a study trip they took to Tanzania. In the second article Guy Pfeffermann, chief executive of the International Finance Corporation, a member organization of the World Bank, argues that focusing on economic growth is the key to reducing poverty.

CLASS WARS
Oliver Robertson, Amina Kibria, et al.

Until the 1980s primary education in Tanzania was free and compulsory. In the 1980s the system began to decline as government trade revenues fell and debt repayments increased. Fees were introduced, but the income was often absorbed by general expenditure without benefiting education. See www.worldbank.org/wbi/attackingpoverty/events/Tanz_0602/casestudy_tanz.doc for further background.

Compare this to your own school situation. Is sports equipment a necessity for a good education? What difference does graffiti make?

YES

Kasim Masu is nine years old and sleeps on a step outside a shop. When we caught up with him at 7am in the Youth Cultural and Information Centre (YCIC), set back from the dusty streets in downtown Dar-es-Salaam [capital of Tanzania], he was ironing his uniform for school. Funded largely by overseas agencies such as Christian Aid and Comic Relief, the Centre aims to develop sufficient confidence, trust and skills in young people to enable them to take control of their lives.

Kasim is just one beneficiary of the project's pre-school literacy booster classes and their bursaries for school fees. Faced with fees of at least 10,000 Tanzanian shillings ($16) a year for primary schooling, street kids and other children living in poverty have a fight on their hands to secure a way in. One of the most valuable aspects of YCIC is that it acts as a bridge, enabling vulnerable kids to make the transition to school.

Like all the young people we spoke to, getting a decent education was top of Kasim's list of wants. His personal ambition? He wanted to be clever so that he could become a pilot. Oliver [Robertson] commented: "It was as though it was his dream literally to fly away from his current life, and he saw education as the way to do it. At one point, he felt he'd be able to do it, and then he said he wouldn't, and then he said he would again. I don't really know what to think of his chances."

Education without resources

Though stoical, Kasim points out how a lack of funds for state schooling undermines children's own efforts: "There are about 40 children in my class. We have some pencils, chalk and exercise books. But we have no sports equipment, the toilets are graffitied and there is no glass in the windows."

"We don't have enough, but we just keep going with what we have. Parents pay for some things, but the Government should pay for it all because they have more money than parents like mine. If your parents can't pay for equipment, you get expelled from school. I have friends who haven't been able to pay their fees. That makes me feel bad."

But the cost of schooling is not the only factor inhibiting the capacity of children like Kasim to learn. He told us that he has only one simple meal each day: "I eat nothing until I go home when I have ugali [a stiff porridge made from flour and water]. I would like to eat more, but that's what I get so that's enough. I eat the same thing every day with seven of my friends. If I can't pay, sometimes my friends share. Otherwise, I go without."

Do you think it is possible to benefit from education if you are malnourished? If not, does this mean that food is a more basic priority than education?

To people living in the developed world, the enormity of improving the education system in a country such as Tanzania, where six times the education budget is spent on debt repayments, may seem overwhelming. But Kasim's suggestions were modest. "I would like a bigger classroom with an electric fan and more desks. I want to be more comfortable," he shrugged.

His school's problems made the constant complaints we hear about British schools seem distinctly less significant. Kierra said: "We moan when we have to share a textbook between two of us, but in Tanzania, there's only one book to a class and it's often outdated."

What should be the priority in education? Is there any point in learning from outdated textbooks?

Lost legacy

On the other side of town, we talked to half-a-dozen teenage girls who lived in rusting iron container ships in the Ferry area of the harbour. They scrape together a living through prostitution and feel their lives are the legacy of an education system that has failed them. When asked if there is a way out of prostitution, they said, "There isn't, because we haven't been to school. We can't do anything else."

Some had their education terminated at an early age when a parent died. Others came from families who simply didn't have the money to send them to school. One girl told us: "When we did go to school, we didn't have uniforms, we didn't have books, we didn't have pencils. We didn't have anything to make us happy. We wanted to be like the others. We wanted to be able to compete with the others who go to school with uniforms and things like that."

Yet, despite the great sadness we felt listening to the girls' stories, we discovered that their enthusiasm to learn how to better their lives wasn't dampened by the obvious lack of opportunities to do so. They said: "We would like to proceed with our schooling. We would like to study in America. We don't know anything about it. We just know the white people we see coming from America have a good life. It would be better if we were there. Here it is a hard place, a horrible place."

Do you think that people from overseas have an oversimple view of countries such as the United States? Would studying in the United States be the answer to their problems?

The second stage of our journey saw us travel to Morogoro, a large town about four hours' drive north-west of Dar-es-Salaam. There we discovered that fee-charging isn't the only major barrier to education. If a child isn't enrolled in school by the time they are seven or eight, it turns out they don't get another chance. We couldn't find out why the Government is so inflexible on this issue, but it doesn't seem unreasonable to guess that the policy is a cock-eyed mechanism for reducing the national education bill.

Another reason for this policy might be that the older a child gets, the more likely it is that their parents (and perhaps the government) expect them to start contributing to the economy by working.

Streetside schooling

Fortunately, for some kids in Morogoro, there is an alternative. Psychologist and social worker Victor Mulimila runs the Streetside School, which guarantees a primary education for around 60 children. There is now enough money to pay Victor and when we met him and his pupils, they were about to move from an open-air yard, where breeze blocks were the only furniture and the seasonal rains would frequently wipe out lessons, to a purpose-built classroom.

As we had found in Dar-es-Salaam, the pupils were motivated and hard-working. Comparing their attitude to those of his own classmates, Duane was in awe. He commented: "They know what to do and how to get on with their work. I looked at their maths books and they had so many ticks! You can see from what they do and the way they speak that they are learning."

Overcoming suspicion

Things weren't always so. Prospective pupils and their relatives initially shunned Victor's attempts to recruit them. "We would walk the streets looking for kids and people shouted at us," he explained. "People said we were thieves, that we wanted to keep their kids. The children would run away and cry, thinking we wanted to take their lives. Now all that's changed, but there are still lots of kids to help. We've also noticed that, slowly, some kids have stopped coming. When you make enquiries, you find that most are breadwinners. They are sent to the streets to look for whatever they can find to feed the family at home. We want to find money to provide loans to the parents so they can start their own income-generating activities. This would enable the children to come to school instead of going back on the streets to beg."

Parents might have been hostile because they would lose the income their children would otherwise earn, and because they would have to pay fees for their education. Can you think of any other reasons why they might be hostile?

The Streetside School, like YCIC, is funded by foreign aid agencies. Victor is angry at the Government's lack of involvement. "It seems as if the Government has withdrawn its obligation to these people as far as social services like education are concerned."

Ethics vs. economics

But he saves his greatest criticism for rich countries which continue to demand debt interest payments at debilitating levels. "What we collect from taxes and other sources of income, we use to pay back our debts. Social services have been deteriorating because all the money which is supposed to pay for them is being paid to rich countries. The way I see the future, it's getting worse. We will be dying. The rich countries have to forgive all the debts—not just of Tanzania, but of all Third World countries. If they want to help, they shouldn't apply conditions that exploit us."

Victor and the other Tanzanians we spoke to may well ask whose interests the international community and its agents have at heart. When we asked Ronald Brigish, the country representative of the World Bank, what would happen were Third World debt to be cancelled, he simply said: "Very little one way or the other. The finances of the Bank would be very badly affected and we would eventually cease to exist." Nothing then, about the likes of Kasim and the girls at the Ferry. Nothing about ethics—only economics.

We probed what impact he thought the Bank's policies have on street kids. "We don't know, quite frankly," he said. He felt it was up to a community to decide whether to waive school fees for those who cannot afford to pay, that this process was "equitable in a way that protects the poor." However, he later conceded that kids like Kasim can fall through the cracks. We said surely every one of the large and growing number of street kids will fall through the cracks, and he replied: "Apparently."

The World Bank's apparent unconcern notwithstanding, the prostitutes we spoke to were clear that something had to change. "We would like to move on, but we don't have the chance to," said one. "We don't know how we see our future. The way we live means we can't predict it."

It is estimated that poor countries owe a total of about $300 billion in debt. The Jubilee 2000 campaign succeeded in getting about 15 percent of this debt canceled. Some governments, such as that of the UK, have canceled all debt owed to them, but much debt is owed to institutions such as the World Bank, which have not yet been willing to cancel what is owed to them. See www.jubileeusa.org for information on the continuing campaign to reduce or cancel this debt.

Do you think there is a danger that the world bank will block proposals that might reduce its influence even if they benefit the poor?

POVERTY REDUCTION IN DEVELOPING COUNTRIES: ... PRIVATE ENTERPRISE
Guy Pfeffermann

In the late 1990s and early 21st century people gathered to protest a broad range of ecological and antiglobalization causes at meetings of the organizations they considered responsible for the poverty of the developing world. They included the World Trade Organization and the World Bank. In 1999–2001 there were protests in Seattle, Washington, D.C., Prague, Czech Republic, and Davos in Switzerland.

In 2002 the income per head of these countries was: Norway, $31,800; Finland, $26,200; Sweden, $25,400.

NO

The positive contribution that private enterprises can make to development and poverty reduction is likely to be obvious to most readers. They would agree that, in the long term, economic development cannot occur without dynamic private companies. They would also agree that good government and efficient public administration are equally necessary. The success of Singapore shows what such a combination can achieve. Then why write an article on the subject? Many of the Seattle, Washington, D.C., Prague, and Davos protesters blame multinational corporations for retarding development, despoiling nature, and keeping wages down...

Escaping from poverty

There can be no doubt that, in today's affluent countries, poverty is far less widespread than it was in earlier times. In 1820, the average income per head in Finland, Norway, and Sweden was less than $1,000 at 1990 prices; hundreds of thousands of people emigrated from those countries to the United States, where income per head was $1,300. Today, these three countries are among the richest in the world.

It is also important to consider intergenerational changes, because income mobility can be high from generation to generation. In Brazil, for example, more than half of the persons surveyed recently who had grown up in poor families moved out of poverty. The majority of those who started their working lives in agriculture as unpaid family workers, or at age 10 or younger, are now living above the poverty line.

What has happened in Brazil has happened in the developing world as a whole. Income mobility is high, but this fact has not received much public attention. According to household income and expenditure surveys, the total number of persons whose incomes are less than $365 a year worldwide—those the World Bank calls the "absolute poor"—has not changed much since 1987. Considering the efforts made by governments and aid organizations, the stagnation of the very lowest incomes is disappointing and seems to indicate that no progress has been made in reducing poverty. However, since 1987 the population of the developing countries has increased by about one billion people. It follows that the number of persons living above the absolute poverty line has increased very substantially during the last 15 years; these persons either had never been among the "absolute poor" or had somehow succeeded in escaping absolute poverty. Examining how one billion people in the developing world stayed out of poverty or escaped it should teach us a lot about what is necessary to achieve large-scale poverty reduction.

Do you think the number of "absolute poor" today would be even lower if population growth was controlled? See Topic 13 Is population control essential in poor nations?

How do people manage to escape absolute poverty? Household surveys show that the answer, in large part, is found in each country's rate of overall economic growth. Recent research confirms beyond doubt that economic growth is a necessary condition for poverty reduction. The impact of national growth on the incomes of the poorest 20 percent of the population is about the same as it is on society as a whole. That is, a doubling of GDP over 25 years—annual growth of 2.9 percent—was found to be associated with a doubling of the poor's incomes. This robust finding is drawn from 80 countries over a period of 40 years. A sobering corollary of the analysis is that the distribution of income within these 80 countries, which is mostly highly skewed, has hardly changed in 40 years.

The data also indicate that poor people do not suffer the biggest falls in income during economic crises and that openness to foreign trade benefits poor people as much as it does other economic groups, as do respect for the rule of law and fiscal discipline. Interestingly, the data suggest that curbing high inflation benefits the poor more than the rest of society. Furthermore, contrary to the view that the poor may have benefited from growth in the past but no longer do so in today's "globalized" world economy, the analysis shows that the positive relationship between growth and poverty reduction has not changed.

This does not mean that economic crises do not affect the poor hardest. Since the poor live on incomes closer to the minimum needed for survival, a person earning $10,000 will be harder hit by a 20 percent drop in income than a person earning $100,000, even though the latter is losing ten times as many dollars.

The role of private firms

Some of the events most closely related to economic improvement are finding a job, or a relative's finding a job, or moving to a better job. Indeed, job creation is a major—probably the major—path out of poverty. The most sustainable job creation is by firms, whether they are new, very small firms or larger enterprises expanding in a growing economy. In almost all developing countries, including China, private enterprises are the main source of new jobs. These include firms in all sectors of activity, large and small firms, domestic and foreign firms. Although government jobs also contribute to income mobility, attempts at deliberate job creation, whether by central governments or by state-owned enterprises, have nearly always been unsustainable. Public enterprises tend to lose money; eventually, many either collapse or become a drain on public resources...

Private firms also contribute to development in other ways that are crucial to economic development and poverty reduction:

Public enterprises tend to lose money if they are competing with private enterprises that are more easily able to lower their costs. Natural monopolies, however, have been run profitably as public enterprises in many countries.

* In most developing countries, they generate a large portion of government tax revenues, without which there would be no sustainable base for funding public health care, education, social safety nets, agricultural research, and other critical expenditures.

This is the focus of the author's argument: Economic growth funds other social improvements, including education. But can economic growth be sustainable or effective without an educated workforce?

* In countries with competitive economies, leading private firms will constantly seek out information that has practical local uses; to remain competitive, other firms will emulate their behavior. In the process, executives and employees upgrade their human capital, productivity, and incomes, contributing to the diffusion of useful knowledge and techniques.

* Over time, competitive firms improve the quality of products and make them more affordable, thereby boosting the purchasing power of consumers, including poor consumers. Indeed, in countries such as India and Brazil, some private companies have begun to focus on the poorer segments of the population as promising new markets...

Macroeconomics is concerned with whole economic systems and the relationships between different sectors of the economy,

Business environment

What can governments do to support the creation and expansion of companies that are financially, economically, socially, and environmentally sustainable? Besides improving health care, education, and macroeconomic conditions, and encouraging competition, governments can undertake institutional reforms that ... lower the costs of doing business and thus create a more favorable business environment. Such reforms encourage activities not only by foreign investors but also—and more important—by the thousands of local entrepreneurs who want to start or expand small businesses in agriculture, services, and manufacturing.

More broadly, the pace of long-term economic progress is intimately related to the costs of doing business. So, for example, some East Asian countries have developed successfully in part because it is cheaper to ship manufacturing components by air to the east coast of the United States via Singapore than it is to ship the same components from the Caribbean, even though the Caribbean is much closer. Air freight from Singapore is extremely competitive, while governments in the Caribbean have restrictions on shipping capacity. In short, governments that improve institutions and welcome competition enhance the poverty-reducing impact of private firms.

A common policy among developing countries has been that a certain proportion of goods shipped abroad must travel on ships registered in that country to encourage the development of a domestic fleet.

The small companies—and start-up firms, in particular—that are crucial to long-term economic and social development are especially vulnerable to bad government. Poor policies and weak institutions hurt these companies more than they do others. Larger firms can better afford to protect themselves, even though protection comes at a cost. For smaller firms, "exiting" into the unregistered informal sector is often the only refuge. By discouraging enterprise creation and forcing small firms to go underground, many governments limit job creation and chances for upward social mobility. Furthermore, start-up and small enterprises are the seedbed of the middle class; the weakness of the middle class in the majority of low-income countries hampers economic and social progress.

The idea that the development of a middle class is essential for the economic growth of a country is something on which almost all economists—from Marxists to neoliberals—agree. Since one of the hallmarks of middle classes everywhere is the importance they attach to education, does that mean that education is also essential to a developing country's economy?

Making life easier for businesses

Surprisingly, business environment surveys have not been used systematically by governments and international organizations until recently, yet they map out in considerable detail "where the shoe pinches" and what concrete steps could be taken to enhance the developmental and poverty-reducing impact of private firms. Indeed, international institutions providing financial assistance to developing countries might find sectoral adjustment loans designed to improve business environments to be useful tools in poverty reduction. Such loans would support governments willing and able to invigorate their economies by taking on vested interests and so give more people opportunities to escape from poverty. Indeed, the steps required to improve the business environment offer a practical framework for examining the particular development challenges faced by individual countries. They therefore constitute an essential component of a holistic approach to development, along with macroeconomic and social policy agendas.

Summary

Reducing poverty in developing countries is a stated key aim of international agencies such as the World Bank. Is education the most essential factor in poverty reduction, or are issues like water and food security, investment, or overall economic growth more important? The preceding articles examine the debate further.

The authors of the first extract interviewed children in Tanzania to give concrete examples of how education has helped keep children off the streets and given them hope for the future. They also interviewed children whose lack of education has trapped them in a life of prostitution. The authors claim that funds are being diverted from sectors such as education in developing countries to repay their debts to rich nations. As one interviewee says: "The rich countries have to forgive all the debts … of all Third World countries. If they want to help, they shouldn't apply conditions that exploit us."

The second article is by Guy Pfeffermann, chief economist of the International Finance Corporation, an organization promoting private sector investment in developing countries. He argues that private enterprise will help reduce poverty by encouraging growth. He says that private business is "an essential component of a holistic approach to development, along with macroeconomic and social policy agendas." By focusing on private enterprise as the single most important element in economic growth, he implies that it is more fundamental to poverty reduction than education.

FURTHER INFORMATION:

Books:

Black, Richard, and White, Howard (eds.), *Targeting Development: Critical Perspectives on the Millennium Development Goals*. New York: Routledge, 2003.

Colclough, Christopher (ed.), *Marketizing Education and Health in Developing Countries: Miracle or Mirage?* New York: Clarendon Press, 1997.

Schiffer, Mirjam, and Beatrice Weder, *Firm Size and the Business Environment*. Washington, D.C.: World Bank, 2001

Useful websites:

www2.gol.com/users/bobkeim/money/debt.html *New Internationalist*'s introduction to the debt crisis.

www.uis.unesco.org/pagesen/ed.htm UNESCO's database of global education statistics.

www.oxfam.org.uk/policy/papers/educationforall/eduafr.htm Oxfam's background on the Education for All initiative.

econ.worldbank.org/files/1696_wps2587.pdf An article by David Dollar and Art Kraay.

The following debates in the Pro/Con series may also be of interest:

In this volume:

Topic 10 Are protectionist policies essential to economic growth in developing nations?

In *Human Rights*:

Topic 12 Is the UN an effective advocate for children's rights?

WOULD INCREASED INVESTMENT IN EDUCATION REDUCE POVERTY IN DEVELOPING COUNTRIES?

YES: Education enables people to learn professions, to join unions, and to earn higher wage rates and generally improve their standard of living

YES: According the World Health Organization, far fewer women receive schooling than men in developing nations. Education would go a long way to reducing inequality.

PAY
Does better education lead to higher rates of pay?

INEQUALITY
Would education reduce gender inequality?

NO: Research shows that in developing countries even people who have been schooled earn far lower incomes than people doing their equivalent jobs in industrialized nations

NO: Other factors are important in maintaining gender inequality. The Taliban's banning of women from most professional work and schools in Afghanistan shows that politics and religion play an important role too.

WOULD INCREASED INVESTMENT IN EDUCATION REDUCE POVERTY IN DEVELOPING COUNTRIES?

KEY POINTS

YES: This just fuels the divide between the educated rich, who get richer, and the illiterate poor, who are paid poor wages and live in dreadful conditions

YES: An education that emphasizes literacy, numeracy, and life skills teaches people to think for themselves

BUSINESS
Does too much investment go to private business in developing nations?

DEFINITION
Does the western idea of education apply to developing countries?

NO: The development of commerce and trade benefits all sectors of society, not just those directly involved

NO: Many jobs in the developing world are manual, so education programs should be more practically based

Topic 9

HAVE PERSISTING GENDER INEQUALITIES HINDERED GROWTH IN LATIN AMERICAN COUNTRIES?

YES

"LATIN AMERICA AND CARIBBEAN COUNTRIES MAKE PROGRESS IN GENDER EQUALITY BUT CONTINUE TO LIMIT PARTICIPATION OF WOMEN IN THE LABOR MARKET"
NEWS RELEASE NO: 2003/242/LAC, WORLD BANK, MARCH 5, 2003
DEVNEWS MEDIA CENTER

NO

FROM "WANTED: A NEW LATIN AMERICAN AGENDA FOR ECONOMIC GROWTH"
HISPANIC NEWS, APRIL 26, 2003

INTRODUCTION

Latin America is a region with valuable natural resources, yet it suffers from low economic growth and great inequality. The World Bank reported that at the beginning of the 21st century the bottom 20 percent of Brazil's population received only 2.6 percent of total national income, compared with 5.2 percent in the United States, 7.5. percent in Taiwan, and 8.2 percent in Germany.

Women in Latin America are particularly affected by inequality. In 1999, according to the UN Economic Commission for Latin America and the Caribbean, half of the female-headed households—around 20 to 30 percent of all the households in Latin America and 40 percent of those in the Caribbean—were living at or below the poverty line. Some commentators suggest that there is a link between gender and economic inequality in Latin America. "Gender disparities are very closely associated with poverty," says Elizabeth King, coauthor of a World Bank report *Engendering Development—Through Gender Equality in Rights, Resources, and Voice* (2001). The report states that countries which promote women's rights and increase their resources and schooling have faster economic growth, lower poverty rates, and less corruption than those that fail to.

More Latin American girls are receiving education than ever before, and a growing number of women are employed in the labor force. However, some critics claim that these women suffer from discrimination in the workplace and are paid lower wages than their male counterparts.

But does gender inequality hinder growth in Latin American countries? Some critics argue that ensuring

110

women have equal rights to education, jobs, pay, and land will help eliminate gender inequality and therefore foster economic growth. Furthermore, they claim that gender bias affects everyone in society, not just women.

"Societies that discriminate on the basis of gender pay a significant price—in greater poverty, [and] slower economic growth.... Societies progress more rapidly if they also adopt specific measures to narrow gender gaps."
—ANDREW MASON, COAUTHOR OF

ENGENDERING DEVELOPMENT

Some educationalists and aid agencies believe that greater investment in education would help Latin American countries improve their economic position. They assert that this correlated with better labor-enforcement laws would help reduce the incidence of child labor in the region, which the Economic Commission for Latin American Statistics estimated in 1998 totaled around 17.5 million; statistically, girls earn less than boys of the same age and suffer a greater degree of abuse.

Many economists, however, believe that gender inequality is secondary to other more important issues that prevent Latin American countries from reaching their full potential.

The economic closeness of countries in the region means that major changes in one economy can affect—adversely or beneficially—the economies of neighboring countries. In 2001 Argentina, Uruguay, and Venezuela all suffered major recessions, which, some commentators believe, resulted in the Gross Domestic Product—the total value of the goods and services produced by a country—in Latin America and the Caribbean contracting by 1.3 percent in 2002. In addition, internal economic events, including a severe banking crisis, resulted in Argentina experiencing a greater contraction (10.9 percent) in 2002. This crisis affected the exports and tourism of neighboring Uruguay, Paraguay, and Bolivia. In Venezuela, meanwhile, an unstable political situation caused a major drop in investment, high capital outflows, and a national strike at the end of 2002, all of which had a detrimental effect on its economy.

Latin American countries also suffer from external factors. Direct foreign investment fell by over $25 billion from $69 billion in 2001 to $42 billion in 2002. Economic problems in Europe and the United States also substantially reduced demand for Latin American exports between 2000 and 2002, pushing the region's export growth down substantially. Some commentators argue, however, that Chile, Colombia, Mexico, Peru, Ecuador, and most Central American countries were not as severely affected, despite low commodity prices and higher borrowing costs.

The following two articles examine in detail the question of whether gender inequality has hindered economic growth in Latin America.

LATIN AMERICA AND CARIBBEAN COUNTRIES ... PARTICIPATION OF WOMEN IN THE LABOR MARKET
DevNews Media Center

Go to www.worldbank. orglacgender for more information about the World Bank's work in the Latin America and Caribbean region.

Every year International Women's Day (IWD) is celebrated on March 8 around the world. IWD dates back to 1910, but it was influenced by the first national women's day held in the United States in 1908. The United Nations also recognizes and celebrates IWD.

YES

☑ Women in Latin America and the Caribbean have made significant advances with regard to equality but traditional social patterns continue to undermine their participation in the labor market, and hinder the ability of households to escape from poverty, a new study of the World Bank indicates.

Still much to be done

According to *Challenges and opportunities for gender equality in Latin America and the Caribbean*, prepared to commemorate International Women's Day on March 8, women have made significant improvements in education and access to the labor market. However, the report indicates that there is much to be done with regard to poverty and social exclusion, reproductive health care and protection from domestic violence. "In spite of the significant progress over the past 20 years, gender inequalities remain an obstacle to the full development of the countries in the region," said Maria Valéria Pena, Leader of the World Bank's Gender Unit for Latin America and the Caribbean.

Inequality translates into losses resulting from the unrealized potential of women's full integration in the economy, the social and economic cost of violence against women, and the loss in human capital from maternal mortality and pregnant girls, and boys who drop out of school.

The study, which describes the most important changes in the condition of women in Latin America and the Caribbean over the past two decades and the challenges, both by region and by country, points out that even though the participation of the women in the formal economy has continued to increase, there are still obstacles—especially those in rural areas and affecting indigenous women.

Have persisting gender inequalities hindered growth in Latin American countries?

A woman searches a garbage dump in Mexico City hoping to find items of value to sell.

Overall, the participation of women in the labor market continues to be much lower than that of men. In Brazil, 56 percent of women take part in the labor market; in Chile, 44 percent; Colombia 56 percent, Mexico 43 percent and Peru 55 percent, while in all of these countries the participation of men is over 88 percent.

Costa Rica is one of the most stable countries in Latin America. It is still mainly an agricultural country, but it also has strong tourism and technology sectors. The standard of living is relatively high, and land ownership is widespread. See Topic 5 Is tourism consistent with sustainable development? for further information on the influence of tourism on developing nations.

Women earn less than men

Although the salary divide between genders has narrowed considerably in many countries such as Honduras, Venezuela, Brazil, Colombia, Argentina and Mexico, women earn less than men in all countries of the region with the exception of Costa Rica. In Argentina, women earn 98 percent of what men earn, in Mexico 89 percent, in Colombia 84 percent, in Peru 80 percent, 77 percent in Brazil and Chile, in El Salvador 74 percent, and in Nicaragua 64 percent.

Factors contributing to this phenomenon include the large-scale participation of women in the service sector, which is generally the most poorly paid sector of the economy. What's more, women are generally the ones who are responsible for caring for their families, often leading to a higher turnover rate in the labor force and a preference for part-time work. "Even though Latin American women have almost reached the same level of education as men ... they continue to participate less in the labor market and earn less than men", writes María Elena Ruiz Abril, author of the report. "This is a fundamental issue that should be addressed by public policies".

If education helps improve economic position, why are women in some Latin American countries worse off than men despite being educated to the same level?

This situation is all the more acute for rural women, since they also deal with high fertility rates, a high number of dependents and lack of access to land. Although access to land has significantly increased in countries such as Colombia, Costa Rica, Honduras, Nicaragua, Chile and El Salvador, Mexico is the country with the region's biggest gender gap in land ownership, with women only holding 21 percent of all land titles.

Why do you think older women and those heading households suffer more from poverty? Go to www.census.gov to find out if the situation is the same in the United States.

The report shows that women, especially older women and heads of household, are more vulnerable to poverty. Discrimination concerning access to education and to health care puts indigenous women at a disadvantage at the same time they are fighting against poverty and social exclusion.

"In order to address poverty in Latin American households, we need policies and programs aimed at redressing gender inequalities, since they will benefit not only women, but their families and the Latin American society as a whole," said Ernesto May, World Bank Director for Poverty Reduction and Economic Management in Latin America and the Caribbean..

To do this, the report recommends labor policies aimed at reducing the barriers that women face, particularly, poor women, when attempting to enter the job market. These policies include increasing the number of daycare centers, providing family planning services, and a more equitable distribution of the workload at home.

With regard to health care, the document points out that even though maternal mortality has decreased in most countries, it continues to be women's principal healthcare problem, above all in Bolivia, Peru, Ecuador, El Salvador and the Dominican Republic. AIDS, in turn, has become one of the most serious problems in the Caribbean, where men and women suffer from a similar level of infection.

Closing the education gap

In education, the gap between men and women has been closing in all countries ... and in some, women have reached a higher level of education than men, such as in Brazil, Costa Rica, Venezuela, Argentina, Jamaica, Nicaragua and Colombia. This is due to the fact that fewer boys enroll in school and leave school more frequently in order to help their families economically. However, during economic crises, it is the daughters that parents are more likely to take out of school.

For its part, the study emphasizes that domestic violence "remains a challenge for countries across the region", with Haiti being the country with the highest rate of the female population affected (70 percent). According to the report, "the risk of physical abuse for women decreases with household income level and years of completed schooling, and increases with marriage and, disturbingly, with women's independent income in certain countries."

The document explains that even though there are some gender problems that are shared in most of the countries in the region, such as maternal mortality, these same countries often have their own unique development challenges related to gender. While access to the labor market is the main problem for Mexico, Chile, Uruguay and Venezuela, in Colombia it is domestic violence, and in Guyana, French Guiana and Surinam, maternal mortality. Argentina has problems related to the job market and teenage pregnancy; in Brazil, the labor market and maternal mortality are the foremost problems; in Central America, Ecuador, Peru and Paraguay, the main problems are maternal mortality and domestic violence; in Bolivia, they are maternal mortality and teenage pregnancy and in the Caribbean, AIDS and domestic violence are the greatest problems.

Do you believe that public policy can really influence the workload in the home?

Go to www.overpopulation.com/faq/health/mortality/maternal-mortality/latin-america.html for a list of the maternal mortality rate by country in Latin America and the Caribbean.

Are you surprised that levels of domestic violence are higher among married couples? What can be done to help eradicate domestic violence?

115

WANTED: A NEW LATIN AMERICAN AGENDA FOR ECONOMIC GROWTH
Hispanic News

NO

Luiz Inácio Lula da Silva, leader of the Workers' Party, was elected president of Brazil in 2002. Brazil's first left-wing president for four decades, da Silva pledged to fight hunger and unemployment as a priority during his presidency. Go to www.worldpress. org/Americas/ 1417.cfm for an article about Brazil's president.

Six months ago, such was the gloom about Latin America investors and international finance officials were asking whether it would be Brazil, the region's giant, or one of three or four of its neighbors, that would be next in line to follow Argentina into debt default. Now, that pessimism looks wildly overdone. Brazil has stepped back from the brink: its currency and its bonds have rallied strongly, after its new center left government committed itself to tight fiscal and monetary policies. With risks and sluggishness elsewhere in the world economy, money has trickled back into Latin America. Taken as a whole, the region should grow by at least 2% this year and 3.5% next year, according to the World Bank. Even Argentina, after a four-year slump, is growing again. So panic over—but not the debate about what has gone wrong.

A brighter outlook

For an explanation of Gross Domestic Product (GDP) go to page 111.

Mexico—a country with high levels of poverty and inequality— announced in 1982 that it was going to default on its international loans. Go to http://historicaltext archive.com/ sections.php?op= viewarticle=330 to view an article on the 1982 financial crisis.

Officials at the IMF and the World Bank caution that while the short-term outlook has brightened, Latin America faces deep-rooted obstacles before it can achieve high and sustained growth. And a still-anemic recovery cannot assuage the deep sense of dissatisfaction left behind by Latin America's recent travails. Last year, the region's GDP shrank by 0.6%, after growth of just 0.4% in 2001. Income per person in Latin America now stands 2% below its level of 1997, according to the UN Economic Commission for Latin America (ECLAC). Progress in reducing poverty has halted). This amounts to a "lost half-decade", says ECLAC, harking back to the "lost decade" unleashed by Mexico's 1982 debt default.

This slump has been all the more painful because of high hopes that Latin America was finally on course to catch up with the rich world. The region grew fast in the 1960s and 1970s, when many countries industrialized; but most Asian countries grew faster still. In Latin America, the growth was marred by exaggerated protectionism and bloated, but inefficient, states, culminating in the debt crisis. But a dozen or so years ago, most Latin American countries, many of them newly democratizing, changed course: they implemented a set of free-market policy reforms. These came to be known as the "Washington consensus" (a term coined in 1990 by John Williamson, of the Institute for International Economics, a think-tank in that city). At first, the results were promising: inflation, a chronic Latin vice, was slain; growth surged again, and poverty began to fall.

The necessity for free-market reforms

Subsequent recessions and financial crises, especially severe in South America, have wiped away some (in places much) of those gains. They have also prompted much heart-searching as to what has gone wrong. Many Latin Americans conclude that the answer is the "neo-liberal" reforms themselves. These are held not just to have failed to deliver sustained growth, but to have made the region more vulnerable, and to have increased unemployment, poverty and inequality. Privatization in particular has become deeply unpopular: privatizations of a water firm in Bolivia in 2000, and of an electricity generator in Peru last year, were scrapped after riots. ...

In Chile, an early reformer, fast growth saw poverty halved, to 23%, between 1987 and 1996. Overall, macroeconomic management in the region improved dramatically compared with, say, the 1970s. There was social progress, too. Partly because governments pulled back from running steelworks and factories, they spent more on education and health. In some countries, such as Brazil and Mexico, new, targeted, anti-poverty programs were introduced. Where income inequality worsened, it was mainly because of recession, not reform.

Privatization was not the blanket failure painted by the critics. There is little argument over the sale of state industries. Public utilities are more controversial. In some countries, their sale was badly handled: either tainted by corruption, or by private monopolies, or because regulation has been poor. But private provision of telephones, electricity and water has vastly increased their coverage and quality....

None of this is to deny that, overall, the return from reform has been disappointing. There were several reasons for that. Most relate to long-standing Latin American weaknesses. First, there was the region's chronic vulnerability to balance-of-payments crises. Second, the basic macroeconomic reforms were not fully implemented. In particular, most governments failed to save in good times, and piled up debts. Third, it was quickly accepted that if macroeconomic reforms were to produce higher investment and thus more jobs, they needed to be complemented by "second-generation" or institutional

The phrase "Washington consensus" is a popular and often ridiculed term in debates about trade and development. Williamson says he first used the phrase to refer to "the lowest common denominator of policy advice being addressed by the Washington-based institutions to Latin American countries as of 1989." These policies included fiscal discipline, tax reform, trade liberalization, and privatization.

Macroeconomics is a branch of economics that studies the overall working of a national economy.

Balance of payments is a system of recording a country's economic transactions with the rest of the world over one year. A favorable balance of payments exists when more payments are coming in than going out.

reforms. These range from improving education to bankruptcy proceedings. They are easy to list but hard to do. And fourth, some reformers, as well as critics, argued that in a region of deep income inequality, growth alone would not swiftly reduce poverty.

Capital flow refers to the private capital that is invested in a country or region. Developing countries depend on sustained capital flows to help economic growth, to protect against economic crisis, and to reduce poverty.

The single most important failing was the region's dependence on volatile capital flows. Growth before 1997 coincided with record capital inflows, some attracted by privatization. As a result, currencies became overvalued, hurting exports and local producers, and leading to big current account-deficits … To compensate, governments had to adjust the real exchange rate…

Lessons from the adjustment

Now, most Latin countries have competitive exchange rates. "The adjustment has happened. It was very powerful, but it's over," says Mr. Calvo. The challenge, he adds, is to develop institutions and mechanisms to allow the orderly transfer of capital from north to south. One answer would be a central bank for emerging markets, to ease adjustment by providing liquidity. But there is no political will for that.

So attention is focusing on other "crisis-proofing" measures. Exports are vital. Mexico and Chile were the only two of the region's larger countries to register double-digit annual increases in the volume of their exports throughout the 1990s. Not coincidentally, they escaped the worst of the turmoil of 1998-2002. So further trade opening would help. But the United States is offering less generous terms in the talks on a 34-country Free-Trade Area of the Americas than it did to Mexico in NAFTA.

The Free-Trade Area of the Americas (FTAA) is a plan to unite 34 economies of the Americas into a single free-trade agreement under which barriers to trade and investment will be eliminated. Negotiations are hoped to be completed by 2005. Look at www.ftaa-alca.org/alca_e.asp, the official FTAA website, to learn more.

For export growth, maintaining a competitive currency is important. So most countries are likely to stick to floating exchange rates.…

Another priority is to stimulate saving and borrowing in local currencies. The main hope here is pension reforms, which have created growing investment funds in Latin American countries. Again, Chile and Mexico are leaders.…

The second aspect of "crisis-proofing" concerns fiscal policy. Governments have begun to write fiscal discipline into law. But many are poor at restraining spending in good times.… It also requires reforms of tax and provincial finance. In many countries, local governments depend not on local taxes but on transfers from the center, which rise along with government revenues.…

The second item is institutional reform. Many economists now argue that institutions are crucial for growth.…

Thirdly, the "new Washington consensus" includes some policies designed to reduce inequality. Recent research suggests that inequality in developing countries itself tends to reduce growth: savings and investment become the preserve of a small rich elite. While warning of the potential cost to economic efficiency of actions to improve income distribution, Mr. Williamson concludes that "in a highly unequal region such as Latin America, opportunities for making large distributive gains for modest efficiency costs deserve to be seized." To that end, he suggests more effort to collect income tax, and higher property taxes. But more emphasis goes to helping the poor gain assets, such as education and property titles, and through land reform and micro credit programs.

Which way forward?

The way forward, Mr. Williamson concludes, is to "complete, correct, and complement the reforms of a decade ago", not to reverse them. But can this new formulation command a consensus? However cautious, references to selective capital controls, the role of the state, and income distribution all point to the reform agenda moving towards the center. Some free-marketers will object.

On the other hand, the region's new center-left governments, such as that of President Luiz Inácio Lula da Silva in Brazil, might agree with much of this new agenda. One interpretation of the past six months in the region is that the left has signed up to the "Washington consensus", at least in practice. ...

But there is still plenty of room for disagreements. Perhaps the biggest is on the role of the state. "We don't want to renationalize anything, nor strengthen the state in a traditional sense, but we do want a state that plans things that are fundamental for a development project," says José Genoino, the president of Lula's Workers' Party....

Few argue for turning the clock back to the 1970s. But there is a risk of re-regulation by a thousand obscure decrees and of incremental government hand-outs in the name of industrial policy, aggravating the low productivity and lack of competitiveness that dog the region. On the other hand, by grounding its recommendations more clearly in the region's economic history and institutional realities, the "new Washington consensus" has moved closer to becoming a Latin American product. How much of a consensus it will command, and whether it will guide the region back to growth, remain to be seen.

Microcredit programs are those in which people—usually women—are granted small, collateral-free loans for use in income-generating activities. They are designed to help women and their families work their way out of poverty and empower them in ways that may also reduce their fertility.

Look at www.iadborg/ idbamericalindex. cfm?thisid=2229 to read an article about the "new Washington consensus." How does this differ from the original Washington consensus?

Summary

In the first article, published by the DevNews Media Center, the author focuses on a World Bank report that argues that although there have been significant developments for women in recent years, gender inequalities are still holding back Latin American countries. In the article Maria Valéria Pena, leader of the World Bank's Gender Unit for Latin America and the Caribbean, states that "In spite of the significant progress over the past 20 years, gender inequalities remain an obstacle to the full development of the countries in the region." The study recommends that changes in labor policies would help reduce gender differentials.

The second article, from *Hispanic News*, however, examines other factors that have affected the region's growth. It argues that economic slumps, Mexico's debt default in 1982, currency crises, and problems associated with newly democratic nations have had major effects on Latin America's growth. The article looks at the "Washington consensus"—a list of financial policy advice, including fiscal discipline, tax reform, and privatization, given to countries of the region—to see how Latin America's economic problems have been addressed. The authors of the article concede that while free-market reforms have had success in reducing inflation in Latin America, overall economic growth has been disappointing. However, many Latin American leaders are now prepared to adopt a "new Washington consensus," revised in the light of the region's economic history, as a way forward to economic growth in the region.

FURTHER INFORMATION:

Books:

Williamson, John (ed.), *After the Washington Consensus: Restarting Growth and Reform in Latin America*. Washington, D.C.: Institute for International Economics, 2002.

Useful websites:

www.library.yale.edu/socsci/egcrla.html
Yale University Library guide to sites relating to economic growth in Latin America.
www.iadb.org/sds/doc/845eng.pdf
Conference paper on "Growth, Poverty, and Inequality in Latin America: A Causal Analysis, 1970-94."
www.unfpa.org/profile/overview_latin.htm
Profiles of 30 Latin American and Caribbean countries on the United Nations Population Fund site.
www.iie.com/
Site of the Institute for International Economics.

The following debates in the Pro/Con series may also be of interest:

In this volume:
Topic 8 Would increased investment in education reduce poverty in developing countries?

Topic 13 Is population control essential in poor nations?

Topic 14 Is the protection of indigenous people more important than economic development?

HAVE PERSISTING GENDER INEQUALITIES HINDERED GROWTH IN LATIN AMERICAN COUNTRIES?

YES: Fewer women than men work, they have fewer paid work opportunities, and they earn less than men. They are prevented from fulfilling their earning potential.

YES: Although many women have reached the education levels of men, they still have a long way to go. In economic crises girls are more likely to be taken out of school than boys.

DISCRIMINATION
Are women discriminated against in the labor market?

EDUCATION
Have unequal rights to education affected women?

NO: The percentage of Latin American women participating in the economy has grown considerably in the last 20 years. Women's pay has also improved.

NO: Many women are now as educated, if not more educated, than men. They do not work for other reasons.

HAVE PERSISTING GENDER INEQUALITIES HINDERED GROWTH IN LATIN AMERICAN COUNTRIES?

KEY POINTS

YES: Women's traditional social role keeps them from paid work. Women also suffer from high maternal mortality rates and domestic violence. They also have less access to education and land ownership. Rural and indigenous women are particularly affected.

YES: Research shows that countries with fewer gender inequalities are more likely to have lower poverty rates and experience better economic growth

POVERTY
Are women more likely to suffer from poverty?

GENDER VS. ECONOMICS
Is gender the most important factor in preventing growth?

NO: Both men and women are vulnerable to poverty if they live in countries that are plagued by economic crises

NO: Recessions, trade problems, and financial crises have been more important in the economic problems of Latin America

PART 3

TRADE

INTRODUCTION

International trade is considered by many to be the "engine of growth" which stimulated the economic and industrial advancement of many countries in the 19th and 20th centuries. Historically the economies of many rich nations were made and sustained by trading in goods, services and people, including the United States, Britain, and the Netherlands. However, as some nations became wealthier, the economies of others dwindled and the divide between the industrialized rich nations and the developing poor countries increased. The existence of trade barriers and protectionism, some critics argue, exacerbated this divide, while those using free trade practices prospered.

During the 20th century some poor countries were able to use trade to promote growth, notably South Korea, Taiwan, and Singapore; others, however, have found it difficult to generate growth through world trade. Critics comment that although poor nations have most of the world's population they receive only a tiny fraction of the world's income from trade.

Problems

Some economists believe that there are several factors responsible for the problems that developing countries have experienced regarding trade.

The terms of trade (the price received for exports in relation to the price paid for imports) for many developing countries have declined. One reason for this is that many such countries are dependent on the export of primary commodities—such as sugar, palm oil, and rubber—for their main foreign earnings. For many of these goods there is limited potential growth for demand, and synthetic cheaper substitutes have been developed. At the same time, many poor countries rely heavily on imports, such as machinery and consumer goods, to fuel their industrial development. Frequently, their import costs exceed their export payments, resulting in a deficit on their balance of payments. Some poor nations also face difficulties in trying to diversify production to create other goods for export, such as processed and manufactured goods.

Trading systems

Some commentators argue that rich countries have an advantage over poor nations since they can use their advanced technology and political and economic power to get preferential loan rates to develop new products and remain competitive. They claim that if developing countries successfully produce low-cost products they often find that developed countries protect their markets by erecting barriers to trade, such as tariffs and quotas. For example, raw cocoa beans can be imported into the European Union or the United States without tax. But if the exporting country processes the beans into cocoa butter themselves, the import tariff is 10 percent. If they turn it into chocolate, the tariff rises to 20 percent. As a result, developing countries produce 90 percent of the world's cocoa beans but only 5 percent of the chocolate.

Should developing countries then develop more inward-looking protectionist policies rather than focusing on trade liberalization? Proponents of free trade claim that by opening their economies to global trade, developing countries can allow in new organizational systems,

believe such agreements have helped trade relations between rich and poor countries, critics claim that organizations like the WTO are unfair since their policies often favor developed nations. They argue that by forcing open markets onto developing countries and promoting trade liberation regardless of individual circumstances they ignore the sometimes dire consequences of such action on the economies of poor nations.

In response to such criticism the WTO negotiations of 2001 in Doha were aimed at placing developing countries at the heart of trade

---

"Men cannot not live by exchanging articles, but producing them. They live by work not TRADE."
—JOHN RUSKIN (1819–1900), BRITISH SOCIAL THEORIST

---

information systems, technology, and the values and ideas of the developed world. But protectionist policies placed against foreign imports may enable local industries to develop and mature enough to be able to compete in international markets. Topic 10 examines whether protectionist policies are key to economic growth in developing nations.

Trade agreements

Many modern economists believe that international trade has benefited from agreements like the General Agreement on Tariffs and Trade (GATT), which was set up to remove barriers to trade after World War II, and was replaced by the World Trade Organization (WTO) in 1995. While advocates

negotiations. Agricultural products have been central to the Doha round of talks since 70 percent of the world's poor work in agriculture, and a large number of existing trade barriers are directed at agricultural products. For example, despite agreeing to cut agricultural subsidies both the European Union and United States have increased subsidies to their own farmers. Such action has, some commentators argue, helped depress world cotton prices by an estimated 10–20 percent and created surpluses. Topic 11 discusses what effect agricultural subsidies have on developing nations.

Topic 12 looks at drug patents and their effect on health care in poor nations. Critics believe patents are a form of protectionism and are unfair.

Topic 10

ARE PROTECTIONIST POLICIES ESSENTIAL TO ECONOMIC GROWTH IN POOR NATIONS?

YES

FROM "FINDINGS IN DETAIL: THE U.S. AND CHIQUITA AT THE WTO"
WWW.ROSRO.COM/CH3.HTM
IBRAHIM J. GASSAMER

NO

"DEVELOPMENT DIMENSIONS OF THE WORLD TRADE ORGANIZATION"
A NOTE OF THE HOLY SEE ON THE PREPARATION FOR THE DOHA MINISTERIAL CONFERENCE
THE HOLY SEE (THE VATICAN)

INTRODUCTION

"Protectionism" refers to the practice of insulating a nation's firms or workers from foreign competition. It is the opposite of "free trade," which is based on unrestricted commercial interaction between all nations. Any government policy that discriminates against foreign products is protectionist.

Protectionism can be implemented in many ways. One method is through quotas, whereby countries impose limits on the amounts or values of goods that they allow to be imported in order to protect their own producers. Another method is the imposition of special taxes known as import tariffs. Tariffs can be applied to foreign goods on their arrival at the port of entry, on their delivery to the retailer, and at their point of sale. A further method is via subsidies, grants of money to encourage domestic industries that would otherwise be unprofitable.

In the United States protectionism was the dominant trade doctrine for over a century, reaching its height in 1930 with the Smoot–Hawley Act, which set tariff rates at an average of 60 percent. During the years after World War I (1914-1918) governments around the world adopted similar policies as they aimed to rebuild and stimulate their national economies. Until this time free trade, as advocated by the Scottish economist Adam Smith in 1776, had underpinned the economies of western Europe following their rapid expansion in the Industrial Revolution.

After World War II (1939-1945) there was a consensus among governments that a return to free-market principles would be beneficial to the world economy. Many economists wanted to avoid the contraction in world trade that had contributed to the Great Depression in the 1930s after the

Smoot–Hawley Act. The General Agreement on Trade and Tariffs (GATT), set up in 1947, and the World Trade Organization (WTO), which succeeded it in 1995, were both established to facilitate international trade, economic growth, and stability through policies with a basis in free trade. The WTO has pledged itself to support trade in developing countries not through protectionist policies but multilateral measures that take into account their different levels of natural resources and modernization.

> *"Developing countries are ... asking for ... a fair chance to trade their way out of poverty."*
> —KOFI ANNAN, SECRETARY-GENERAL OF THE UNITED NATIONS (SEPTEMBER 10, 2003)

However, although international organizations such as the WTO advocate free-market economics in theory, many of its member countries continue to use protectionist policies. In the context of development one of the most publicized issues is the detrimental effect that subsidies and tariffs imposed by wealthy nations are having on poor countries. Many nongovernment organizations and development campaigners criticize the European Union (EU) and the United States for the policies with which they protect their markets from imports. They claim that their subsidies and tariffs—some of the most contentious

are on wheat, rice, and cotton—prevent poorer countries from developing viable production and trade by excluding them from export markets and flooding their own domestic markets with cheap surpluses. These restrictions prevent poor nations from developing their often already limited resources and marketable commodities.

On the other hand, some people think that developing countries would benefit from applying protectionist policies themselves. Poor nations could use tariffs and subsidies to protect their producers and encourage new business and trade, while increasing national economic self-sufficiency. In this way they could build up strong national industries that would then be able to compete in a global market.

Some developed countries assist poor countries through protectionist measures, such as the European Union's preferential import arrangements with its member countries' former colonies on goods such as sugar and bananas. Advocates argue that these policies support production and trade in regions that have no other viable source of income and are a means of development preferable to aid. Opponents argue that that is not the way to develop the economies of poor countries. They claim it leads to higher consumer prices and, in most instances, lower welfare for the country as a whole, because inefficient domestic industries are favored, and gains from international trade are reduced. They believe that protectionism leads to economic stagnation rather than development and makes countries more prone to collapse in times of recession.

The two following articles examine the issues in more detail.

FINDINGS IN DETAIL:
THE U.S. AND CHIQUITA AT THE WTO
Ibrahim J. Gassamer

This extract comes from a report by Ibrahim J. Gassamer, an academic who specializes in law and development. It is posted on the website of Ross Robinson Associates, a U.S. organization that aims to promote awareness of foreign policy issues. Go to http://www.rosro. com/cover.htm to find out more about the organization. See page 143 to find out more about the banana war.

YES

☑ …About 40,000 Jamaicans earn their living from the banana trade. The banana industry is second only to sugar as an agricultural export commodity, and last year, banana exports provided Jamaica with about U.S. $51m in foreign exchange. For Dominica and St. Lucia, the industry is even more important, employing more than 30% of Dominica's total workforce of 35,000 people, and about 25% of St. Lucia's. Banana exports bring in, on the average, about 60% of these nations total export earnings.

Moreover, the banana industry has a multiplier effect on the economy of each country and on the region as a whole. Since banana is harvested weekly, it provides family farmers, many of whom are women working small acreages, with a regular source of income. Furthermore, without the weekly banana exports, the shipping industry that is crucial for the transportation of other exports would virtually cease to exist.

Survival of the banana industry

The European assistance program incorporated in the banana regime is crucial to the survival of the Caribbean banana industry and it does so without causing any significant effects on other banana exporters. Caribbean exports represent only a tiny portion of the European Union market—about 8 to 10%. This represents an even smaller percentage—about 3%—of the global market. A 1994 World Bank report concluded that without the program, the industry would shrink, with disastrous consequences:

> …Apart from the farmer, the industry provides employment and income to a large segment of society. The cost of banana industry compression would be high. It would not only adversely affect the national economy but would affect the living standards of farmers and all those associated with the banana industry. A compression of the banana industry could deprive up to 50% of the farmers of their livelihood.

None of these Caribbean countries can compete successfully in the world banana market without the kind of support provided by the European regime. Dominica, for example[,] yields five tons per acre while its Latin American competitors yield thirty tons per acre. Production costs for Caribbean banana exporters are considerably higher than those of Latin American producers....

The E.U. banana regime will review its banana commitments in the year 2001, one year before the current regime expires. In anticipation, the Caribbean banana industry, supported by national governments, has worked to reorganize itself comprehensively to reduce costs, improve productivity, and diversify to the extent possible. This reorganization is being funded partly by grants from the E.U. ... The delegation saw evidence of this new commitment in visits to farms in Dominica and St. Lucia, and to the port of Castries. In discussions with farmers and banana workers, the delegation found a spirit of determination and pride that went beyond purely economic calculations....

The process of reform

Learning from its more successful international competitors, new managers of the industry in the Windwards have restructured it to make it more vertically integrated. Now, the industry profits not only from production of bananas, but also from shipping, ripening, marketing and distribution. Unfortunately, the U.S. challenge to the banana regime has hampered this reform process by fostering uncertainty in the industry and undermining the morale of farmers and workers to a significant degree.... The stability provided by the European banana regime is vital to the survival of the industry and the economic well-being of these countries. The U.S. challenge to this well-established policy has already exacted a huge cost, economically, socially, and politically from these countries. If the U.S. complaint before the WTO succeeds, there will be significant costs to the region and to U.S. interests, but no benefits in terms of either jobs or exports for the United States.

With regard to calls for reform and diversification, the delegation concluded that there is a limit to what can be accomplished through reform and diversification. The plain fact, as the delegation found, is that no other industry can substitute for bananas in these countries. Economically, it produces a weekly cash flow for the independent family farmer that no other agricultural product can match. Bananas are also the only crop resilient enough to suffer through

In July 2001 the EU revised its quota system in line with U.S. and WTO rulings. Go to http://www. guardian.co.uk/ netnotes/article/ 0,6729,515822,00. html to learn more.

The report refers to a U.S. delegation— drawn from the labor, public policy, and academic sectors—that visited Jamaica, Dominica, and St. Lucia in 1996 to assess the effect the U.S. challenge to the EU quota program would have.

The Windward Islands are a group of islands in the East Caribbean including St. Lucia, St. Vincent, Grenada, and Dominica. In 1998 income from the banana trade with Europe accounted for about half of the Windwards' export earnings.

If there was no likely benefit for the United States in terms of jobs or exports, what prompted it to complain to the World Trade Organization? Go to www.google.com and see if you can find out.

perennial devastation inflicted by storms and other natural disasters and produce again for export within months of destruction. ... [D]espite vast sums spent by development agencies to encourage diversification, no viable alternative crop to bananas has been found.

Considering some vague U.S. suggestions that the European banana regime could be replaced by some sort of direct aid programs, the delegation found that, to the contrary, the current European banana regime is crucial to survival of the banana industry and cannot be replaced by a direct aid program. Direct aid, as an alternative to the European banana regime, would leave the Caribbean banana industry at the mercy of the three giant multinational companies which already control 65 percent of the global banana market. Furthermore, it was the firm view of the delegation formed from talking to ordinary citizens and government officials that direct aid to these countries, as currently advocated by some in the United States, would mean not only the end of the banana industry but also the beginning of a welfare-type dependence on foreign assistance by people who would much rather work for their living.... [T]he cost to U.S. tax payers of any new aid program and the cost to people of the Caribbean in terms of loss of national pride, self-sufficiency, and social stability would, combined, far exceed any potential benefits that could be presumed for the United States....

Banana trade vs. the drug trade

One very clear consequence of an end to the European banana regime is that the Caribbean banana industry will shrink drastically, throwing thousands of farmers and others who make their living in the banana industry out of work. Massive unemployment will not only devastate the economy of the region, it will certainly lead to social disorder....

Assuredly, many of those facing a lifetime of destitution will head for the United States, employing legal as well as illegal means. The impact on already-strained U.S. social services will be tremendous. Even worse, many others will reluctantly be drawn to the drug trade, either growing marijuana or servicing Columbian cocaine cartels always on the lookout for new transshipments points to United States markets.... It was readily apparent to the delegation that the U.S. posture on bananas was weakening the bonds ordinary citizens in these countries had with the United States, thus threatening to undermine U.S. effort to engage them as well as their governments in a concerted effort against drug trafficking. The delegation came back convinced that ... [c]ontinued U.S.

opposition will worsen an already tense situation; economic uncertainty will grow, fostering social disorder and endangering our national struggle against drug trafficking....

Another certain consequence of the current U.S. approach would be sharply increased legal and illegal immigration. Without a strong banana industry and the jobs it provides, many Caribbeans will flee to the United States in search of work ... [I]n 1995 ... when banana prices hit a 22 year low that year, at least 4000 illegal immigrants from these densely populated islands landed on the shores of the U.S. With the widespread unemployment that would surely result if the U.S. challenge to an industry that employs over 30 percent of the population in some countries succeeds, the 1995 illegal immigration figure would certainly multiply astronomically....

Do you find the author's argument about illegal immigration persuasive? Would it help if he compared the 1995 statistic to those of other years?

The delegation was convinced that harmful social, economic, and political consequences that would very likely arise if the U.S. challenge to the European banana regime proves successful, far outweigh any potential benefit. The devastation caused to the Caribbean economy would be felt in the streets of American cities which would be flooded with new drug supplies. It would also be felt in the boardrooms of corporate America as American investors in the region suffer from the shockwave that would accompany the collapse of the banana industry. And American taxpayers in general would suffer as tax dollars get diverted to help stem escalating drug flows, increased illegal immigration, and the spread of misery from the region....

The author uses powerful statements and language to make his point about the possible effects of Caribbean economic failure on the United States. Do you think he is exaggerating?

Preserving their heritage

In discussions with government officials and other national leaders, as well as with ordinary citizens, the delegation was reminded of the critical role played by the numerous small independent banana farmers in preserving the democratic heritage and social stability of these small islands. Unlike their Latin American counterparts who work in large, company-owned plantations, these hardy independent farmers generally own their relatively small five to ten acre plots which they work generally with their families. Banana workers in the Caribbean also, on the average, were paid twice as much as their Latin American counterparts working in large plantations owned by multinationals like Chiquita....

A central point of the author's argument is that the culture of the Caribbean banana industry differs from that of Latin America, partly because it is based on local rather than foreign ownership. Do you agree that these factors contribute to social well-being and development more than achieving maximum economic efficiency?

[O]n the vital importance of the European banana regime to the survival of their societies there was no disagreement. As St Lucia's opposition leader, Velon John put it, "We are at one with the government; it is the fight for St. Lucia, a fight for the survival of our country and people."

DEVELOPMENT DIMENSIONS OF THE WORLD TRADE ORGANIZATION
The Holy See (The Vatican)

The Fourth Ministerial Conference of the World Trade Organization (WTO) took place in Doha, Qatar, in November 2001. The Holy See prepared this note to make its own contribution to the ongoing debate on the draft of the Final Declaration of the Ministerial Conference—a document defining WTO policy. The Final Declaration was adopted in February 2003. Go to http://www.wto.org/english/thewto_e/minist_e/min01_e/mindecl_e.htm to read the declaration.

NO

The Doha Conference is planned to take place at a moment in which the world is challenged by new tensions. It is thus more urgent than ever to ensure that the outcomes of the Conference mark a clear step on the path to a new and more inclusive vision of world trade, in which all can take part effectively on an even footing. This can only be achieved by gestures of flexibility and solidarity, recognizing also that the enhanced development of the poorer countries is a contribution to global economic progress, international security and peace.

Failure to give such a clear signal can only worsen already deep-felt sentiments of exclusion which many communities harbour today. The credibility of the WTO and of a universal multilateral trading system is at stake.

Within this general framework, the Holy See would like to draw attention to some factors that the Ministerial Conference in Doha should address in order to give greater focus and impetus to the WTO's developmental agenda in the future, while maintaining focus on its specific trade-related mandate.

1. Unsatisfactory progress for the poorest countries

The Uruguay Round was the final set of GATT (General Agreement on Tariffs and Trade) negotiations that took place in 1986. It established the trade principles adopted by the WTO when it replaced GATT in 1995.

Despite the opportunities offered by the Uruguay Round the least developed countries and other poor countries still have only a marginal and diminishing share in world trade. Progress in the equitable integration of the poorest countries into the global market has been unsatisfactory.…

A fair integration of the least developed countries into the global economy will only be achieved by an integrated approach. Trade liberalization is a means, and must be implemented in such a way that there is sufficient flexibility to adopt fundamental development measures. The goal and dimension of development must be central in WTO rules and in the assessment of proposals.

Fair trade relations certainly constitute an essential component of economic and human development, but, as

Pope John Paul II has stressed, "economic freedom is only one element of human freedom" and "the economy is only one aspect and one dimension of the whole of human activity" (*Centesimus Annus*, n. 39). Economic life cannot be absolutized. Economic activities must be pursued within the broader context of human development, the promotion of human rights and especially the overarching policies and targets of the family of nations aimed at eliminating poverty.

2. The development framework of the WTO
Trade liberalization and developmental concerns are not only not incompatible, moreover, they should go hand in hand.

The opening paragraphs of the Marrakesh Agreement establishing the World Trade Organization set out the [basic] framework within which its activities in the field of trade and economic endeavour are to be conducted. This framework requires the Organization to look at its activities within the context of a broad range of human, social and environmental aims, which have the objective of sustainable development. It recognizes the need to ensure that the developing countries, and especially the least developed among them, secure a share in the growth in international trade commensurate with the needs of their economic development....

3. Eliminate trade-distorting protections
The application of the WTO's rules has resulted in a wide opening of the domestic markets of developing countries, often with heavy adjustment costs. The wealthier countries, however, have been able to maintain strong legal protections precisely in those economic areas in which poor countries could be competitive (e.g. agriculture, textiles and other labour intensive industries).

Even where quota-free and duty-free market access has been widely opened to the least developed countries, many developed countries continue to prolong high levels of protection especially in agriculture and textiles, claiming that they need additional time to adjust. They thus constrain poorer countries to share the burden of their own domestic protection through unfavourable trade conditions and dumping measures. Both justice and long-term economic efficiency require that the international trade system restore to all its participants the highest achievable equality of opportunity by eliminating, within the shortest possible period, trade and production distorting export subsidies, and providing ample market access on a sure and predictable basis to products in which the poorest countries have

Do you think that a single organization like the WTO can successfully further both trade and development? Is international trade based on commercial gain and competition fundamentally incompatible with development goals?

Go to www.wto.org/english/docs_e/legal_e/legal_e.htm to find out more about the Marrakesh Agreement.

Do you think governments should put the prosperity of their own countries before that of other countries? Do you think there is a conflict of interest?

"Dumping" refers to the practice of developed countries selling large surpluses of goods to developing nations. Because these products—which are often agricultural—have been produced with subsidies, they can be sold more cheaply than those produced locally without such financial support.

comparative advantage. It is important to be attentive to the possibility of new protectionist measures being introduced, disguised under various titles.

4. The developing countries should adopt consistent development policies

The developing countries should, however, avoid the temptation of taking a crude protectionist path. There have been occasions in the past in which protection of certain sectors, at times of vital national importance, has been advantageous in specific circumstances and for a determinate period of time. This can still be true today. However, a correct balance must be attained, keeping in mind that in today's circumstances, generally, protectionism can be of only limited value to developing economies.

The developing countries need rather a solid and viable path to free trade that permits them to enter into an equitable dialogue with international markets. The existing WTO special and differential treatment principle in favour of the least developed countries should, therefore, be fully implemented and operationalized and new measures should be considered as an integral part of future negotiations....

The food security concerns of net food importing countries and of the least developed countries are obviously of legitimate concern and must be addressed in trade negotiations. It has been proposed that a specific "development box" to address such concerns should be elaborated. The suggestion merits close attention. Careful research should be carried out in order to provide a clear analysis of the concrete effects of implementation on food prices and food security for the poorest countries.

5. Implementation and technical assistance

The rigid application of the same rules to economies that start out from different development levels and different capacities tends to create further inequities and asymmetries. It is thus essential to address urgently the uneven trade capacities of countries. For a free trade system to be fair, it must not only guarantee legal equality among countries, it must also redress, as much as possible, the disadvantages, in terms of economic and negotiating power, of less industrialized economies and of commodity producer economies.

The accession process for poorer countries should be tailored to their special economic conditions and commensurate with the level of development. Due

Food security is when a nation's population has unhindered physical and economic access to enough safe and nutritious food to meet its dietary needs. A net food-importing country is a country that relies on imports for the majority of its food. See Topic 15 Have measures to improve food security been successful?

The paper acknowledges that different countries have different resources and trade potentials, as well as being at different stages in development. Is it possible to legislate effectively for this diversity? How does this "positive discrimination" differ from protectionism?

Is free trade the same as fair trade?

extensions should be given to the transitional periods for implementation when needed.

WTO technical assistance must be improved and sustainable financial support for such assistance be solidly integrated into the budget, at levels sufficient for the task in hand. Such technical assistance should focus, in the first place, on assisting developing countries to implement existing WTO obligations. In those areas where developing countries face persistent problems in implementing their obligations, a systematic exercise to review, to apply more flexibility and, where necessary, to amend the existing rules or procedures should be carried out....

Beyond the implementation subjects, poor countries also require urgent technical assistance from appropriate agencies, to help broaden and diversify their production and export base and their trade promotion efforts....

7. Increased transparency

The majority of the members of the WTO are developing countries that have as much—or even greater—stake as the developed countries in a truly fair and balanced multilateral system. The developing countries must be able to attain adequate means to voice their interests and exercise their rights. The WTO must portray itself clearly as a trade body working for the interests of all countries.

The very nature of a free trade system entails the full ownership of the trade decisions by all the participating States ... The special negotiating difficulties of the least developed countries, and especially of countries which can afford only a minimal representation at the WTO headquarters, must be continuously addressed.

Do you think the WTO presents itself as a body working for the interests of all countries? See Volume 3, Economics, Topic 11, Is the World Trade Organization fair to poor countries?

8. Towards a broader development agenda

Naturally, the World Trade Organization cannot address all the development challenges of today's world. Attempts to overstretch its mandate should, indeed, be resisted.

A well-prepared and balanced trade negotiation, which goes hand in hand with continuous verification of the ability of the poorest countries to implement past and new WTO agreements, is an important element in a broad new development scenario, in which different international organizations can mutually enhance one another's contribution, so that other outstanding issues—such as the protection of fundamental labour standards, environmental protection and the establishment of global anti-trust norms— can be adequately addressed in the most appropriate forum.

Some people view the breakdown of the Fifth Ministerial Meeting of the WTO held in Cancun, Mexico, September 10–14, 2003, as evidence that the WTO is failing to conduct balanced trade negotiations. Go to http://www. guardian.co.uk/wto/ cancun/0,13815,101 8998,00.html to find out more about the collapse of the Cancun talks.

Summary

The first article, written by Ibrahim J. Gassamer, advocates protectionist policies in the context of the Caribbean banana industry. The report states that the European Union's quota policy—which has been revised since the report was written—benefited the Caribbean by providing small producers in the region with a guaranteed market share, while having little adverse effect on the global banana trade. It makes the case that the EU's quotas were beneficial not only economically but socially, contributing to development and stability in the Caribbean. The report also points out that U.S. proposals to remove the EU quotas—proposals supported by the World Trade Organization—will result in poverty and increased drug production and migration, which will directly affect the United States.

   The second article, by economists at the Vatican, supports free trade and the removal of protectionist policies. However, it notes that while advances toward achieving this goal have been made under the guidance of the World Trade Organization, developed countries continue to maintain protectionist policies—particularly in the form of agricultural subsidies. It stresses that this protectionism is placing severe and unfair constraints on developing countries and must end. The paper also advocates commitment to a multilateral policy that aims to redress the inequities faced by different nations with differing natural resources and levels of development. The article concludes that a balanced approach to free trade, which responds to the needs of developing countries, is an important part of development.

FURTHER INFORMATION:

Books:

Gomory, Ralph E., and William J. Baumol, *Global Trade and Conflicting National Interests*. Cambridge, MA: MIT Press, 2000.
O'Brian, Robert, et al., *Contesting Global Governance: Multilateral Economic Institutions and Global Social Movements*. New York: Cambridge University Press, 2000.

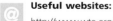

Useful websites:

http://www.wto.org/english/tratop_e/devel_e/devel_e.htm
Trade and development section of the WTO site.
http://www.bananalink.org.uk/trade_war/trade_war.htm
Site of Banana Link, a nonprofit company that promotes sustainable international banana trade.
http://www.cato.org/dailys/09-04-03-2.html
Discussion of negative effect U.S. and European protectionism is having on developing countries.

The following debates in the Pro/Con series may also be of interest:

In this volume:
   Topic 1 Do rich countries have a duty to give financial help to their former colonies?

In *Commerce and Trade*:
   Topic 1 Is a free market the best way to organize world trade?

   Topic 14 Is protectionism good for U.S. trade?

ARE PROTECTIONIST POLICIES ESSENTIAL FOR ECONOMIC GROWTH IN POOR NATIONS?

YES: Protectionist policies have the potential to increase income by generating jobs and self-sufficiency and reducing expenditure on imported goods

YES: The removal of external competition enables nations to build up their businesses and trade, and to create more jobs and stronger economies

WEALTH
Do subsidies, tariffs, and quotas increase poor countries' income?

COMPETITION
Is it beneficial to remove competition from trade and industry?

NO: Protectionism can be too aggressive; it can provoke retaliatory action from other countries, reducing potential export markets

ARE PROTECTIONIST POLICIES ESSENTIAL FOR ECONOMIC GROWTH IN POOR NATIONS?

KEY POINTS

NO: The removal of competition leads to inefficient companies and a lack of innovation and diversity, which are vital to a healthy economy

YES: Poor countries often have few resources and marketable commodities, and are a long way behind developed nations in terms of modernization; protectionist policies can help redress the imbalance

YES: Protectionist policies enable industries to operate in an artificial environment; when governments are no longer able to subsidize them, for example, in times of recession, their economies will collapse

EQUALITY
Do protectionist policies create a fairer environment for poor countries?

SUSTAINABILITY
Do protectionist policies create unsustainable economies?

NO: Protectionist policies obstruct poor countries' access to the world market; multilateral agreements are a fairer and more effective means of promoting growth

NO: Protectionist policies allow businesses and producers in poor countries to establish themselves and compete effectively in the world market

Topic 11

HAVE HEAVY AGRICULTURAL SUBSIDIES DAMAGED THE ECONOMIES OF POORER NATIONS?

YES

"THE DISASTER OF INTERNATIONAL FOREIGN AID PROGRAMS"
INTERNATIONAL SOCIETY FOR INDIVIDUAL LIBERTY PAMPHLET SERIES
ORIGINALLY PUBLISHED IN 1988, REVISED MAY 1998
KEN SCHOOLLAND

NO

"EU'S VOW ON CARIBBEAN BANANAS HARD TO KEEP"
WWW.SUNSONLINE.ORG, JULY 7, 1998
SOUTH–NORTH DEVELOPMENT MONITOR (SUNS)

INTRODUCTION

The developed world spends billions of dollars each year on agricultural subsidies. In the United States agricultural subsidies ran to some $19 billion in 2000, and in 2002 President George W. Bush signed a bill increasing this amount by some $6 billion a year.

Developed nations have adopted a number of steps to keep the price of agricultural produce above what the market would otherwise have yielded. Direct cash incentives are used to maintain prices on the domestic market so that farmers are guaranteed a return above world-market levels. Export subsidies are used alongside import regulations to control the price of agricultural produce. Domestic consumers pay more for the produce than foreign purchasers as a result of export subsidies, and the import regulations keep cheap foreign produce

off domestic markets, which would otherwise drive prices down.

In the European Union (EU) subsidies are distributed under the Common Agricultural Policy (CAP), amounting to some $43 billion in 2000. Instituted in 1962, when memories of wartime hunger were still fresh, the CAP aimed to make volatile food prices more stable by giving farmers a reliable income for their produce. Forty years later, with hunger a distant memory and surpluses rather than shortages a problem, the CAP is widely criticized both inside and outside Europe.

Under the CAP every milk-producing cow earns a European dairy farmer $720 a year in EU subsidies. This figure is four times as much as a typical dairy farmer in Senegal earns in total every year. Once their cows have produced milk, EU dairy farmers then receive another subsidy for exporting excess produce to other countries. Meanwhile, the dairy farmer in Senegal is often stuck with his milk because there is a limited market for it.

In September 2003 the objections of developing countries to agricultural subsidies were among the issues that caused the breakdown of a negotiating round of the World Trade Organization (WTO) in Cancun, Mexico. A coalition of developing nations suggests that rich nations should remove or reduce agricultural subsidies to ease the burden on the world's poorest farmers. However, these plans met with fierce opposition from those against agricultural reforms.

"Rich countries spend more than $300 billion a year on agricultural subsidies, an amount roughly equivalent to the entire gross domestic product of sub-Saharan Africa."

—BENJAMIN MKAPA, PRESIDENT OF TANZANIA, SEPTEMBER 30, 2001

Supporters of agricultural subsidies argue that they bring many benefits. They stabilize prices and the supply of food. They also lead to an increase in the yield of food crops by encouraging farmers to use new pesticides and fertilizers, and by encouraging wider cultivation, for example, on flood-prone land, which again increases crop yields. In addition, subsidies maintain rural communities that would otherwise become depopulated, provide surplus produce that can then be sold cheaply or given to poor countries as food aid, and reward good farming practice.

Critics of subsidies point out that subsidized food is used directly as foreign aid by the United States, further undercutting local producers in poor countries (the EU has stopped this practice and now buys food aid in the countries receiving aid, thus supporting local producers).

Others contend that the surplus food benefits the developing world directly by reducing famine and poverty. How can developed nations be accused of being concerned with profit when they invest so heavily in farming and then give the produce away as foreign aid?

Critics claim there is a double standard in the agricultural policy of the developed countries. While these countries continue to export food as aid, they maintain some of the strictest import regulations in the world, citing food safety as their concern. While it is obvious that food imports should be safe to eat, many people think that the restrictions are unnecessarily stringent.

The following articles examine the issues behind the subsidies and their effects on the developing world. In the first article Ken Schoolland, a director for the International Society for Individual Liberty, argues that developed countries do great harm to the economies of poorer countries by subsidizing their own farmers. The second article, from the South-North Development Monitor, argues that the preferential trade treatment given by the EU to their banana-producing former colonies (which effectively acts as a subsidy) is vital to protect the economic interests of those countries.

THE DISASTER OF INTERNATIONAL FOREIGN AID PROGRAMS
Ken Schoolland

YES

Feast and famine: an age of irony

Conscience money, popularly known as "foreign aid," cannot undo the harm that is done to developing countries by the trade and agricultural policies of industrial nations. While millions of people are starving across Africa, it is not uncommon to read about tons of food being stored or destroyed in the United States, Western Europe, and Japan. These reports seem as if they were coming from different planets: an impoverished Third World suffers while a prosperous First World disposes of surplus food.

The food being destroyed is not just the accumulated discard from schoolchildren's lunch plates. Instead, the great destruction of food is the result of an official agricultural program to keep food off the domestic market in order to raise farm prices.

Planned waste

Not long ago, Japanese officials announced plans to destroy 8,600 tons of cabbages and radishes because their prices slumped below "acceptable" levels. West European officials are reported to have stocked away mountains of butter and lakes of milk for the same reason. And U.S. officials ordered 3.5 billion oranges, two-fifths of all production, to be removed from the California market in order to raise prices.

One farmer in California, Carl Pescosolido, faced hefty fines because he chose to give two million oranges to the poor people of San Francisco rather than let them rot in the field. The authorities do not always look kindly on charity, unless it fits their own assistance plans. Emergency assistance in the form of famine relief grabs the headlines, but these paltry sums are dwarfed by the massive government programs that created the conditions of poverty in the first place.

Nearly $100 billion is spent annually by governments to subsidize farmers in the developed countries. Over the long run, these massive subsidies to First World farmers have had a deleterious effect on the ability of Third World nations to develop a sound agricultural base and to become economically self-sufficient. This occurs in two important ways.

Ban trade—give aid
In order to maintain high domestic food prices, First World nations usually use one, or both of these techniques:

1. Prohibit the importation of many agricultural products from the developing countries and/or
2. Dump crops abroad under the guise of "foreign aid."

Such policies serve to obstruct or ruin farm investment and production where it is needed most. It is no accident that, while First World nations restrict access to their markets, they like to boast of helping their desperate neighbors with generous shipments of aid. The Japanese government will herald its new ties with Southeast Asia by offering economic assistance, but will curtail the importation of rice and boneless chicken. The U.S. government will fortify its Caribbean allies with military and economic aid, but will restrict the importation of sugar and tomatoes. And Western European governments will offer similar policies to their former colonies in Africa.

This apparently inconsistent behavior, banning trade while giving aid, is frequently part of the same agricultural policy. Politicians, especially in the U.S. and the European Union, are always in the awkward position of having to dispose of vast quantities of "surplus" food that their domestic subsidies have generated. This must be done with finesse so that these "surpluses," or subsidy crops, won't reach the domestic consumer and reduce local food prices. Thus Americans and Europeans must pay five to seven times as much for sugar as they would have to pay on the world market. And the Japanese must buy domestic rice at five to seven times the price of rice which is produced by farmers in Thailand. Since the Third World nations are prevented from selling these products to the First World, they are not able to earn much of the foreign exchange which is necessary to repay development loans or to purchase vital fertilizers, tractors, petroleum, and education. As the opportunities for self-generated earnings are diminished, developing nations remain eternally dependent on their benefactors.

THE MAKING OF SUBSIDY CROPS
In America, this agricultural policy began in 1929. Under the Farm Stabilization Act, the Hoover administration first bought

The World Trade Organization (WTO) has encouraged countries to replace restrictions on imports in the form of quotas with tariffs instead (a process called tariffication). This is regarded as an interim goal on the way to eliminating such restrictions altogether.

Since the Japanese see rice as an essential part of their diet, they have always insisted on maintaining self-sufficiency in rice production. Since land is expensive in Japan, and rice produced there is up to seven times the average world cost, in a completely open market Japan would import all its rice and produce none itself. To maintain self-sufficiency, it banned all rice imports until 1995, when trade negotiations forced it to allow a minimum amount to be imported. Do you think it is reasonable for a country to seek to maintain self-sufficiency in some foodstuffs?

The Great Depression of the 1930s was perhaps the most serious and disruptive economic depression since the beginnings of industrialization. Do you think it is legitimate for governments to take actions that stabilize prices and guarantee income for farmers in such circumstances?

The Farmers Home Administration was founded in 1946 as an agency of the U.S. Department of Agriculture, to provide small farmers with credit to construct or repair homes and farm buildings, improve farming operations, or become farmowners.

Food for Peace was established by President Eisenhower in 1954. It is still the program under which the U.S. Agency for International Development (USAID) distributes food aid.

up and stored 257 million bushels of wheat in order to please the farm bloc.

During the Great Depression, while the hungry and unemployed were lining up at soup kitchens, the Roosevelt administration tried to save on storage costs by paying farmers to plant fewer crops, to plow under millions of acres of cotton, and slaughter several million pigs and cows. It has been an expanding bipartisan boondoggle ever since. In 1983, U.S. government subsidies nearly equaled the total of net farm income. In 1984, the US government succeeded in removing 82 million acres of prime land from cultivation. This idled 36 percent of the land devoted to corn, wheat, cotton, sorghum, and rice. Still, new subsidies always brought on new surpluses. While the U.S. Department of Agriculture (USDA) was holding land and commodities off the market, various branches of government were simultaneously increasing farm yield and opening virgin territories to even more subsidized farming.

With truckloads of pesticides and fertilizers at hand, the USDA conducted research and training programs to help farmers increase their crop yields. The Farmers Home Administration (FHA) provided low-interest loans, and the U.S. Congress underwrote the construction of mammoth pork-barrel irrigation projects in the desert. Disaster insurance even encouraged farming in drought-prone and flood-prone areas.

So the embarrassing surpluses continued to mount. There was, however, one last option for the disposal of subsidy crops. What couldn't be stored or destroyed could be sent abroad.

What helps farmers at home can hurt farmers abroad

The Food for Peace program was established in the 1950s to get rid of unwanted farm surpluses, to build new markets for American products, and to reward favored Third World regimes. … Logic suggests that if American farmers benefit when the U.S. government purchases their crop, then small, marginal farmers in developing countries can be devastated when those crops are unloaded on Third World markets. In a report from the British magazine *The Economist* (February 2, 1985), "This dumping has allowed shortsighted local governments to keep the price of foodstuffs for the urban proletariat so cheap that native farmers are ruined, and dependence on imported foods become a drag on development."

Farmers in many Third World nations don't always have the clout that farmers have in developed nations. Many repressive Third World regimes, along with some international bureaucracies and political lobbies, owe their continued existence more to aid programs than to indigenous popular support.

Autocratic rulers can more easily hold on to the reins of power when there is abundance of wealth to distribute among corrupt power brokers. In this sense, foreign aid is more likely to retard development. Over the decades of Eastern and Western programs, Ethiopia has virtually become a textbook case.

It is simply not enough to measure a nation's concern for the poor, as many analysts are prone to do, by examining the annual increase in foreign aid. As economist Thomas Sowell reveals in his book *The Economics and Politics of Race: An International Perspective* [1983], Tanzania has received more foreign aid per capita than any other nation, yet its output per worker has declined 50 percent over the period of a decade and it has turned from an exporter of corn to an importer. In fact, food production all across Africa has been declining in the past decade despite continued aid programs.

According to the UN's Food and Agricultural Organization, food production per person in Africa declined consistently from the mid-1970s to the mid-1980s. Since then the trend has been upward.

Matching practice with ideals

Japan, Western Europe, and the United States have more to offer the world than restrictive trade barriers and the persistent custom of protecting the domestic farm at all costs. As a lesson from their own history, the First World nations know that an export potential is crucial to developing economies. They could foster greater investment and growth in the Third World by simply living up to their frequently-espoused ideals of free trade.

The citizens of the First World nations should be proud to be able to feed the impoverished Third World, and much of the formerly communist Second World, but they must recognize that this abundance is not due to the competitive strength of the agricultural sector as much as it is due to those businesses, workers, customers, and taxpayers who must shoulder the burden of subsidies and high prices. This represents a tremendous misallocation of resources and lost productivity for both the developed and the undeveloped nations. The poor in all nations, First and Third, suffer as a result.

It is time that the United States, Western Europe and Japan set a better, more consistent model for the Third World to emulate.

Since the 1980s governments in the West (particularly in the United States and Britain) have tended to allow market forces free rein in the manufacturing sector. Why do you think they have considered agriculture to be more deserving of support and subsidy?

EU'S VOW ON CARIBBEAN BANANAS HARD TO KEEP
South–North Development Monitor (SUNS)

NO

X Plans to revise Europe's banana trade deal with developing nations, so as to fit the world trading rules, mean only bad news for the Caribbean. Whatever the EU decides, the islands' small farmers and their families will be worse off.

"The EU made a commitment to protect our banana market until the new millennium. Instead, it has turned its back on us," accuses Renwick Rose, coordinator of the Windward Islands Farmers Association.

EU agriculture ministers last week announced a complete overhaul of the EU's banana trade "regime", part of the bloc's massive Lomé Convention trade and aid programme, to bring it into line with World Trade Organisation (WTO) rules by January 1999.

The WTO has ruled against the EU banana regime's system of import preferences for banana produces from the Africa–Caribbean–Pacific (ACP) group of nations. Following complaints by the U.S. and Central American nations, the WTO said that parts of the regime, such as trade import licensing agreements and the dividing up of quotas among ACP states, breach free trade rules.

Now the EU, which consumes some four million tonnes of bananas a year, must open up a market worth some two billion dollars to all exporting nations—or, theoretically, face trade sanctions.

The new pact, which must withstand any further challenges from the WTO, does not change existing tariff quotas, one of 2.2 million tonnes and the other of 353,000 tonnes, with a duty of 75 ECUs ($83) per tonne for non-ACP bananas and duty-free entry for ACP bananas.

The main changes proposed involve the setting up of a new licence distribution system, an aid package to be worth about $400 million to assist producing countries during a 10-year transition process, and the end of country-specific quotas for ACP states.

In 1975 the Lomé Convention was signed in Lomé, capital of Togo (formerly French Togoland in West Africa). It provided access to European markets for goods from 46 of Europe's former colonies. Its fourth extension was signed by 71 nations in 1989 and ran until the end of 1999. The new ruling described here therefore came into force when Lomé IV still had a year to run.

The effect of the proposed change was that each ACP country would no longer have a specific quota of European imports it could fill (the main basis of the U.S. complaint). However, an overall quota level would remain for the ACP group as a whole.

COMMENTARY: The banana wars

Several member states of the European Union (EU) were former colonial powers, and the EU's trading arrangements have often reflected those countries' ongoing relationships with their former colonies, the so-called Africa–Caribbean–Pacific (ACP) group of countries. For example, the EU gave the banana-producing former British and French colonies in the Caribbean and West Africa preferential access to European markets by allowing them to export a certain quota of bananas to Europe free of duty. The European countries saw this as a way of maintaining their financial and moral responsibilities to their former colonies, while the producing countries could count on a secure source of income.

However, this arrangement involved "discrimination"—treating ACP countries differently than other banana-producers. The World Trade Organization (WTO) was set up in 1995 to eliminate such discrimination. Transnational corporations (TNCs) based in the United States, such as Del Monte and Chiquita, grow bananas (known as "dollar bananas") on a huge scale—and lower cost—on plantations in Central American countries such as Honduras and Ecuador. Although these countries already had the largest share of the European banana market, they and the United States lodged a complaint with the WTO that European tariffs discriminated against their bananas. In a series of reforms between 1999 and 2001 the EU was forced to give these countries a larger quota of the market and pledged to eliminate all quotas by 2006 and ACP duty-free privileges by 2008.

The effect of these changes is likely to be that bananas will be sold more cheaply in Europe, and in this sense it is a classic demonstration of the efficiency of the market in ensuring that goods are produced for the lowest cost, giving the consumer the greatest benefit. But the effect is likely to be disastrous for the small ACP banana farmers who cannot hope to compete with the TNCs. In terms of development there will also be disadvantages. Since most banana production is in the hands of U.S.-owned TNCs, more profits will end up in the United States and less in the developing world. Wages and labor standards are lower in the dollar-banana countries than in the ACP countries; so while the banana industry in many ACP countries is likely to be destroyed, there is little or no chance of a corresponding increase in income or living standards in the dollar-banana countries.

Classical economics suggests that the ACP countries that lose out in the banana wars should do something else instead. Dominica has been relying on Europe's preferential banana imports for up to half its income. Wouldn't it be better to follow the example of countries such as Barbados in building up tourism and banking to make its economy less vulnerable? Others argue that a secure income from commodities such as bananas is essential to achieving this aim—without the money to invest in education and infrastructure the transition to a diversified economy cannot take place.

But the UK Presidency project, an association of British development NGOs, says the EU's decision "imposes one single 'block' quota for all the 71 ACP states. That quota will be dominated by the big transnationals, who can produce bananas at half the cost of the Caribbean fruit."

Already unable to compete against the massive industrialised banana plantations run largely by U.S. TNCs [transnational corporations] in Central America, the Caribbean states could find themselves competing against the same giants in their protected markets.

Banana TNCs are already moving into ACP countries, in West Africa, where they will be able to take advantage of a future block quota. "The TNCs have already increased production and are gearing up to push the smaller producers out," the co-president of the ACP–EU Joint Assembly, Glenys Kinnock, recently warned.

> *Do you think trade rules should distinguish between small producers and TNCs as a way of preventing the TNCs from dominating the whole market?*

The new system, as announced last Friday, sets itself the major objective of guaranteeing that "no ACP state... will be placed in a less favourable situation than in the past or present," a commitment that will be hard to meet.

About 20 percent of the bananas consumed in the EU every year are supplied by producers within the EU—in Madeira, the Canary Islands, and the French Overseas Departments. The remaining 80 percent are imported.

Of EU banana imports from outside, 21 percent come from twelve ACP countries: Cote d'Ivoire, Cameroon, Surinam, Somalia, Jamaica, St Lucia, St Vincent and the Grenadines, Dominica, Belize, Cape Verde, Grenada and Madagascar (known in EU terminology as "traditional" ACP countries). Three percent come from other "non-traditional" ACP states and the rest, 76 percent, come from third countries, mainly Ecuador, Colombia, Costa Rica and Honduras.

> *"Dollar bananas" are so called because they come from countries traditionally within the U.S. dollar sphere of influence, and because U.S. TNCs control most of the banana production in those countries.*

Small banana farmers in the Caribbean say that without preferential agreements they cannot compete in an open market against the cheaper "dollar bananas" grown industrially in Central America. They are well placed to scoop up the rest of the market.

"Windward Island farmers may be out of business within the next two years," says Elias John of the Windward Islands Farmers' Association. A third of the labour force in the Windward Islands is dependent on the production of bananas, with 70 percent of their land area devoted to their production.

Guaranteed access to the European market is seen as the key to the livelihoods of thousands of farmers in the Caribbean, sustaining the economies of several countries in the region. Many believe that if the banana industry collapses, social unrest and economic decline could follow. Many warn that the only other export crop that could provide them with a living is cannabis.

"Take away the (Caribbean) banana industry and the economy collapses. There will be mass poverty. It's a simple equation", said Phil Bloomer of the British NGO Oxfam.

Britain's agriculture minister, Jack Cunningham, says the deal on bananas meets WTO obligations. "I personally have been very concerned to ensure that the revised arrangements secure continuing stability in the Caribbean as well as being fully defensible in the WTO", said Cunningham, after chairing a meeting of EU agriculture ministers last week. EU spokesman Gerry Kiely said the new banana regime will be "fully compatible" with the WTO ruling.

But Dutch agriculture minister Josef van Aartsen, who opposed the adoption of the new regime, said that in his view it did not.

More importantly, the governments of Ecuador, Guatemala, Honduras, Mexico, and Panama, which initially brought the complaint against the EU's original banana regime to the WTO, and the United States, home to the trio of multinationals that dominate Central America's banana industries, Dole, Del Monte and Chiquita Brands, all say the new proposal does not meet WTO rules.

Independently from that, a major stated objective of the banana regime, the maintenance of the EU commitment that "no ACP state … will be placed in a less-favourable situation than in the past or present" will become more and more difficult to reach.

If banana growers turn to growing cannabis, most of it will end up in the United States. Should that be considered the responsibility of the TNCs that have pushed for the change in quotas? If not, whose responsibility is it?

Ecuador alone was awarded 26.2 percent of the EU's banana market in the 1999 proposals —more than all the ACP countries put together—but still continued its protest at the WTO. In 2001 it secured the transfer of a further 100,000 from the ACP quota to the "dollar" quota.

Summary

In the first article Ken Schoolland argues that subsidized agriculture—a favored policy of western countries—is damaging the lives of people in the developing world. He argues that subsidized agriculture creates huge surpluses of food in the developed world. While farmers in the developing nations struggle to survive, millions of tons of food are being destroyed or distributed to poor nations as foreign aid. Dumping tons of food on the developing world in this way means that farmers in poorer countries suffer: Their market is swamped by foreign food that is cheaper not because it has been more efficiently produced, but because it has been subsidized. Schoolland also believes that strict import regulations go against western ideals of free trade by preventing farmers in the developing world from exporting their own produce. In conclusion, Schoolland contends that everyone suffers as a result of this misdirected agricultural policy. People in the developed world continue to shoulder the burden of subsidies and high food prices, poor farmers go out of business, and poverty and famine persist.

The second article, from the South–North Development Monitor, examines EU plans to overhaul its banana trade with the Africa–Caribbean–Pacific (ACP) group of nations in response to a ruling by the World Trade Organization (WTO). The ruling follows complaints from the United States and some Central American nations, which argue that country-specific EU import quotas for ACP bananas breach free-trade rules. The ruling effectively forces the EU to impose a single "block" quota from ACP countries. The article suggests that small banana farmers in ACP nations, such as those in the Caribbean, will be forced out of business as large transnational corporations, such as Chiquita, Del Monte, and Dole, dominate the new block quota, just as they already dominate the production of dollar–bananas. The authors fear that the EU's promise that no ACP state will be harmed by the ruling will be hard to keep. The banana industry sustains the economies of several Caribbean countries, which face ruin if banana farmers go out of business.

FURTHER INFORMATION:

Books:

Clegg, Peter, *The Caribbean Banana Trade: From Colonialism to Globalization*. New York: Palgrave Macmillan, 2002.

Ingco, Merlinda D. (ed.), *Agriculture, Trade, and the WTO: Creating a Trading Environment for Development*. Washington, D.C.: World Bank, 2003.

 Useful website:

www.bananalink.org.uk/trade_war/trade_war.htm
Banana Link's page on the history of the banana dispute.

The following debates in the Pro/Con series may also be of interest:

In this volume:

Topic 1 Do rich countries have a duty to give financial help to their former colonies?

HAVE HEAVY AGRICULTURAL SUBSIDIES DAMAGED THE ECONOMIES OF POORER NATIONS?

YES: They promote unnecessary surpluses that consumers have to pay for; only rich farmers benefit

YES: If food aid is sent from the West instead of being bought in the region, it destroys the agricultural economies of the regions receiving it; they can't compete with subsidized prices

SUBSIDIES
Do subsidies always have a bad effect on agriculture and trade?

AID
Is using surplus food as emergency aid a bad idea?

NO: They can be used to stabilize prices in times of uncertainty, ensure everyone has enough to eat, and promote national self-sufficiency in food

HAVE HEAVY AGRICULTURAL SUBSIDIES DAMAGED THE ECONOMIES OF POORER NATIONS?
KEY POINTS

NO: Food aid supports starving people who would otherwise die. It also helps build markets for the future.

YES: Quotas based on colonial history only perpetuate the dependence of poor countries on former colonizers, instead of letting them move on

YES: This is a great opportunity for ACP countries to move away from cheap commodity agriculture and develop higher-value goods and services

QUOTAS
Should countries be barred from giving preference to goods from some countries over others?

DIVERSIFICATION
Should ACP countries leave bananas to more efficient growers and do something else instead?

NO: Countries with a responsibility to ex-colonies should be allowed to favor those countries in trade

NO: The idea just salves the conscience of big transnational companies, which are going to take away their business

147

Topic 12

DO PATENTS LEAD TO HIGHER-PRICED DRUGS?

YES
"MAKE AIDS DRUGS AVAILABLE TO ALL"
NEW INTERNATIONALIST, ISSUE 346, JUNE 2002
MATTHEW FLYNN

NO
"PATENTS AND AIDS DRUG RESEARCH"
LETTER TO *THE WASHINGTON POST*, OCTOBER 11, 2002
ALAN HOLMER

INTRODUCTION

The drug industry is one of the most profitable in the world, with profits around 20 percent of a multibillion dollar turnover. Despite this there are millions of people suffering from HIV/AIDS and other illnesses who do not have access to medications and treatments: The high cost of patent-protected anti-HIV/AIDS drugs puts them beyond the reach of patients and governments in the developing world. Manufacturers claim that patents (the mechanism by which inventors protect their ideas from being copied or stolen) are necessary to recover high research and development costs. Others say that manufacturers are able to charge exorbitant prices because patents prevent cheaper versions of drugs from being produced. Is that really the case?

When inventors or companies come up with ideas, they submit a description of their invention and how it works to a patenting office. If the idea is judged to be original, then a patent is granted, which prevents anyone else from legally making and selling the invention for a certain period, usually 20 years. The inventor's description of the idea is also made public for others to use in their own research and development.

Patents ensure that those who invest in expensive research reap the benefits of a successful invention. Drug companies typically invest $800 million and 15 years' effort into developing a new drug, and only one in five new drugs makes it to market. If another company could just copy it, then there would be no incentive to carry out the research, and many existing medicines and technologies would not have been developed. Conversely, the patent gives companies the sole right to price and distribute their products, a position that critics argue companies might abuse.

Because a patent is a legal device, its effect differs between countries. India, South Africa, and Brazil have laws that allow local manufacturers to make their own cheaper versions of drugs, called "generics," or import cheaper generic versions from other countries. Drug companies have opposed these laws— for example, 39 pharmaceutical corporations tried to sue the South African government over patents in 1998. International pressure forced them to drop the lawsuit in 2001.

"Drug companies are in the awful spot of having to balance the needs of their shareholders against the needs of the dying."

—MICKEY SMITH, DIRECTOR

OF THE CENTER FOR

PHARMACEUTICAL MARKETING,

UNIVERSITY OF MISSISSIPPI (2001)

Critics believe the drug companies are abusing the patent system to charge artificially high prices. However, the drug companies accuse makers and buyers of copies of patented drugs of effectively stealing from them and thus hindering the development of new treatments. It is a difficult moral issue, since the availability of these drugs can determine whether people live or die.

In support of patents the United Nations Secretary-General Kofi Annan said, "Intellectual property protection is key to bringing forward new medicines, vaccines and diagnostics urgently needed for the health of the world's poorest people." Drug companies have paid for the training of personnel and built medical facilities in poor areas.

They have agreed to provide certain drugs at cost price or free to several countries. Many medicines are not patented anyway, including 95 percent of those on the World Health Organization's list of essential drugs.

Yet the South African government defended its legislation to ignore patents as part of its constitutional obligation to provide health care through affordable drugs. After the laws were passed, Cipla, an Indian drug manufacturer, offered a generic "cocktail" of anti-AIDS drugs for $350 a patient per year; the same drugs cost $12,000 in the United States. Soon afterward, almost every drug company announced drastic cuts to their prices in Africa. The generic drug manufacturers say their drugs are cheap because they spend much less on marketing and make less profit than the major drug companies, such as Pfizer. As an example, Pfizer's research and production costs were 31 percent of its sales, whereas marketing was 39 percent and profit was 30 percent.

The following articles are from both sides of the debate. The first is a report for the *New Internationalist* in which journalist Matthew Flynn discusses how ignoring patents increases the availability of drugs in poor countries. Taking Brazil as a case in point, Flynn argues that the generic anti-AIDS drugs produced in government laboratories have led to a successful HIV/AIDS treatment program. The second article is a letter to *The Washington Post* from Alan Holmer, the president of the Pharmaceutical Research and Manufacturers of America (PhRMA). He claims that PhRMA has contributed billions in aid, and that to continue essential research into new drugs, patents need to be protected.

MAKE AIDS DRUGS AVAILABLE TO ALL
Matthew Flynn

YES

☑ For one week, normal life stops and parades, floats and dancing take over. Behind the scenes, however, carnival has a serious side: it is also the time when Brazil's Health Ministry redoubles its efforts to educate party-goers about the risk of AIDS. Billboards, t-shirts and television commercials encourage young and old alike to have safe sex and use condoms—"the party gowns of life." The message could not come at a better time. In a culture famous for its libidinous ways, carnival is the wildest time of all.

Nearly a decade ago, the World Bank warned that Brazil would have over a million AIDS cases by the turn of the century if action were not taken. Today, while the country has lost 100,000 people to the deadly virus, infection rates remain a low 0.6 per cent and the predicted epidemic has been avoided.

The author uses some startling facts about Brazil's successful fight against an AIDS epidemic to gain the reader's interest.

Successful strategies

Prevention is one of the pillars of Brazil's successful AIDS programme. But treatment and human rights are also key.

Brazil began investing in drug therapies in the early 1990s, even though aid agencies argued that drug therapy was not "cost effective" and that scarce resources should be concentrated on prevention.

Antiretroviral drugs (ARVs) slow down the development of AIDS. They are most effective when taken in a "cocktail," or combination of several drugs. See page 151.

But, says Paulo Teixeira, head of the government AIDS programme, the Brazilian thinking was different: "It is impossible to mobilize a society, to mobilize people—infected or not—for a national effort if you do not provide what they are expecting to receive: support and clinical treatment."

Brazil's commitment to providing affordable drug therapy is abundantly clear. Last year, the health ministry distributed antiretroviral (ARV) drugs to 110,000 registered HIV patients —free of charge.

Go to www.who.int— the site of the World Health Organization—and find out how this figure compares to other developing nations.

"Access to free medication encourages more people to test themselves and helps curb the spread of the disease," explains Veriano Terto, general co-ordinator of the Associação Brasileira Interdisciplinar de AIDS [Brazilian Interdisciplinary AIDS Association]. ABIA is a non-profit organization which conducts research and provides counselling to HIV-positive people.

COMMENTARY: Anti-HIV/AIDS drugs

Antiretroviral drugs (see pages 160–161) are the primary treatment for HIV/AIDS. They do not kill the virus, but they can dramatically slow its growth. HIV invades and takes over a type of cell in the body's immune response system known as a CD4 cell, which it uses to replicate itself and spread into other cells. HIV weakens the body's immune system, making sufferers more susceptible to illnesses that will eventually kill them. Antiretroviral drugs work by targeting HIV at specific points in its life cycle. They suppress the activity of one or both of two viral enzymes essential for HIV to reproduce. This slows down the development of HIV into AIDS and can prolong the life of an HIV-positive person for years. The first antiretroviral, known as AZT, or zidovudine, was developed in the 1980s. Since then several other effective drugs have been developed, with the result that the effect of HIV/AIDS in Europe and the United States has been greatly reduced. But drug patents have, critics argue, prevented the treatment of the virus in developing nations.

Taking anti-HIV/AIDs drugs
When taking the drug therapy, patients have to follow a regimen (or systematic plan) closely. At the same time, safe-sex methods need to be followed both to avoid reinfection or catching other infections. Taking the wrong dose or the wrong combination of anti-HIV/AIDs drugs can be very dangerous. Incorrectly treated HIV can reproduce itself rapidly and mutate to produce new strains that are resistant to the drugs prescribed. The new drug-resistant strains can be passed on to other people in the same way as ordinary HIV. The drugs can also have side effects, such as diarrhea and anemia; they do not work for everyone.

Reducing mother-to-child transmission
Following a regimen of antiretroviral drugs in combination has been shown to be much more effective than following a single antiretroviral course. Dual therapy—when two antiretrovirals are taken in a regimen—is better than one, but the most effective treatment (and also the most expensive) is the triple combination. An exception to this is the application of single antiretrovirals in the treatment of pregnant HIV-positive women. The chances of an HIV-positive mother passing on the virus to her child during pregnancy, childbirth, or while breastfeeding are about 25 percent without treatment. Taking AZT or nevirapine can virtually eliminate the chances of passing on the infection to newborn babies if taken correctly; in this case single-drug regimens can play an important role in preventing the transmission of the disease from mother to baby. Several developing countries have begun such programs of treating pregnant women and have successfully cut transmission rates.

Terto, who learned that he was HIV positive in 1996 and began treatment the following year, says that in a developing nation like Brazil drug therapy needs to be available and affordable.

"Like most other Brazilians I would not be able to afford the high price of the medication." Since learning of his illness Terto has been able to continue working normally and was able to finish a doctorate in public health.

Like other cash-strapped developing countries, Brazil was faced with the problem of providing a growing number of AIDS patients with expensive treatments sold only by large, international drug companies.

Go to the World Trade Organization website— www.wto.org—for information about the TRIPS agreement.

Brazil's answer: manufacture the drugs locally

"We started producing those drugs before the country signed the WTO [World Trade Organization] trade-related intellectual property agreement (TRIPs) in 1996," recalls Teixeira. "The first consequence was that the price dropped tremendously—some 80 per cent." While treatment in the United States costs $12,000, in Brazil it is $2,500 and falling. With most ARVs already on the market before the country adjusted its patent laws to WTO requirements, Brazil could sidestep steep royalties to the companies when making generic copies.

Government labs currently produce 8 of the 14 ingredients that make up the so-called AIDS cocktail. The government saves $250 million a year by not paying for the high-priced, patent-protected imported drugs, and it avoids the additional expenses of hospital care for untreated patients.

"The reduction in the incidence of AIDS-related diseases has saved us $670 million over 3 years," reports Dr Marco Antônio Victória, chief medical advisor to Brazil's AIDS programme.

See page 155 for details of Big Pharma's legal fight with the South African government regarding its laws allowing the importation of generic drugs.

Government participation in Brazil's $6.5 billion domestic drug market was not cheered by everyone. The giant multinational companies, collectively known as Big Pharma, were angered by the cheaper, generic drugs. More recently, their ire has focused on government research into newer ARV treatments. Unlike generics, Efavirenz (sold by Merck) and Nelfinavir (made by Hoffmann-La Roche) are protected by Brazilian patent legislation.

The United States, pressured by Big Pharma, threatened a WTO investigation of Brazil's breach of the TRIPs accord. But unlike smaller nations that often back down in the face of pressure, Brazil rallied international support for its case. Both the UN Commission of Human Rights (UNCHR) and the World Health Organization (WHO) approved Brazilian-sponsored motions supporting access to life-saving drugs as a basic human right. The country then scored another small victory at the WTO's annual meeting in Doha, Qatar last November where the US—partially owing to the Anthrax scare—offered lukewarm support to a similar measure.

Meanwhile, the government lab FarManguinhos was diligently working to crack the secret of Efavirenz and Nelfinavir.

After learning how the drugs were manufactured, Brazil would be in a position to threaten to break their patents and produce them locally—or negotiate better prices with suppliers Merck and Hoffmann-La Roche.

Eloan Pinheiro, director of the state-owned FarManguinhos lab, adds that after discovering the make-up of a drug it is possible to compare the cost of production to the retail price. "It was easy to calculate the profit margin. It was enormous and continues to be exorbitant," she says.

With the drug companies stripped of their clothes, the Health Ministry negotiated price reductions of 58 per cent for Nelfinavir (from $1.53 a capsule to $0.65) and 64 per cent for Efavirenz (from $2.32 a capsule to $0.84).

Despite the success of Brazil's generic programme, it is far from perfect. The country has 110,000 HIV-positive patients who receive the drugs, but another half-million people are estimated to be infected who don't benefit from government programmes.

"We still have AIDS being contracted by socially excluded, more marginalized people," says Veriano Terto of the ABIA. "And while the conditions of poverty, unemployment and violence that create such marginalization are not combatted, it will be difficult to control the spread of AIDS in these populations."

Brazil remains a highly stratified society and its public-health system continues to be underfunded. But whatever its shortcomings, the country has made significant progress despite limited resources.

In fact, one of Brazil's newest exports is its expertise in dealing with HIV/AIDS. Médecins Sans Frontières (MSF) recently signed an agreement with FarManguinhos to use their generic antiretrovirals in MSF projects. In return, MSF helps fund FarManguinhos' efforts to find new cures for diseases ignored by Big Pharma.

Brazil has also signed technical co-operation agreements with four African countries—Angola, Mozambique, Guinea Bissau and São Tomé. And several others, including Namibia, Zimbabwe, South Africa, Kenya, Nigeria and Botswana are said to be interested in the country's AIDS drugs.

This article was published in June 2002. The WTO meeting was held from November 9 to 13, 2001, in Doha. The conferences are held every two years and are attended by member states. This particular conference drew criticisms from developing nations, environmentalists, labor unions, and NGOs, among others, who claimed northern industrialized nations have too much control over world trade.

Who do you think these marginalized people might be? Go to www.un.org/ news/briefings/ docs/2001/BrzlAIDS. doc.htm to find out more.

MSF, also known as Doctors Without Borders, is an independent humanitarian medical-aid agency committed to providing medical aid wherever it is needed. Visit their website www.msf.org for more information.

PATENTS AND AIDS DRUG RESEARCH
Alan Holmer

NO

 Letter to the editor of *The Washington Post*

While we [the pharmaceutical industry] don't expect *The Post* to share all of our views, we were surprised that a column would focus on a critique of an individual staffer speaking for the industry rather than on the issue at hand— AIDS in the developing world ["Talking Cadillacs to Rickshaw Riders," op-ed, October 7, 2002].

The author argues that patents are not the real problem in African health care. He tries to shift the central issue of the debate. Is this an effective technique?

Phony issue
Patents are a phony issue when it comes to AIDS treatment in the developing world.

A study published in the *Journal of the American Medical Association* last October found that antiretroviral AIDS medicines are patented in few African countries. Throughout Africa, countries are free to import generic versions or to make the drugs themselves. Yet AIDS deaths keep rising because the true barriers to treatment are not patents but poverty, neglect and the lack of sustained international aid.

The writer stresses the importance of actions over words. He mentions PhRMA members' donations to aid to head off criticism that the companies are only concerned in making large profits.

The position of U.S. pharmaceutical companies
America's pharmaceutical companies, many of which have worked in Africa for decades, long ago moved beyond rhetoric to action. In the past five years, members of the Pharmaceutical Research and Manufacturers of America [PhRMA] have contributed more than $2 billion in overseas aid.

They have made available at heavily discounted prices, or for free, millions of dollars' worth of AIDS medicines to Africa. They also have sponsored projects to improve the health infrastructure and to train doctors, nurses and other medical personnel.

No cure for AIDS
As yet, there is no cure or preventive vaccine for AIDS— although drug companies have about a hundred medicines in the pipeline.

COMMENTARY: Big Pharma vs. South Africa

Big Pharma vs. South Africa was a court case in 2001 in which pharmaceutical companies tried to sue the South African government for allowing the use of cheaper versions of drugs in South Africa. South Africa's 1997 Medicines Act contained several important measures relating to patented drugs. It legally obliged pharmacists to prescribe cheaper generic drugs instead of patented drugs where possible and provided for the establishment of a pricing committee to ensure a more transparent pricing system for all medicines. The act also provided for parallel importation: allowing patented drugs to be imported from abroad. Patented drugs are often cheaper in countries such as India because the production of local generic drugs there has forced down the price of brand-name drugs. The measures were planned to ease the pressures on the overloaded public-health system struggling with the huge numbers of HIV/AIDS patients in South Africa.

Legal challenge

Thirty-nine of the world's largest pharmaceutical companies challenged the legality of the Medicines Act under the World Trade Organization's (WTO's) trade-related intellectual property agreement (TRIPS). The pharmaceutical companies feared that if patents were not respected in South Africa, it could lead to other countries ignoring patents and importing or making generic drugs. The South African government, however, held that the act was an acceptable and lawful response to a crisis in access to drugs. The pharmaceutical companies first brought the action in 1998 and obtained an interim interdict preventing the South African government from implementing the Medicines Act until the case had been decided.

South Africa's leading AIDS activists, the Treatment Action Campaign (TAC), launched in 1999, together with the international aid agencies Doctors Without Borders, Oxfam, and other groups, campaigned to raise international condemnation of the court case. They gained global support from those who saw the case as an attempt to protect the commercial interests of transnational companies at the expense of the constitutional rights of South Africans to adequate health care.

The U.S. government gave its support to the pharmaceutical companies at first but withdrew it in 2000 in response to public pressure. The case was heard in March 2001 in the South African High Court. The court decided to accept evidence from TAC as a "friend of the court." TAC represented people living with HIV. On April 19, 2001, the pharmaceutical companies dropped the lawsuit. Campaigners saw this action as an important step on the road to establishing a legal framework for ensuring that medicines in South Africa are affordable. In August 2003 the WTO approved a deal allowing certain poor countries, such as India, Brazil, South Africa, and Kenya, access to cheaper drugs.

Supporters of South Africa's leading HIV/AIDS campaign group, Treatment Action Campaign, call for access to affordable anti-HIV/AIDS drugs at a rally in Cape Town, February 2002.

To continue this expensive, high-risk research, we need patent protection in the developed world and movement toward patent protection in the poorest countries.

This may not be a fashionable view, but it has the virtue of being true.

ALAN F. HOLMER
President and Chief Executive Officer
Pharmaceutical Research
and Manufacturers of America

Is the author implying that patents protect people from using high-risk drugs on a mass scale? Do you think most people would be willing to take the risk?

Summary

The issue of whether or not patents lead to higher-priced drugs has become more pressing in the context of the HIV/AIDS pandemic sweeping through the developing world, where millions of HIV/AIDS-infected people cannot afford patented drugs. In the first article Matthew Flynn cites Brazil as an example of how ignoring patents and allowing generic drugs to be produced results in a significant reduction in cost. In Brazil government manufacture of many generic anti-AIDS drugs has drastically cut the spread of HIV infection over the last decade. Drug treatment costing $12,000 in the United States now costs $2,500 in Brazil, and the price is still falling. With its expertise gained in treating its HIV-infected population Brazil is also in a position to help other countries with similar problems.

In the second article Alan Holmer puts forward an opposing view held by the major pharmaceutical companies. He argues that the use of patents is a "phony issue" that obscures the real barriers to treating HIV/AIDS in the developing world—poverty, neglect, and a lack of international financial aid. To support his view, he points out that HIV/AIDS medicines are patented in few African countries, yet the number of deaths continues to rise. Pharmaceutical companies have given billions of dollars to these nations and provided medicines at heavy discounts or even for free. He asserts that to continue the expensive and risky research into a cure for AIDS, these companies need protection of their patents.

FURTHER INFORMATION:

Books:

Jaffrey, Zia, *The New Apartheid: AIDS in South Africa.* New York: Verso Books, 2002.

Kalipeni, Ezekiel, et al. (eds.), *AIDS in Africa: Beyond Epidemiology.* Oxford: Blackwells, 2003.

Mahlangu-Ngcobo, Mankekolo, *AIDS in Africa: An African and Prophetic Perspective.* Mahlangu-Ngcobo, 2001.

World Bank, *Intensifying Action against HIV/AIDS in Africa: Responding to a Development Crisis.* Washington, D.C.: World Bank, 1999.

Articles:

Goldberg, Robert M., "Fight AIDS with Reason, not Rhetoric," *Wall Street Journal*, April 23, 2001.

Useful websites:

www.unaids.org

Joint UN program on HIV/AIDS site.

www.cptech.org/ip/health/

Site of the Consumer Project on Technology, an antipatent activist site with links to all sides of the argument.

www.fda.gov/cder/ogd/

Site on generic drugs by the U.S. Food and Drug Administration (SDA).

www.who.int/m/topics/hiv_infections/

World Health Organization pages on HIV/AIDS.

> *The following debates in the Pro/Con series may also be of interest:*
>
> In *Health*:
>
> Topic 3 Should there be mandatory testing for AIDS?

DO PATENTS LEAD TO HIGHER-PRICED DRUGS?

YES: Not all products and ideas should be protected by patents. Some, such as life-saving drugs, help people and should be readily available to everyone.

YES: Generic drugs or copies save money and sometimes help advance science

INTELLECTUAL PROPERTY
Is it wrong to protect the intellectual copyright of drugs?

GENERICS
Should developing countries be allowed to develop generic drugs?

NO: If someone has worked hard and invested a lot of money in developing a successful drug, they should receive the benefits

NO: Patent protection laws exist for a reason. They must be observed, otherwise research and development will suffer.

DO PATENTS LEAD TO HIGHER-PRICED DRUGS?
KEY POINTS

YES: Increasing prices in rich countries provide the income necessary to fund research and development and also to subsidize low-cost drugs in poor countries

YES: Pharmaceutical companies will have no incentive to invest in research and development for new drugs unless they can recoup the money through patents

PRICE DIFFERENTIALS
Is it ethical to have different prices in different countries?

RESEARCH AND DEVELOPMENT
Is the investment in research and development argument for patents a viable one?

NO: Not everyone in rich countries is necessarily able to afford expensive drugs

NO: Pharmaceutical companies are already very rich. They do not need to get richer at the expense of poor countries.

159

DRUG PATENTS AND HIV/AIDS: THE CASE OF SOUTH AFRICA

"Sixty million Africans have been touched by AIDS in the most immediate way."

—DR. PETER PIOT, EXECUTIVE DIRECTOR OF UNAIDS (2003)

South Africa has the largest number of HIV/AIDS sufferers in the world. In 2003 the Aids Foundation of South Africa estimated that 4.74 million South Africans of a total population of 43.3 million are HIV positive. In a country where most people live below the poverty line, HIV/AIDS is a devastating killer. In 2001, 360,000 people died from AIDS—a rate of nearly 1,000 per week. Very few South Africans have access to the drugs developed to tackle HIV/AIDS available in the developed world. Some critics claim this is not just because of insubstantial government policies toward HIV/AIDS prevention and treatment, but because of drug patent laws that make adequate treatment too expensive.

The disease and treatment

AIDS (acquired immune deficiency syndrome) damages the body's immune system, leaving sufferers open to infections that will eventually kill them. AIDS is caused by a virus called HIV (human immunodeficiency virus). Since the first reported case in 1981 HIV/AIDS has spread rapidly across the world. Sub-Saharan Africa is today the worst hit area, with more than 70 percent of cases. HIV/AIDS is incurable, but drugs have been developed that can minimize the impact of HIV on the immune system. These drugs, known as antiretrovirals (ARVs), can improve an HIV/AIDS-infected person's quality of life and help them stay well longer. The drugs slow down the progress of the virus into AIDS and reduce the chances of the disease being transmitted from mother to child.

High drug prices

The first antiretroviral drug, AZT (zidovudine, commercially called Retrovir), was approved in 1987 by the Food and Drug Administration. Other antiretrovirals (ARVs) were quickly formulated, patented, and authorized. As a result, the number of deaths from AIDS has been dramatically reduced in developed countries. But the U.S. patented price for the most effective combination of ARVs is $10,000 per patient per year—a price far beyond the reach of millions of people in South Africa, where the epidemic is most severe. Although pharmaceutical companies dropped their prices to $1,000 for HIV/AIDS patients in Africa, this is still three times the cost of generic drugs (cheaper copies of brand-name patented drugs). Drugs companies argue that issues other than high prices restrict access to HIV/AIDS drugs in Africa such as the lack of international aid, transportation and storage problems, and the difficulties of implementing a complex drug regimen. They argue that apart from South Africa, few African countries have patent laws.

Court case

Patent laws protecting intellectual property allow pharmaceutical companies to have a monopoly on selling drugs that they have developed over a number of years. The protection gives them an opportunity to sell drugs at high prices to recoup costs and acts as an incentive to conduct further research and development. Some countries, notably India and Brazil, have been able to produce generic HIV/AIDS drugs because they have only recently adopted patent laws.

In 1997 the South African government passed an act permitting pharmacists to bypass patent laws and buy generic drugs. As a consequence, 39 pharmaceutical companies brought charges of piracy against the South African government in 1998. President Bill Clinton supported the pharmaceutical companies' court case until public protest led him to deny the pharmaceutical companies patent protection and issue an executive order in May 2000 to make inexpensive ARVs more widely available in Africa. Due to international pressure the case was eventually dropped in 2001.

Government policies

South Africa's HIV/AIDS campaigners calling for cheaper ARVs have also had to fight their own government. President Thabo Mbeki and health officials have cast doubt on the effectiveness of ARVs, declaring them unproven and difficult to take. Activists have long accused the government of inaction. Instead of introducing drug therapies, government ministers have prioritized the improvement of the overall state of the health care system. However, in August 2003 the South African government finally agreed to implement a public program of administering ARV drugs to its HIV-positive citizens as a matter of urgency. This new attitude could secure better and longer lives for the millions of South Africans living with HIV/AIDS.

In December 2002 the United States government declared that it would permit developing countries to override patents on drugs for HIV/AIDS, malaria, tuberculosis, and other infectious epidemics. Two months later it pledged $15 billion dollars to HIV/AIDS programs in Africa and the Caribbean. Meanwhile, the World Trade Organization's (WTO) agreement on trade-related aspects of intellectual property rights (TRIPS) allows companies to make a profit trading a drug for 20 years, enforceable by trade sanctions from 2006. The WTO agreement will end the production of cheaper generic drugs, which in turn will drive up the price of new medicines. Many health campaigners see this provision as overly generous toward drug companies in the face of the public health crisis caused by HIV/AIDS. They are calling for an urgent revision of the WTO agreement.

PART 4
POPULATION, FOOD, AND WATER

INTRODUCTION

In the last 50 years or so there has been a dramatic increase in global population levels. Whereas in 1950 there were just over 2.5 billion people—1.8 billion of whom lived in developing countries—in 2003 there were just over 6 billion—4.9 billion of whom lived in developing countries. The United Nations has estimated that by 2050 global population levels will have reached 9.3 billion and that most of this growth will occur in Africa and India. Critics argue that these regions can ill afford to experience such growth since they already have the highest rates of famine, chronic undernutrition, poverty, and water and food security problems. Others claim that these problems are ones that the international community must address quickly since resources are already overstretched and overexhausted. But what, commentators ask, can be done to improve conditions? Are governments really doing enough to prevent population exploding out of control?

How many is too many?

Some scientists have theorized that the Earth has a natural "human carrying capacity"—that is, the maximum number of people the Earth can sustain in the long term. Experts have estimated that this may be around 40

billion people, taking into account current technology. Others argue that the Earth's carrying capacity is infinite. Critics of this theory claim that it is obvious that the planet is near, or has already exceeded, its carrying capacity, and that a large population is overstraining an already overtaxed environment.

Population control

Population grows when birthrates exceed death rates. In Europe the populations are actually going down because deaths currently exceed births. Some demographers have estimated that the world population would stabilize if there was a "replacement level" fertility rate of around two children per couple. However, the average in most developing countries is around 3.6 children, compared with only 1.6 children in more developed countries.

Some health experts argue that natural events will intervene to curtail growth. Famine and disease, for example, have historically decimated populations in Africa and India. Experts estimate that despite high birthrates Botswana, South Africa, and Zimbabwe will all experience population decline in the next 50 years or so due to the incidence of HIV/AIDS in these countries. In 2003 around 36 percent of Botswana's 1.6 million adults had been infected with the HIV/AIDS virus. Whereas in 1990 the average life expectancy there was 62 years, in 2000 this had fallen to 36 years.

But some people argue that scientific and medical advances are happening at such a rate that diseases like HIV/AIDS will soon be curable. They argue that the population rate and the exhaustion of resources is such that something must be done to curtail population growth and that the governments of poor nations in particular have a duty

source of income and labor. They claim that as more people in these communities are encouraged to stay in school or go to college, and more receive skills training, their economies will develop. Some critics thus argue that protecting the culture and lifestyle of indigenous peoples can prevent vital economic development. Topic 14 examines this issue further.

Food and water security
International agencies claim that monitoring population levels and

---

"Water, taken in moderation, cannot hurt anyone."
—MARK TWAIN (1835–1910), AMERICAN AUTHOR

---

to discourage citizens from having children. Population control policies are one way to do this. Advocates cite the example of China, which initiated a government program to control the birthrate with varying levels of success. Critics, however, argue that such policies infringe on basic human rights and that population control is not a solution to the problems of the developing world. Topic 13 in this section examines whether population control is essential in poor nations.

Others argue that economic development helps reduce population levels. Historically as women entered the workplace they tended to get married later, if at all, and have fewer children. Some critics argue that indigenous peoples, who largely still live in traditional agrarian societies, tend to have larger families, partly because children are a fundamental

indigenous populations are both largely irrelevant if essential water and food supplies are exhausted. The UN Food and Agriculture Organization (FAO) estimates that approximately 800 million people are chronically undernourished. The world's hungry are predominantly located in South Asia and sub-Saharan Africa. War and political instability have added to existing problems caused by drought and environmental changes.

Similarly, clean, adequate water supplies have been a major concern for centuries. Water is an essential resource, but the World Bank estimates that 12 million people die from unsafe drinking water each year. Water is also essential for growing crops, clean sanitation, and in the development of industry, among other things. Topic 16 assesses whether water scarcity prevents sustainable development.

Topic 13
IS POPULATION CONTROL ESSENTIAL IN POOR NATIONS?

YES
"POPULATION CONTROL: GOOD STEWARDSHIP?"
TRIPLE HELIX, WINTER 2000
JOHN GUILLEBAUD

NO
"DON'T FUND UNFPA POPULATION CONTROL"
CATO INSTITUTE, MAY 15, 1999
STEPHEN MOORE

INTRODUCTION

During the 20th century the number of people in the world rose from around 1.6 billion in 1900 to 6 billion in 1999. Much of this population growth has taken place in the developing world, a situation that has resulted in a heated dialogue between those people who believe that population control must be encouraged in poorer countries and those who oppose such action as unfair or impracticable. The debate over population control covers a wide range of issues, from fears about the planet's capacity to support life to questions of human rights.

Among the arguments that advocates of population control put forward is that unchecked population growth will lead to catastrophic environmental damage. They cite the loss of forests in poor countries as trees are cut down to create farmland and provide wood both to burn and export. As more and more forest is felled, these people claim, the soil the trees once held in place is

washed away or blown away, turning the land to desert and causing further trees to be felled to create yet more farmland. Furthermore, they say, destroying trees, which absorb carbon dioxide, increases the greenhouse effect. An excessive buildup in the atmosphere of so-called greenhouse gases, of which carbon dioxide is one, is cited as a cause of the widely accepted process of global warming.

Supporters of population control also contend that food and water supplies, already stretched to the limit in places, simply cannot expand to satisfy unbridled growth in human numbers. One person who shared this view was British economist Thomas Malthus (1766–1834), who wrote about the importance of population control as early as 1798 in *An Essay on the Principle of Population*. Malthus believed that population, unless checked, would eventually outstrip the food supply.

Some commentators link population control in the developing world to women's rights. They argue that if women in poorer countries gain access to birth control, education (general and on reproductive issues), and jobs, then evidence suggests a decline in the birthrate will follow as these women choose to have smaller families. The introduction of such measures was endorsed by the 1994 International Conference on Population and Development (ICPD). Held in Cairo, this meeting was the latest in a line of United Nations population conferences that have taken place each decade since 1954.

"Population growth is the primary source of environmental damage."

—JACQUES COUSTEAU (1910–1997), FRENCH OCEANOGRAPHER

Critics of population control take issue with the notion that it necessarily gives women more control over their lives. The Committee on Women, Population, and the Environment (CWPE), for instance, asserts that "Most demographically driven population control policies and programs are deeply disrespectful of women, particularly women of color and their children. Such policies disempower women...."

Birth control programs can also be coercive, anticontrol commentators argue, citing China's one-child policy as an example. Introduced in the 1970s, in an attempt to place a check on the growth of the Chinese population, the policy has been accused by critics of leading to forced sterilizations and to the killing of unwanted female babies.

Others oppose population control on ideological grounds, seeing it as racism or an extension of western imperialism, or as a violation of religious law or as morally unacceptable. The United States government, which has generally been in favor of population control, has refused aid under the Republican administrations of the 1980s and of President George W. Bush (1946–) to organizations associated with voluntary abortion.

Opponents of population control also argue that it simply is not necessary. Far from running out, they say, food supplies are increasing, and any shortages are caused by problems in distribution or poor management. They claim that technology will provide solutions that will allow the world's population to keep on growing. One of the major proponents of the view that the population is not reaching crisis point was U.S. economist Julian Simon (1932–1998), who said, "There is no meaningful limit to our capacity to keep growing forever."

The two articles that follow examine the population control debate from different perspectives. Gynecologist John Guillebaud argues that population growth needs to be slowed through a combination of the relief of poverty and "the means for women to achieve their human right to control their fertility." In the second article economist Stephen Moore, on the other hand, claims that the "population bomb hysteria" has passed, and that the United Nations Population Fund should be "condemned for the evil acts in which it has participated."

165

POPULATION CONTROL: GOOD STEWARDSHIP?
John Guillebaud

YES

The author, gynecologist John Guillebaud, is a noted advocate of planned parenthood and was formerly professor of family planning and reproductive health at University College, London (UK).

The "IPAT equation" was formulated in the early 1970s by biologist Paul R. Ehrlich (born 1932). Ehrlich is the author of The Population Bomb (1968), which predicted that overpopulation would lead to food and resource shortages. His principal adversary on population matters was Julian Simon (see page 165).

The environmental cost of population

Unremitting population growth is not an option on a finite planet. We have just celebrated 2,000 years since Jesus' birth. Then, world population was around 200 million. Continuing to grow exponentially for just 2,000 more years would lead by one calculation to the mass of human flesh equating to the mass of the earth. By 2025, centuries before such reductio ad absurdum, our species will eliminate an estimated one fifth of all the world's life forms. Most of this destruction is not so much wanton as thoughtless. It occurs through competition from sheer numbers of humans, leading to the destruction of other species' habitats (wetlands, woodlands, coral reefs).

Too often the 'P' factor is overlooked in the IPAT equation as follows:

$$I = P \times A \times T$$

WHERE: I is the impact on the environment of a given society/civilisation
P is population, the number of individuals in that society
A is their per capita affluence (with consequential invariable 'effluence' = pollution and resource/energy consumption per capita)
T is a composite factor accounting for the per capita impact of the technologies in use (lowered by 'greener' technologies, with lower energy use and maximum recycling)

The need to stabilise population

In many resource-poor countries the people deserve that the A-factor, affluence, should significantly increase, along with an increase in per capita disposable income. Although this will mean greater energy consumption and adverse effects on the local and global environment, this is something the 'haves' of the world must accept—and Christians rightly take a lead here. But it makes global reduction in the average per capita A-factor even less probable. There are strict scientific limits to the reductions possible in the T-factor, so it would seem logical that Christians should have a positive view on stabilising (rather than just adapting to) the P-factor, population, the only other factor in the IPAT equation.

Fortunately, birth rates are declining in most countries (small thanks to the opponents of voluntary birth control services). But all of tomorrow's parents are already born, so many in number that even if their family sizes were improbably to average two, population growth would not cease until about 9 billion. This is a 50 percent increase on October 1999's 6 billion and it will occur despite the ravages of AIDS. The choice about stabilisation is not whether, but when—and at what total. If we wish to preserve a halfway tolerable global environment, and achieve a halfway decent life for those in degrading poverty, this must be as little above that unavoidable 9,000 million as possible.

The vicious cycle of population and poverty

If we see population growth just as something to adapt to, a vicious circle emerges: population increase maintains poverty, and poverty maintains population increase.

Population increase maintains poverty, because the finite 'cake' of any resource-poor country has to be divided amongst ever more individuals. Without stabilising the number of individuals to share it, an increase in a country's GDP can produce (as in my home country of Rwanda) a fall in the per capita GDP and more poverty. The increase in population keeps wiping out the gains, whether in agriculture, education and literacy, or health care.

> A country's GDP (gross domestic product) is the total value of goods it produces and services it provides, usually calculated each quarter or each year.

In turn, poverty maintains population increase, because in rural poverty 'every mouth has two hands'. The labour of each new child in the family is welcomed, especially in the absence of social security for sickness and old age. High child mortality also tends to reduce interest in birth planning.

Ultimately, the medical and social consequences could be catastrophic. Hence my Kew Gardens 2044 Time Capsule, which included an apology. We have not inherited the world from our grandparents, we have borrowed it from our grandchildren. My prayer is that they should not need to accuse us of damaging their loan beyond repair.

> The author coordinated the Environment Time Capsule project in 1994, in which capsules containing various objects were buried in several locations around the world to be opened in 2044. Go to www.ecotime capsule.com to find out more.

Short of that, while definitely not the cause of all major world problems, increasing population is the unrecognised multiplier of most. Some were in our recent BMJ [*British Medical Journal*] editorial: 'poverty and malnutrition, resource shortages and pollution, the loss of bio-diversity and wildlife habitats, increasing global inequality, and conflict and violence'. Medical consequences are obvious within that list, others are predicted from global warming (more humans burning ever more fossil fuels).

Not coercion, but planning and social justice

I doubt Maurice King's notion that the USA is in some kind of alliance to downgrade the importance of population so as to continue, as now, profligately consuming resources. However I am perturbed by the prevalence of ostrich-like laissez-faire views, given the 200,000 additional individuals that humankind somehow has to care for with each new day. The notion that we need do nothing to regulate population is dangerously complacent.

On the other hand, I am strongly opposed to every agency, government or individual that practises or permits compulsion, whether overt or covert, regarding birth planning methods or family size. I therefore teach avoidance even of the word 'control', after 'population' or 'birth'. I reject one-child policies and coercion in any form. We should not so much count people as ensure that people count.

I believe the best way for the world to deal with the 'problem' of population is through the relief of poverty and all its consequences combined with the means for women to achieve their human right to control their fertility. In short, we must work for birth planning and social justice with equal vehemence! Wealthier smaller families mean less population growth, fewer to share the 'cake', and hence still less poverty and even smaller families. The vicious cycle of population causing poverty and vice versa can then become a virtuous, upward spiral—as has happened, with average family sizes dropping below three in countries as different as Thailand and Costa Rica.

'Social justice' includes many components: education, reproductive health care, and women's empowerment. If we take care of the people, the population will take care of itself. But part of that 'taking care' involves ensuring that people can enjoy God's gift of sex within marriage while at the same time being able to plan the number and spacing of their children. For this they need universal, easy access to culturally appropriate reversible contraception methods through subsidised user-friendly services. We know from … social surveys of 240,000 women in 38 countries that it is now a myth that most women in the South do not want to plan their families. We are failing to push at an open door! Doing so could greatly reduce both maternal mortality and the abomination of 50 million induced abortions annually.

Do you think it is justifiable for the rich countries of the world to urge population controls on poorer countries when wealthy nations consume the majority of the world's resources?

Is it realistic to "stabilize" population without some element of force? See Volume 11, Family and Society, pages 200-201.

The Catholic Church forbids contraception. What impact might that have on Guillebaud's goals?

In the real world it is medically necessary to make methods of contraception available to unmarried as well as married people. However I dissociate myself from any agency or individual which promotes intercourse outside marriage, and from policies or practices that undermine the family as our Designer's intended setting for child-rearing.

Sensible stewardship

Many non-Christians see Christianity as the problem—seeing in Genesis 1:26,28 a biblical justification for riding roughshod over the biosphere—a licence for humankind to exercise 'dominion over' the world rather than (the more correct) 'stewardship for' the world.

Genesis 1:28 is as follows: "God blessed them, saying: 'Be fertile and multiply; fill the earth and subdue it. Have dominion over the fish of the sea, the birds of the air, and all the living things that move on the earth.'" How would you interpret this passage in a modern context? Do you feel it should be viewed "a licence for humankind to exercise 'dominion over' the world"?

Yet if one looks again it is striking that God exhorted plants and animals to be fruitful and multiply before giving that instruction to us humans. The Creator did not and does not intend us to multiply so much that we prejudice the fruitfulness of all his other creatures. This would be contrary to his immanent nature.

I believe there is implicit in the Bible another attribute of our God, additional to his omnipotence, omniscience, and omnipresence; namely omni-common sense! Population growth has happened as a result of vastly improved survival through modern medicine but without adequate birth planning. If obeying the 'multiply' instruction would lead to human numbers which exceed the carrying capacity of the land available—and so wipe out millions by starvation, disease or violence—godly common sense suggests this is not obeying his other instruction to us and the rest of creation to 'be fruitful'! Christians should be enthusiastic supporters, often through their own tithing, of voluntary birth planning within God's ordinance of marriage—worldwide. I believe this is squarely within God's plan for these times....

Critics of the Bible point out that it often seems to contradict itself. Does that make it any less reliable as a guide to the Christian faith?

We must ask ourselves new questions relating to the two great commandments of Jesus:

First, 'Love the Lord, your God': are we really doing that if we do not cherish and care for his creation—just as we would for something made by a human loved one? Our love for God should surely ensure inter alia that there are not more of one species (humans) than can possibly live full lives, while permitting the survival of all his creatures.

Second, 'Love your neighbour as yourself': should we not as well as loving our overseas neighbours, also love our future neighbours? And doesn't this involve helping to ensure that there are not ultimately so many future neighbours that God's world becomes uninhabitable?

DON'T FUND UNFPA POPULATION CONTROL
Stephen Moore

Stephen Moore is a
senior fellow at the
Cato Institute
(www.cato.org),
a public policy
research
organization, and
was formerly its
director of fiscal
policy studies. In
1999 Congress
voted to reinstate
funding to UNFPA
for the fiscal year
2000. See also The
United States and
UNFPA (page 171).

NO

Within the next week or so Congress will vote on whether to restore $60 million of U.S. taxpayer funding over the next two years for the United Nations Population Fund (UNFPA). For at least 30 years the UNFPA has been a complicit partner in some of the most unspeakably brutal population control programs around the globe—including China's genocidal one-couple, one-child policy. Almost universally, women and children—at least hundreds of thousands of them—have been the victims of this fanatical crusade. The UNFPA should not be re-funded. It should be universally condemned for the evil acts in which it has participated.

Discredited predictions
These days almost no sane person gives any credence to the population bomb hysteria that was all the rage in the 1960s and 1970s. Every prediction of massive starvations, eco-catastrophes of biblical proportions and $100 a barrel oil has been discredited by the global economic and environmental progress of the past quarter century. Intellectually, the Malthusian limits-to-growth menace is stone dead.

But within the Clinton-Gore State Department, Malthusianism flourishes. The Clinton administration still allocates almost $300 million a year to international population control—or what is euphemistically described these days as "family planning." In countries ranging from India to Mexico to Nigeria to Brazil, the basic human right of couples to control their own fertility and determine their own family size has been trampled upon by the state, thanks in larger part to flows of dollars and deluges of false limits-to-growth propaganda supplied by the American government.

The UNFPA, however, has had a particularly demon-like presence in developing nations. Back in the Reagan years, Congress sensibly pulled out of the UNFPA because of its complicity in some of the most inhumane forms of population containment. Today the UNFPA ludicrously

This article was
written in 1999.
The U.S. allocation
to population aid
for fiscal year
2003 (beginning
October 1, 2002)
was $465 million,
of which $34
million was
earmarked for
UNFPA. See
also The United
States and UNFPA
(page 171).

COMMENTARY: The United States and UNFPA

The United Nations Population Fund (UNFPA) was set up in 1969, with U.S. help, as the United Nations Fund for Population Activities; the UN changed the organization's name in 1987 but retained the original abbreviation. According to its website, UNFPA supports "programmes that help women, men and young people: plan their families and avoid unwanted pregnancies; undergo pregnancy and childbirth safely; avoid sexually transmitted diseases (STDs)—including HIV/AIDS; combat violence against women." UNFPA operates in some 140 countries and is financed mainly by government contributions rather than from the UN budget. From UNFPA's beginnings until the mid-1980s the United States provided up to half the organization's annual funding. The U.S. allocation to UNFPA is separate from USAID, the United States Agency for International Development, a U.S. body that funds bilateral population assistance projects.

The first defunding

As part of its funding program for fiscal year 1984 (beginning October 1, 1983), the administration of President Ronald Reagan (1911–) held back 50 percent of the U.S. funding allocation to UNFPA pending evidence that the organization was not associated with "abortion or coercive family planning programs." The money was eventually released, but in 1985 an amendment to an appropriations act was signed into law, disallowing funding to "any organization or program which, as determined by the President of the United States, supports or participates in the management of a program of coercive abortion or involuntary sterilization." The so-called Kemp-Kasten Amendment was invoked to suspend funding to UNFPA for fiscal year 1986 because the organization operated in China, which had a coercive population control program. There was to be no more U.S. money for UNFPA during the remainder of Reagan's administration or that of his successor, George H. W. Bush (1924–).

Clinton, George W. Bush, and the second defunding

When President Bill Clinton (1946–) took office in 1993, he determined that to be in violation of Kemp-Kasten an organization must directly support or take part in coercive birth control programs. Under this reinterpretation UNFPA once again began receiving U.S. funding, but there were provisos, among them that none of the money was to be used in China. With the exception of fiscal year 1999, U.S. funding for UNFPA continued through the Clinton administration and into the first year of the presidency of President George W. Bush (1946–). In July 2002, however, the $34 million allocated to UNFPA for that year was withheld, with Kemp-Kasten cited as grounds, and a similar amount allocated for fiscal year 2003 was also withheld on the same basis.

maintains the fiction that the agency has fought coercive policies. How does one explain then, that UNFPA once gave an award to the Chinese government for the effectiveness of its genocidal one child per couple policy?

China introduced its one-child policy in the 1970s. Go to www.refugees.org/world/articles/women_rr99_8.htm for background on the subject.

To this day no one knows precisely how many babies and women have died at the hands of the population control fanatics in China. What we do know is that this program will go down in history as one of the greatest abuses of human rights in the 20th century (see table). The Chinese government's birth control policy has already claimed an estimated 5-10 million victims. I say already because this is an ongoing genocide. An estimated 80-90 percent of the victims have been girls. UNFPA still spends millions each year on population control programs in China.

Where's the choice?

Incredibly the members of Congress leading the campaign to restore funding for the UNFPA tend to be "pro-choice" women—principally Carolyn Maloney of New York, Cynthia McKinney of Georgia and Connie Morella of Maryland. But how in the world can an agency that participates in programs that sterilize women against their will or that tells women they have an ecological responsibility to have only one or at most two children possibly be called pro-choice? Last year the U.S. Senate Committee on Human Rights heard from witnesses of the China population program, who related how rural women are forcibly strapped to steel tables in "hospitals" and their babies aborted—in some cases in the 7th, 8th and 9th months of pregnancy. Ms. Maloney may fantasize that the UNFPA promotes "reproductive rights," but there are quite literally millions of women in China, India and Mexico who would beg to differ.

The author cites reasons why UNFPA cannot be regarded as "prochoice." Why then do you think the "prochoice" women he lists above might want to see U.S. funding of the organization reinstated?

These programs were never about giving women reproductive choice. Just the opposite. Population control programs have been from their inception about preventing couples from having "too many" babies. Moreover, these "family planning" services do not promote women's and children's health; they come at its expense. There are many Third World hospitals that lack bandages, needles and basic medicines but are filled to the brim with boxes of condoms—stamped UNFPA or USAID.

Rep. Maloney believes that population control is necessary to "stop hunger and preserve our world's resources." In Maloney's dim world view, human beings are not resources. They are destroyers of resources. Yes, the spirit of Malthus is alive and well in the U.S. Congress.

A vote for the UNFPA is a vote for a fanatical anti-people creed that holds that we should celebrate the planting of a tree, or a litter of three baby seals, but that we should regard the birth of a human couple's third baby in China or India or even the United States as eco-terrorism. This is a fundamentally anti-Christian philosophy and it explains why groups like UNFPA, Zero Population Growth and Planned Parenthood view the Catholic Church as "the evil empire."

Would this argument be more convincing if Moore gave some evidence? What about the Exxon Valdez oil spill off the coast of Alaska in 1989 or the overfishing of cod in the North Sea?

The cause of world hunger and environmental disasters in the world today is not too many people. It is too much statism. Almost all of the greatest ecological damage of the past 50 years was perpetrated by the socialists behind the iron curtain.

Reagan had it right when he declared 15 years ago that economic growth is "the best contraceptive." The UNFPA is at best irrelevant to economic development and probably a deterrent. To help women and children in the developing world, the United States should be exporting capitalism, not condoms.

Greatest Genocides of the 20th Century

Turkey's Slaughter of Armenians	0.5–1.0 million
Hitler's Holocaust	6 million
Pol Pot's Killing Fields	1–2 million
Stalin's Extermination of Peasants	10 million
Mao's Great Leap Forward	10–20 million
Chinese One-Child Policy	5–10 million

Summary

The size of the world's population has been a topic of debate for more than 200 years. The two preceding articles look at different aspects of the issue. In the first John Guillebaud, emeritus professor of family planning and reproductive health at University College, London (UK), argues that "population increase maintains poverty, and poverty maintains population increase." He states that population planning is necessary in order to improve conditions and wealth in developing countries. Arguing from a Christian standpoint, he suggests that the commandment to "Love your neighbor as yourself" should involve ensuring that "there are not ultimately so many future neighbours that God's world becomes uninhabitable."

Stephen Moore of the Cato Institute, on the other hand, argues that even though Paul Ehrlich's population bomb theory (see Volume 11, *Family and Society*, pages 200–201) is outdated, the U.S. government of the time was still being asked to contribute to the United Nations Population Fund (UNPFA). He refers to UNFPA programs that "were never about giving women reproductive choice" and claims that "A vote for the UNFPA is a vote for a fanatical anti-people creed that holds that we should celebrate the planting of a tree, or a litter of three baby seals, but that we should regard the birth of a human couple's third baby in China or India or even the United States as eco-terrorism." Moore asserts that too much statism rather than overpopulation is "The cause of world hunger and environmental disasters in the world today."

FURTHER INFORMATION:

Books:

Bulatao, Rodolfo A., *The Value of Family Planning Programs in Developing Countries*. Santa Monica, CA: Rand 1998.

Ehrlich, Paul R., *The Population Bomb*. New York: Ballantine Books, 1968.

Kasun, Jacqueline, *The War against Population: The Economics and Ideology of World Population Control* (revised edition). San Francisco, CA: Ignatius Press, 1999.

Mosher, Steven W., *A Mother's Ordeal: One Woman's Fight against China's One-Child Policy*. New York: Harcourt Brace Jovanovich, 1993.

Useful websites:

www.overpopulation.com
More than 1,000 pages of material dealing with population and overpopulation issues.
www.unfpa.org
Site of the United Nations Population Fund.

The following debates in the Pro/Con series may also be of interest:

In this volume:
    Part 1: Issues in international development, pages 8–9

In *Individual and Society*:
    Topic 15 Is abortion a right?

In *Family and Society*:
    Topic 16 Should government policy dictate the size of families?

IS POPULATION CONTROL ESSENTIAL IN POOR NATIONS?

YES: There is plenty of food, and technology will keep pace with demands for resources

YES: Given control over reproduction, women opt for smaller families and end up with greater disposable income

ENVIRONMENT AND RESOURCES
Can the planet support unchecked population growth?

STANDARD OF LIVING
Does family planning lead to greater wealth?

NO: The increase in numbers has led to environmental degradation, and food and water supplies are stretched to the limit in some places

NO: In poor countries, having more children who can work is often the only way to increase family income

IS POPULATION CONTROL ESSENTIAL IN POOR NATIONS?
KEY POINTS

YES: Such programs empower women. Family planning, education, and jobs give women control over their lives.

YES: Not only is it a basic human right, but in some people's view contraception and abortion are violations of religious law or crimes against the unborn

WOMEN'S RIGHTS
Are population control programs beneficial to women?

HUMAN RIGHTS
Is it a person's right to have as many children as he or she wants?

NO: Population control programs are disrespectful to women and often coercive, racist, and an extension of imperialism

NO: It is selfish to insist on such a right when evidence suggests that population growth needs to be slowed down

Topic 14

IS THE PROTECTION OF INDIGENOUS PEOPLE MORE IMPORTANT THAN ECONOMIC GROWTH?

YES

FROM "ANWR ENVIRONMENTAL ISSUES THREATEN ALASKAN NATIVES"
LAKOTA JOURNAL, 2001
RUTH STEINBERGER

NO

FROM "CANADA CREE NOW BACK POWER PROJECT ON NATIVE LANDS"
NATIONAL GEOGRAPHIC NEWS, JULY 2, 2002
BEN HARDER

INTRODUCTION

The 1948 Universal Declaration of Human Rights (UDHR) aims to protect the rights of all individuals, but the status of the rights of groups is not so clearly defined. This has become a major concern for the world's indigenous peoples, many of whom have suffered for centuries as a result of conquest and colonization. Indigenous people are descendants of the original human inhabitants of a place—in regions such as North and South America, Australia, and New Zealand—where they are no longer the most populous or dominant ethnic group.

Many people believed that human rights legislation and international monitoring would prevent the direct persecution of indigenous peoples on the scale seen, for example, in the United States' treatment of Native Americans in the 19th century. However, more indigenous communities disappeared during the 20th century than ever before. In the Amazon basin of Brazil alone, around 100 indigenous communities vanished over the course of the last century. These communities have disappeared despite the apparent concern of the international community and the numerous treaties prohibiting the persecution of minorities.

Most of the pressure on indigenous communities, however, comes not from direct political persecution but from marginalization. Today we live in a global market in which the dominant communities seek to control the world's natural resources, therefore making it harder for indigenous people to live. Most indigenous peoples still maintain a hunting-and-gathering lifestyle, which requires far more land per person to sustain than an agriculturally based civilization. As the world's population increases, there is pressure for agricultural populations to settle land that indigenous peoples have used for hunting and gathering.

Despite this pressure, some 300 to 500 million indigenous people exist in the world today. While developed countries move toward the accumulation of wealth and the globalization of the world economy, indigenous peoples reject the model of endless economic growth. What binds these communities together are their deep sense of dependence on their immediate environment, their self-sufficiency, and their concern for the preservation of traditional ways of life.

> *"The human family is a tapestry of enormous beauty and diversity. The indigenous peoples of the world are a rich and integral part of that tapestry.... The protection and promotion of their rights and cultures is of fundamental importance...."*
> —KOFI ANNAN, UN SECRETARY-GENERAL, AUGUST 8, 2003

Many people believe that the developed world's exploitation of the Earth's resources has devastated indigenous groups throughout the world. While indigenous peoples hold ancestral claims to around 30 percent of the world's total land area, they now occupy only a small fraction of their former territories. However, those areas

at least partly under their control, such as the Canadian territory of Nunavut, contain some of the last unspoiled habitats on the planet. There resources such as minerals and water abound. By adhering to a sustainable use of renewable resources while retaining some control over income-generating extraction industries, Nunavut enjoys a measure of economic independence and self-sufficiency, while maintaining the delicate balance of resources.

Critics, however, think that the balance is tipping, pointing to the developing world's exploitation of valuable resources on indigenous lands for economic gain. They argue that it is wrong to place more emphasis on wealth than on the culture and livelihoods of indigenous peoples. Are commodities such as oil more important than preserving the right of indigenous people to maintain their chosen lifestyle? Yet it is not only the control of resources and land that affects indigenous peoples. They are also increasingly expected to live according to the norms and values of dominant, western civilization.

Some people argue that indigenous peoples should embrace globalization to improve their standard of living. To finance this, western governments may offer indigenous groups a share of the profits from oil or mineral extraction, giving them a source of income that allows them to enter the money economy. Industrial activities provide indigenous peoples with employment and personal wealth. They also give them access to education and health services that can enable them to participate in the wider world.

The following articles take opposing views on proposals to open up indigenous lands for industrial projects.

ANWR ENVIRONMENTAL ISSUES THREATEN ALASKAN NATIVES
Ruth Steinberger

Ruth Steinberger is an animal rights advocate and freelance journalist.

YES

✓ Native Alaskan villages may be seriously impacted by environmental damage if the exploration and drilling proposed by President Bush's energy plan moves forward. Additionally, claims made by the oil industry and the Bush administration regarding economic incentives for the proposed drilling in the Alaskan National Wildlife Refuge are being questioned by environmental and consumer groups. The Bush administration claims that the exploration and drilling will impact only eight percent of the Arctic National Wildlife Refuge, a refuge containing a total of 19 million acres of Alaskan wilderness.

However, national environmental groups and Native Alaskan tribal members claim that the figure of eight percent is deliberately misleading. National groups voicing opposition to the Bush proposal include the Native American Rights Fund, the National Congress of American Indians, Natural Resources Defense Council, the Sierra Club and numerous others.

Amid fears of a severe energy crisis George W. Bush's administration recommended drilling for oil and gas in Alaska's Arctic National Wildlife Refuge (ANWR). In 2002 the Senate rejected a bill to open up ANWR to drilling. In 2003 a bill was introduced in the House of Representatives to open the refuge to drilling, while two others (in the House and the Senate) were introduced to designate the area a wilderness, thus preventing it from being developed.

The Sierra Club is America's oldest and largest environmental organization.

The last remnant
The 1.5 million acres targeted by the Bush administration is the only area of the Alaskan coastal plains that remains off limits to the oil industry. Sara Chapell, Sierra Club's Alaska Representative, explained that the entire coastal plains are the only area potentially useful to the oil industry. The 1.5 million acres within the refuge is the only portion of the coastal plains to have any legal protection. The remaining 92% is not protected. While the land in question is eight percent of the ANWR, it is only five percent of the coastal plains, the region requiring protection. In a recent interview Chapell said that, "This area, this 'so called 8%,' has been at the heart of the dispute concerning protection of the coastal plains for the last thirty years. The remainder of the coastal plains is available for exploration. The Bush proposal is to remove legal protection from the only region of the coastal plains that is protected. The proposal is to open up 100% of the coastal plains to the oil industry. This region is the

See www.inforain. org/maparchive/ arcticwildlife_ refuge.htm for a map of Alaska showing the coastal plain area in dispute and the complete ANWR of which it is a part.

biological heart of ANWR." The 8% of ANWR proposed for exploration is a region that biologists consistently refer to as the "heart of the refuge." This is the most significant region for maintaining the biodiversity in ANWR, and the impact would be far greater than the figure implies. Much of the ANWR is rocky and too cold, even in summer, for most of the species to use for habitat or for raising their young. The region proposed for oil exploration is where 130,000 caribou return to each year to give birth and to raise their young. It is an irreplaceable sanctuary for white wolves and polar bears.

See www.arctic-caribou.com/faq.html for answers to frequently asked questions about caribou behavior, characteristics, and life cycles.

Caribou—the cultural focus

This region remains crucial to Native Alaskans who depend largely on wildlife and the environment for their subsistence. Native Alaskan villagers and environmental groups believe that the information from the administration and the oil industry is intended to allay fears of damage to the ecosystem, particularly the potential impact on caribou herds. Caribou are the mainstay of Native Alaskan culture. Many Native Alaskans hunt for around 80% of their diet, mainly relying on caribou.

If development happens, will Native Alaskans become rich enough that they do not have to depend on the caribou?

Faith Gemmill, of the Gwich'in Steering Committee of Fairbanks, Alaska explained, "The Steering Committee was formed in 1988 to address the issue of development in the birthplace of the caribou. We have a mandate from our people to protect this area." Explaining that the caribou is critical to the lifestyle of the villages, Gemmill said, "The caribou is the core of our culture, our spirituality, nutrition and is the heart of our social structure. We've always lived this way, and don't want to be forced to change our way of life, and development will change our way of life in every possible way." Gemmill continued, "We use the caribou for food, clothing, we make tools from the bones of the caribou, our songs and our dances center around the caribou. Each year, when the caribou are in the region, families go into the mountains to harvest caribou and there we share our stories with our youth, that's where they learn our traditions. We need that time on the land with the caribou, it's part of us. We need that time to keep our culture alive—if we lose this, we lose our life. We've been offered money and jobs, we don't want that. We want to continue to live our lives. Development in the region is cultural genocide."

See www.alaska.net/~gwichin/nav1.html for a page of links to more information about the Gwich'in and the place of caribou in their culture.

Diabetes danger

A significant loss of the caribou may also be the beginning of physical genocide. Diabetes, and other medical conditions associated with it, has been linked to the introduction of the western diet in Native Americans. Some tribes experience rates of diabetes in as high as 50% of adults, and the onset of this problem has been documented to begin shortly after a change in diet from a traditional diet to a modern western diet. Liz Gray, Cherokee, has compiled research on the health effects of the modern diet on Native Americans. Gray said, "Science and statistics have proven that traditional people, historically living in areas where there may be famine, have developed what is called a 'thrifty genotype.' [Such] people become more susceptible to diabetes when given an abundance of carbohydrates and are forced into a change of lifestyle involving less physical activity. This combination is literally burning the candle at both ends in tempting the onset of diabetes." Gray said that an example of this are the Pima, of Arizona. Gray said, "The Pima are a desert tribe. When the Pima lost the Gila River, they lost their lifestyle as well as their traditional diet. They were forced to rely on government commodities. There was no prior problem with any elevated rate of diabetes. Within three to five years, diabetes was recognized as a growing problem for the tribe. The rate of diabetes immediately shot up dramatically, affecting over 50% of the adult population." Gray concluded, "If health issues that have plagued other tribes across the entire continent are a predictor, a change in the ability of Native Alaskans to continue their lifestyle and diet could have a devastating impact."…

See www.abc.net. au/science/news/ stories/s873893.htm for the scientific background to the high rate of diabetes in indigenous populations.

Why are caribou numbers growing?

Oil industry proponents cite the expanding numbers of a neighboring caribou herd existing in a region that already has drilling to offer proof that caribou are unaffected by drilling operations. Sara Chapell, Alaskan representative for the Sierra Club, points out that the reason for expansion of the numbers is unknown, but what is crucial is the fact that the female caribou in the other herd have moved to a different calving ground, avoiding the oil field activity. Chapell explained that whiie the caribou in the herd that has expanded had the option to move to a different calving ground, there is no such place for the herd that uses the area proposed for drilling by the Bush administration.…

Adam Colton, of the Alaska Wilderness League, said that the proposed area is in precisely the most ecologically sensitive part of the refuge. Colton said, "Known as the biological heart of the refuge, this is where polar bears den in winter, it's the caribou calving grounds, 135 species of

Do you think advocacy groups such as the Sierra Club, which have their base in the dominant community, should be involved in causes such as these? Or should indigenous people themselves be leading the campaign?

migratory birds use this region for nesting or resting along their way to or from nearly every state. There are fifteen Native Alaskan villages along the caribou migratory route that will be impacted by changes in the herd." Colton cites activities peripheral to the drilling likely to have extensive environmental impact. Gravel mining would be needed to build pads for drilling rigs. Fresh water would be needed to build ice roads necessary for travel in the region. Water for these roads would be dredged from local streams, impacting fish and water quality. Colton summed up the impact on Native Alaskans saying, "What this boils down to is that any claims made by the administration are inconclusive and damage will have a major impact on a herd that's vital to the survival of 7,000 native people." Colton concluded that, "Saying that it's only eight percent—this is the entire coastal plains that would become open to the oil industry—it's like loggers saying we only want to log in the national forest where there happen to be trees."

> *Although the Gwich'in live on the affected land, they do not own it. Do you think they should be given ownership of the land or the right to decide on its use?*

Will caribou go the way of the bison?

Gideon James, of Tribal Services of the Ventie Tribal Government explained that this issue is a decisive one for people everywhere. James said, "I was born and raised here. I am an elder and have seen a lot of changes, especially with the weather and the animals that the native people around here depend on. It's hotter, the plants are affected, the colors of the leaves are changing. People that use this land notice this. They [the Bush administration] keep leaving us out of the picture. The administration says we don't have scientific facts…what is this? The scientific facts are already here. It's right in front of us. Bush is an oil man and people have to decide which side they're on, destruction or conservation." Shawn Martinez, of the Ventie Tribal Government, reflected on the agenda of the proposed drilling operations. Martinez said, "Drilling in the caribou calving ground is like forcing a woman to give birth in an automotive shop." Referencing the 1988 gathering to discuss prevention of development in the region, Martinez explained, "We worked together to prevent development and to discuss what the caribou mean to us—spiritually and financially as well. For thousands of years our people have subsisted off the caribou, our culture is based on the caribou and we still depend on the caribou. The same thing was done to the buffalo [American bison], it's beyond me, it's beyond all of us. The oil industry claims they can explore and drill without affecting us, but this will affect us."

> *Since the industrialized world is responsible for most of the greenhouse gas emissions that are the probable main cause of global warming, do you think those societies should be mainly responsible for dealing with its effects? If so, what would that mean in terms of responding to the situation in ANWR?*

CANADA CREE NOW BACK POWER PROJECT ON NATIVE LANDS
Ben Harder

Ben Harder is a freelance journalist who writes about the environment, nutrition, and public health.

Hydro-Quebec is planning to begin construction in 2005 and complete the project in 2010, diverting much of the flow of the Rupert River into the Eastmain and from there into the La Grande, powering the huge hydroelectric generating stations already installed there. See www. hydroquebec.com/ eastmain1a/en/ index.html for more details about the project.

Should governments and indigenous peoples have the right to make decisions about use of their land? Should there be any restrictions on that right?

NO

X Bill Namagoose was just a boy when government-dispatched bulldozers came 30 years ago to bottle up the energetic flow of the La Grande River in the remote region of Quebec where he and his fellow Cree live. Now, long after losing a legal bid to halt that damming—and after decades of fighting alongside environmentalists and concerned citizens to block other hydroelectric projects on native lands—the High Council of the Cree has surprised many people by a recent move: It's supporting a project to divert much of the Rupert River.

The government-owned power company [Hydro-Quebec] that built the La Grande River project now wants to redirect much of the Rupert River's flow to a massive hydroelectric plant that is already underway. The plan would flood 400 square miles (900 square kilometers) of land on which the Cree live and hunt and would reduce the river's flow by at least 80 percent.

Stamp of approval

Despite the impact—and unlike in the past—the tribal leaders have given their stamp of approval. In a new deal dubbed the Peace of the Brave, Hydro-Quebec has agreed to share the profits from the hydroelectric plant with the Cree in exchange for the tribe's acquiescence.

Namagoose, now the executive director of the High Council of the Cree, defends the agreement against some environmentalists' claims that it is a sale to the devil. "They want us to go down fighting for the sake of environmental protection," he said. "[But] every nation should be allowed to benefit from the extraction of its natural resources. That's the concession we see in our present situation."

Surprising development

The alliance between Hydro-Quebec and the Cree's High Council once seemed highly improbable, especially after the Cree's bitter experience from the La Grande River project. After the La Grande dam began operating, it flooded 6,750

Is the protection of indigenous people more important than economic development?

The Crees depend heavily on the natural environment for their way of life. Their territory has been severely affected by the development of mining, forestry, and hydroelectricity.

COMMENTARY: Cree Nation

The Cree belong to the Algonquian language family of Native American peoples (or First Nations, as they are known in Canada). Their ancestral home is the forest of northern Quebec and Ontario, where they have traditionally subsisted by fishing, hunting, and trapping. At some point in the past several Cree bands moved westward and adopted the lifestyle of the plains peoples, based around the bison. Today, these groups are known as the Plains Cree and those in eastern Canada as the Woodland Cree.

In the 1970s the James Bay Project galvanized the nine bands of Cree living on the Quebec shore of the bay to group together to oppose plans to turn most of the river valleys draining into the eastern shore of James Bay into reservoirs for electricity generation. They instituted the office of grand chief in 1974 to act as a political leader in negotiations with the province of Quebec. The James Bay and Northern Quebec Agreement of 1975 allowed the La Grande River to be developed in exchange for investment in infra-structure and services to benefit Cree communities; critics said the compensation was too low and only partially delivered.

There was shock and surprise among the Cree when it was announced in February 2002 that Cree political leaders had negotiated a secret deal with Quebec to allow development of the Rupert River. A Cree referendum only narrowly approved the deal, and in August 2002 Ted Moses, who had negotiated the agreement, won reelection as grand chief by just 34 votes. He defended the deal as a sad but necessary compromise, pointing out that it was the largest compensation package ever negotiated by an indigenous group anywhere in the world. In a speech in London in November 2002 he said: "Aboriginal peoples must ... continue to reinvent themselves to go beyond the stereotypes that curiously reinforce their alienation from their own lands, by proposing that they cannot be the developers of the land but can only ever be hunters or gatherers. It is this notion that condemns aboriginal peoples to lives of poverty and forced assimilation."

Small amounts of mercury that exist naturally in soil are released when the soil is flooded behind a dam and are concentrated in the food chain. See www.idsnet.org/ Resources/Dams/ Development/ impact-enviro.html for some of the environmental impacts of dams.

square miles (15,000 square kilometers) that included vast tracts of prime land in surrounding river valleys. The Cree saw much of their fishing and hunting grounds disappear, and the flooding displaced about a third of the 9,000-strong Cree Nation, which has since grown to 14,000 members.

The effects of the damming and flooding led to high concentrations of mercury in local waters. Fish were found to be heavily contaminated with the toxic metal, forcing the Cree to suspend all fishing in the affected region.

"Fish is really spiritual food in our culture," said Namagoose. "It is the first solid food given to a baby and the last food given to an elder before they pass on."

Cree economy

A third of the Cree economy is still based on fishing, hunting, and trapping—subsistence activities that tribal members said were heavily damaged by the dam's construction.

With that bitter experience behind them, Namagoose and his fellow Cree fought back with renewed vigor when new hydroelectricity plans in the 1980s threatened the Great Whale River and the James Bay, into which the Great Whale flows [as do the Rupert and La Grande].

The Cree sued the government and, aligned with environmentalists, mounted an ambitious public information campaign in Canada and the United States.

New York and some states in New England had agreed to buy power from Hydro-Quebec. A proliferation of "Save the Bay" bumper stickers and other moves to block the project fueled public opposition, however, and the company finally backed off.

"I spent seven years of my life fighting hydroelectric projects on the Great Whale River," Namagoose recalled. "And in the end, it was my river."

Do you think legal challenges and environmental campaigns are the best way to gain concessions from governments, or should indigenous groups seek broader political settlements?

A new deal

Under the agreement in February between the Quebec government and the High Council of the Cree, the tribe will receive up to 2 percent of the revenue generated by Hydro-Quebec's new dam on the Rupert River. The Crees' revenue from this arrangement is estimated at $3.5 billion in Canadian currency (U.S. $2.27 billion) over fifty years.

For its part, the High Council has agreed not to marshal its formidable will to oppose development.

The new deal has drawn criticism from environmentalists and others, even though many people say they understand the High Council's motives for accepting it.

"The Cree people are living in what can only be described as extreme poverty," said David Boyd, a professor of environmental law at Simon Fraser University in Vancouver, British Columbia. "Their leaders made a decision—a very difficult decision, I'm sure—to sacrifice some of the environment to reap the economic benefits of development in their region." ...

Some environmentalists criticized the Cree decision. But do other people have the right to condemn the Cree to poverty in order to promote their own values?

Summary

In the first article Ruth Steinberger discusses plans put forward by the Bush administration to conduct oil exploration in the coastal margin area of Alaska's Arctic National Wildlife Refuge (ANWR), which is currently protected. The remaining coastal edge is already open for exploration, yet the administration insists that the last protected section must also be developed. The author explains that the disputed area is considered the biologicual "heart" of ANWR, providing a vital refuge for herds of migratory caribou and other wildlife. Native Alaskans in the refuge rely on caribou for food and shelter—the animals form a core part of their way of life. The author concludes that the Bush administration's plan will irreparably damage the culture of the Native Alaskans through its effect on the caribou herds.

In the second article Ben Harder discusses the decision by the High Council of the Cree to back a project aimed at diverting the waters of the Rupert River toward a hydroelectric facility. If the project is approved, hundreds of square miles of Cree land will be flooded. Historically, the Cree have opposed similar moves by the Canadian government on other projects. They were unsuccessful in preventing the La Grande project in the 1970s, but in the 1980s a sophisticated public relations plan and alliance with environmentalists enabled them to defeat the Great Whale River project. In an apparent U-turn tribal leaders have now agreed to the Rupert River project in return for a share in the profits from the plant. Harder points out that while many people are critical of the deal, they understand the Cree's motives for accepting it.

FURTHER INFORMATION:

Books:

Howitt, Richard, *Rethinking Resource Management: Justice, Sustainability and Indigenous Peoples*. New York: Routledge, 2001.

Johansen, Bruce E., *Indigenous Peoples and Environmental Issues: An Encyclopedia*. Westport, CT: Praeger, 2003.

Niezen, Ronald, *The Origins of Indigenism: Human Rights and the Politics of Identity*. Berkeley, CA: University of California Press, 2003.

Useful websites:

www.amazonwatch.org

Site monitoring development plans in the Amazon basin.

www.unhchr.ch/indigenous/main.html

UNHCHR resource page on indigenous peoples.

http://arcticcircle.uconn.edu/ANWR/

Background on the ANWR peoples and resources.

The following debates in the Pro/Con series may also be of interest:

In this volume:

Topic 5 Is tourism consistent with sustainable development?

In *Human Rights*:

Topic 14 Is the government doing enough to protect the rights of indigenous peoples?

IS THE PROTECTION OF INDIGENOUS PEOPLE MORE IMPORTANT THAN ECONOMIC GROWTH?

YES: By recognizing group rights, the UN would give minorities greater power to tackle problem areas like discrimination and economic inequality

YES: They rely on their immediate environment for their daily survival, so are much more likely to take better care of it

GROUP AND INDIVIDUAL RIGHTS
Should the UN recognize group rights as well as individual rights?

ENVIRONMENT
Do indigenous peoples take better care of the environment?

IS THE PROTECTION OF INDIGENOUS PEOPLE MORE IMPORTANT THAN ECONOMIC GROWTH?

KEY POINTS

NO: Group rights are a way for minorities to get special privileges. This may foster ethnic resentment.

NO: They are just as likely to damage the environment as others. In the long run technology is what will reduce the human impact on the environment.

YES: Interest in indigenous culture, artifacts, and art can generate millions of dollars in tourist revenue

YES: These companies often have massive political and economic power, and exploit the environment and indigenous peoples

GROWTH VS. SUBSISTENCE
Is it possible to maintain a traditional lifestyle while enjoying economic growth?

FEAR
Should indigenous people fear multinational companies that want to work the natural resources on their land?

NO: The government spends millions of dollars supporting indigenous people, who cannot earn enough money from working in traditional economies

NO: The potential benefits in terms of employment, revenue, and additions to existing infrastructure outweigh any negative effects

187

Topic 15
HAVE MEASURES TO IMPROVE FOOD SECURITY BEEN SUCCESSFUL?

YES
"IMPROVED FOOD SECURITY FOR THE MOST VULNERABLE IN INDONESIA"
HTTP://WWW.USAID.GOV/ID/ACHIEVE-AZIZIAH.HTML
USAID

NO
"GLOBAL FOOD SECURITY"
WWW.USINFO.STATE.GOV/JOURNALS
G. EDWARD SCHUH

INTRODUCTION

A nation is said to have "food security" when all its people, at all times, have unhindered physical and economic access to enough safe and nutritious food in order to meet their dietary needs and food preferences for an active and healthy life.

Having enough to eat is a basic human requirement, yet in many parts of the world it is not fulfilled. Although nearly all the people of North America, Europe, Japan, and Oceania now have food security, famine remains a serious threat to the rest of humankind. The technological revolution has improved the standard of living in rich nations, but its principal effect on poor countries has been to cause an unprecedented rise in population growth rates as access to basic health care has improved.

While lack of food security is clearly an effect of poverty, it is now also believed to be one of its principal causes. Hungry people devote so much of their time and energy to getting their next meal that they have none left to take advantage of the traditional routes out of poverty—education and alternative agricultural techniques—that would, in the long term, help them achieve food security.

Many experts now believe that the developed world's traditional response to food shortages in poor countries—hasty, stop-gap measures such as dropping food parcels by parachute—have treated the symptoms of food insecurity rather than its cause. They have called for a change of emphasis: Instead of "firefighting"—concentrating on the short-term relief of famine and malnutrition—resources should be focused on social initiatives such as direct food assistance for families whose children stay in school. Other economists believe that food insecurity is primarily caused not by a shortfall in food production but by governments that have neglected agricultural development, made ineffective use of food aid, and set up protective trade barriers that fail to stop the hunger of their citizens. To counter such abuses, they argue that Western aid should favor governments that provide legal protection for their citizens, especially rural property rights that would encourage farmers to make the types of investments that would boost food productivity.

"Only 1 percent of the arable land in the Horn of Africa has water control [irrigation]."

—JACQUES DIOUF, HEAD OF UN FOOD AND AGRICULTURE ORGANIZATION (FAO), 2000

The developed world has numerous agencies that work to increase food security, such as the United Nations' Food and Agriculture Organization (FAO) and USAID. While still undertaking emergency relief in times of crisis, they now implement development programs in an effort to ensure predictable and stable food supplies appropriate to local conditions. FAO's Special Program for Food Security (SPFS) aims to help people in developing nations improve their food security through rapid increases in food production and productivity by reducing year-to-year variability in food production on an economically and environmentally sustainable basis, and by improving people's access to food.

USAID's Food for Work (FFW) program not only deals with temporary food insecurity during droughts and other emergencies but also supports developmental projects that, it is hoped, will lead to longer-term, more sustainable food security. They include the construction or repair of roads in towns and from farm to market, schools, health clinics, irrigation systems, public water and sanitation systems, tree planting, and other environmental protection and conservation activities.

Critics argue that these programs currently reach only a small percentage of the world's hungry people, while advocates point to examples in which programs have been successful. Bangladesh, for example, which was once almost entirely dependent on food imports, has transformed its devastated agricultural sector into one of South Asia's most productive farm economies through a global partnership between foreign aid agencies, international research institutions, and indigenous nongovernmental organizations.

The first article describes how USAID helped a destitute family in Indonesia. The mother of the family began working on an FFW-sponsored project to build local pathways and a drainage system: By earning a living, she was once again able to provide for her family, while helping to improve her village. The second article, by G. Edward Schuh, professor of international trade and investment policy at the University of Minnesota, argues that global food security has not improved. He cites the reasons for this as insufficient investment in agriculture, inefficient use of food aid, and failure to make the best use of international trade.

IMPROVED FOOD SECURITY FOR THE MOST VULNERABLE IN INDONESIA
USAID

YES

☑ Aziziah, a widow at the age of 37, and her family sleep on a threadbare carpet that is spread upon the dirt floor of their makeshift home. But she and her family consider themselves fortunate.

Aziziah lives in a squatter's camp in downtown Surabaya, in a simple plywood and tin house dwarfed by neighboring high-rise office buildings, international hotels, and shopping malls. She and her family share a latrine with 20 other families. Feces and waste are discharged into surface ditches. She remarks that when her area of the slum floods, sometimes on a daily basis during the rainy season, floodwaters carry the waste and feces into her house threatening her health and that of her three children.

The city of Surabaya is on the northeast coast of Java in Indonesia.

Living close to the poverty line

Aziziah reminisces and recounts that her life has not always been this bleak. When her husband died four years ago, she took over his business as a food vendor on the streets of Surabaya. Initially she was able to support the family on the Rp. 20,000 to Rp. 30,000 she earned a day. However, with the onset of the economic crisis, profits from food sales dropped. Aziziah had to sell household items in order to provide food for her family. She recounts the items, both big and small: chairs, tables, bowls, mirrors, plates, and clothes.

Rp.20,000 (rupiahs) to Rp.30,000 has the same value as $2.5 to $3.5. In 1985 the World Bank defined poverty as an income level below one dollar per day per person in 1985 prices. In 1999 the Indonesian government set the poverty line for people living in an urban area as Rp.90,000 per month.

When her household items ran out, she used her operating capital from the business to purchase food for the family. When the operating capital ran out, Aziziah sold the food push-cart. With barely enough income to provide for her family, and nothing left to sell, Aziziah, her daughter Fitri and two sons were evicted from the house they were renting. With money from friends to buy plywood, and pieces of tin sheeting she was able to scavenge, she built her "house"—a lean-to against two existing walls.

Aziziah was forced to take Fitri and her boys out of school—she could no longer afford the fees for school, and needed the children to earn extra income for the

COMMENTARY: Famine in Africa

Causes of famine

In the past 100 years the population of Africa has multiplied five and a half times. At the same time, the continent has experienced worsening food shortages. From 1969 to 1973 as many as a quarter of a million people died in the Sahel (the semiarid region south of the Sahara, from Senegal to Sudan); in the 1980s Ethiopia, Eritrea, and Sudan had disastrous food shortages; and since 2000 Zambia, Zimbabwe, and Malawi have been badly affected by shortages of corn. There are many causes of famine, some of them natural, others humanmade. Lack of rain can lead to drought and desertification (land turning to desert). Diseases such as HIV/AIDs can place an additional burden on poor families. Civil wars often force people to leave their land. Corrupt governments can deliberately stop food from being distributed to communities suspected of supporting opposition parties. Shortage of land can lead to overuse and soil degradation. Lack of roads raises the cost of seeds, tools, and fertilizer, and makes it harder for farmers to get their produce to market, while the lack of effective irrigation projects makes it difficult to grow crops.

Famine Early Warning Systems Network

One of the most effective organizations at monitoring famine is the Famine Early Warning Systems Network (FEWS NET). FEWS NET is a USAID-funded activity that works closely with sections of the U.S. government such as the U.S. Geological Survey and the National Aeronautics and Space Administration to monitor crop production and prices, and climate changes. It looks out for particular hazards such as droughts, cyclones, increases in food prices, decreases in food production, desertification, and increases in the numbers of people suffering with HIV/AIDs. In this way it aims to be able to predict when food shortages are likely so that famines can be avoided, and foreign aid can be organized.

FEWS NET receives its information from a number of sources. It has its own field representatives who work in areas of Africa where famine might happen, satellites measure rainfall and assess plant health from space, and other organizations watch for drought and famine. It also works closely with two UN organizations, the Food and Agricultural Organization and the World Food Program, to estimate crop production and food need.

FEWS uses the Internet (www.fews.net) to offer information for free and as a way of educating young people about famine. It supplies a Risk Analysis of the countries that are most at risk from famine, grading countries as Emergencies, Warnings, and Watches. For example, in August 2003 Ethiopia and Zimbabwe were considered the highest priority. Ethiopia had as many as 15 million people at risk of starvation, while Zimbabwe had 5.42 million at risk. Eritrea and Mozambique were in the urgent category.

Children playing in a slum in Jakarta, Indonesia. Jakarta, like Surabaya, has thousands of poor families living in makeshift homes.

family's survival. Even on the income she and her 12-year-old daughter Fitri earned as maids, and her two sons earned on the streets begging and selling newspapers, sometimes it was not enough.

As she continued her story, Aziziah's mood lightened and she related how life has improved.

Food for Work

Six months ago she began her "job" with Food for Work (FFW). For the first time in years, she was able to feed her family.

With Aziziah earning enough to provide food, the money her children earned covered other critical household needs. Fixing the roof in time for the rainy season was her first priority. She can now afford to buy soap for daily personal and household use.

Through FFW projects, Aziziah and her community have paved the major pathways in their neighborhood, and improved the drainage to reduce persistent flooding. FFW activities are also renovating existing latrines and constructing a septic tank.

When asked what impact the Food for Work Program has had for Aziziah, she did not respond in terms of "food security" or "social infrastructure." Aziziah's answer was simple: "Fitri is back in school. Now, Fitri will finish school." FFW programs funded by USAID are improving the lives of Aziziah and others like her throughout the archipelago.

The Food for Work (FFW) program involves poor families receiving staple food such as rice in return for which they agree to do work to help their communities, such as repair roads, bridges, and irrigation canals or build water and conservation systems.

The implication here is that education is key to eradicating poverty. For more on this discussion see Topic 8 Would increased investment in education reduce poverty in developing countries? on pages 98–109 of this volume.

GLOBAL FOOD SECURITY
G. Edward Schuh

NO

From June 10 to 13 [2002], leaders from nations around the world will meet in Rome at the World Food Summit plus 5 to discuss the progress made since the original World Food Summit some five years ago. The results will not be particularly pleasing, since progress is not as great as was expected.

In my view, three issues have contributed to the poor performance in reducing food insecurity in the recent past: (1) the neglect of agricultural development both by governments in developing countries and by the international donor community, (2) the ineffective use of food aid, and (3) the failure to capitalize on international trade as a means to ensure food security.

A basic premise of my thinking is that food security is a poverty problem—the lack of food is due to the lack of the means to acquire it. It is not, in general, due to a shortfall in food production. This is the familiar finding of Nobel laureate Amartya Sen from his studies of famines in China and India.

Another point useful in understanding this analysis is that food security problems can be of a short-term or a long-term nature. In other words, people may suffer either from short-term fluctuations in their incomes, or they may suffer chronically from low per capita incomes. The policy prescriptions for these two problems are quite different.

Lack of attention to agricultural development
Both the governments in developing countries and the international development community have in recent years sorely neglected agriculture as a component of their programs for economic development. This neglect reflects an enormous institutional memory loss: back in the 1960s and 1970s such neglect would have been unheard of.

The apparent logic behind this neglect appears to rest on two perceptions. First, observers of the development scene note that as an economy grows and per capita incomes rise, the share that agricultural employment makes up of total employment declines, as does the share that agricultural gross domestic product (GDP) makes up of total GDP. They conclude from such trends that agriculture declines in importance as economic development proceeds, so one can neglect the agricultural sector.

The difficulty with that argument can be seen by considering the modernization of the production of staple foods by the introduction of new production technology into the sector as the basis for agricultural modernization and development. Staple commodities tend to have low price elasticity of demand, with the result that the introduction of new production technology to the sector will result in a lower price for the staple, other things being equal. That decline in real prices will be equivalent to an increase in real per capita incomes for consumers. This points to the ultimate importance of agriculture in the development process. It is important because everybody consumes food.

Staple food is food for which there is a constant demand, such as rice or bread.

As nations become more industrialized, is it inevitable that agriculture becomes less important? What do you think the status of farmers is in modern U.S. society?

The contribution from modernizing the production of food staples does not stop there, however. It turns out that poor-income groups benefit in a relative sense from the modernization of agriculture, in part because low-income groups spend a larger share of their income on food than do middle- and upper-income groups. It is difficult to find a sector of the economy in which the benefits of the development process will be spread as widely as in the case of agriculture, and so much in favor of the poor.

Similar arguments can be made about the modernization of tradable agricultural commodities. In this case, the price of the commodity does not decline with modernization. However, the sector becomes more competitive in the international economy, and the net result is either an increase in export earnings or an increase in savings of foreign exchange earnings. The benefits will again be widely distributed in the domestic economy, since the foreign exchange can be used either to service international debt or to finance higher rates of economic growth and development.

There is a certain irony in the finding that food insecurity is not due to shortfalls in food production, but that the modernization of agriculture has such an important role to play in alleviating food insecurity. The explanation for what to some might appear to be an anomalous result is that agriculture can be a key to more general economic development of the economy. To be even more specific, the modernization of agriculture contributes to widespread distribution of the benefits of modernization to consumers, with those benefits distributed in a relative sense in favor of the poor.

In what ways do you think the modernization of agriculture might help in the development of a poor economy?

The American economist Theodore William Schultz (1902–1998) studied the problems of developing countries. His special area was low-income groups in agriculture and the agricultural economies of developing nations.

Monetization is the process by which governments sell agricultural commodities to obtain foreign currency for use in aid programs. For example, the U.S. government buys food commodities from U.S. farmers and then sells them. Proceeds from the sale are then used by NGOs to carry out specific activities.

Inappropriate use of food aid

Food aid is one component of foreign aid that continues to garner ample political support in the developed countries. That support reflects in part the strong political constituencies in the agricultural sectors of the developed countries. It also reflects an appreciation of the direct benefits of food aid to its ultimate beneficiaries.

Of course, food aid is not without its problems. Academics such as Nobel laureate Theodore W. Schultz and others were at one time fairly critical of food aid, largely on the grounds that it had strong disincentive effects for poor producers. At one time those critics made substantial progress in addressing these problems, and much care was exercised in how the food aid was introduced into the economy of the recipient country.

Monetization

Later, however, the lexicon of foreign aid was enriched with the addition of a new word and concept—"monetization." This new concept referred to the sale of the food aid in the market for cash, which in turn was used for fiscal purposes in general economic development programs. Regrettably, monetization quickly became popular in the new lexicon, and disincentive effects soon disappeared as an issue of concern. One hardly hears the term "disincentive effects" mentioned in today's policy debates, and monetization has rapidly conquered the day.

Again, there is a serious side to this problem. The political support for monetization comes largely from nongovernmental organizations (NGOs), which still depend heavily on food aid for their financial resources. Their support for food aid and for monetization is obvious. Their livelihood depends on it—never mind the consequences for the poor farmer.

The point to be emphasized is that there are other means of making more effective use of the food aid, and we need to move in those directions. One such approach is to use the food aid to pay the families of school-age children to send their children to school. This will introduce the food aid into the economy as an increase in income to very poor families. In so doing, the disincentive effect will be minimal.

At the same time, children of low-income families are seldom able to go to school, largely because they are needed to earn the income needed to support the family. In rural areas, these children typically work on the farm. In urban areas, such children typically beg on the street corners or sell apples or pencils. In either case, the families need the income the child earns to survive.

The use of food aid to "pay" the family to send the child to school has multiple contributions. The disincentive effects are minimal. The child is able to go to school, thus increasing educational attainment. The health and nutrition of the family is improved. And the per capita income of the family is improved.

The neglect of international trade

International trade can be an important means to promote economic development. The sectoral specialization and division of labor it makes possible lead to increases in per capita incomes. Moreover, it eliminates the limit on economic growth and development that is so characteristic of small countries. Despite the progress of globalization and the growth in international trade in general, protectionism continues to be a problem, especially in the global agricultural sector.

The United States and the European Union are especially protective of their agricultural sectors. Moreover, these countries continue to make effective use of dumping policies, in the form of food aid and in the form of export subsidies—both explicit and implicit.

The developed countries are not alone in having weak economic policies for their agricultural sectors, however. They discriminate against their agriculture by shifting the domestic terms of trade against their agricultural sectors. This leads to premature migration from agriculture and the rapid urbanization of domestic economies that one sees all around the world. The result is a failure to take advantage of the contribution that international trade can make in bringing about balance in the flow of exports and imports, and thus to address the basic food security problem through international trade.

Protectionism is an economic policy designed to protect the domestic economy. Protectionism can take many different forms, such as restricting or taxing foreign imports. For more discussion on protectionism see Topic 10 Are protectionist trade policies ever a good idea? in Economics, pages 130–141.

"Dumping" is the sale of a commodity in a foreign market at a loss.

Concluding comments

Progress will be made in addressing the global food security problem only as progress is made in alleviating global poverty. Poverty, in turn, will be alleviated only as agriculture is modernized and the benefits of that modernization are realized through the liberalization of trade policies and the opening of national economies. Although increased food production is not the means to alleviate food insecurity problems directly, the modernization of agriculture can contribute mightily in alleviating poverty on a global scale.

Summary

The first article is an account written for USAID, describing how the organization helped a poor family rebuild a degree of financial self-sufficiency after an economic recession had forced some of its members to beg on the streets of Indonesia. Supported by reported quotations from the widowed mother, the piece is an outline case history that attempts to illustrate how the Food for Work (FFW) initiative gives ill-fed people employment designed to make lasting improvements to their community that will eventually enable them to achieve food security. While it is clear that Aziziah and her family are still, in western terms, destitute, their conditions have been improved by the aid program, and they consider themselves much better off than they were at their lowest point.

In the second article G. Edward Schuh, professor of international trade and investment policy at the University of Minnesota, suggests that little has been achieved to increase food security in the developing world since the 1996 World Food Summit. He provides three specific reasons for this failure. The first is that agricultural development is neglected by governments that believe, falsely, that the importance of farming declines in a growing economy. The second is that the provision of much food aid is still inappropriate; some governments sell the food provided and spend the money rather than invest it in an infrastructure that would help achieve food security. The third reason is trade protectionism; many western nations impose premium tariffs on foreign goods, and that prevents developing countries from maximizing their export markets.

FURTHER INFORMATION:

Books:

Schultz, Theodore William, *The Economics of Being Poor*. Oxford: Blackwell Publishing, 1993.

Sen, Amartya, *Development as Freedom*. New York: Anchor Books, 2000.

Sen, Amartya, *Poverty and Famines: An Essay on Entitlement and Deprivation*. Oxford: Oxford University Press, 1984.

Useful websites:

www.fao.org/worldfoodsummit/english/index.html
Site on World Food Summit.
www.fews.net
Famine Early Warning Systems Network site.
www.usaid.gov
United States Agency for International Development.

The following debates in the Pro/Con series may also be of interest:

In this volume:

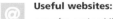 Topic 2 Is corruption a major issue in preventing economic growth?

Topic 10 Are protectionist policies essential to economic growth in developing nations?

Topic 11 Have heavy agricultural subsidies damaged the economies of poorer nations?

HAVE MEASURES TO IMPROVE FOOD SECURITY BEEN SUCCESSFUL?

YES: Modernizing agriculture in developing nations benefits the poorest people

YES: Countries such as Bangladesh have vastly improved their own agricultural systems through such programs

AGRICULTURE
Is investment in agriculture the key to fighting famine?

FOOD FOR WORK
Do Food for Work programs work?

NO: As economic development proceeds, the importance of agriculture declines

NO: These programs only reach a small percentage of the world's hungry

HAVE MEASURES TO IMPROVE FOOD SECURITY BEEN SUCCESSFUL?
KEY POINTS

YES: The UN's Program for Food Security has helped improve food production and productivity and people's access to food

YES: Aid organizations supply vital emergency relief in times of crisis

AID
Are aid agencies a good thing for starving nations?

NO: Aid agencies make poor nations too reliant on handouts, which undermines local agriculture

NO: Often food aid does not reach the starving, but is stolen by corrupt officials or politicians

Topic 16
DOES WATER SCARCITY PREVENT ECONOMIC DEVELOPMENT?

YES
"FRESHWATER"
HTTP://WWW.UN.ORG/ESA/SUSTDEV/SDISSUES/WATER/WATER.HTM
UNITED NATIONS DIVISION FOR SUSTAINABLE DEVELOPMENT

NO
"THE WATER'S RISING—BUY WATER"
WWW.UKCOMMENT.CO.UK
JACOB PRIMLEY

INTRODUCTION

Of Earth's natural resources water is one of the most important; without fresh water there would be no life. Human beings need to drink water—or fluids that contain water—if they are to survive more than a few days. They need water to be safe if they are to avoid catching water-borne diseases such as cholera and typhoid. People also need water for basic sanitation—to protect health by keeping themselves and their environment clean and hygienic. Further crucial uses of fresh water include in agriculture, for irrigation of crops and for livestock, to facilitate various industrial processes, for inland fisheries, and for transportation.

Today one-sixth of the world's people are without access to fresh water, while two-fifths are without sanitation. Most of the Earth's water is oceans—just 2.5 percent is fresh. Of that, 30 percent is underground, while only 0.3 percent can be found in lakes, rivers, and reservoirs. Most fresh water is inaccessible—in glaciers, for instance.

Many economists argue that "water scarcity"—a country's or a group of peoples' lack of access to plentiful supplies of fresh water—can affect that country's economic development. Access to safe drinking water, as well as to water to enable food production and various other economic activities vital to survival and income generation, has been high on the agenda of the United Nations and other international development and health agencies, such as the World Health Organization, for many years. Water was pushed to the fore during the UN Conference on Environment and Development that took place in Rio de Janeiro, Brazil, in 1992. Out of the Rio Earth Summit emerged a global program to promote sustainable development worldwide: Agenda 21. Since then water management has become a priority for international organizations.

In Africa—two-thirds of which is desert or dry land—and in many parts of rural Asia and Latin America people spend several hours each day walking to the nearest water source to fetch water to bring back to their villages. The time and energy spent in fetching water—which after all has to take priority—reduces the time available for other activities such as farming, paid work, or attending school.

> *"Access to safer water is a fundamental human need and, therefore, a basic human right."*
>
> —KOFI ANNAN, UN SECRETARY-GENERAL, MARCH 22, 2001 (WORLD WATER DAY)

Those suffering from water scarcity also often find it impossible to collect enough water to engage in basic sanitation activities such as washing or maintaining healthy living conditions. These factors lead to poor health and disease. About 2.3 billion people worldwide suffer from diseases associated with scarcity of safe drinking water. Some economists believe that this has a severe carryover effect on economic development.

The urban poor find basic survival difficult when they do not have access to piped water supplies. Low-income groups in the city of Jakarta, Indonesia, for example, have to get water supplies from groundwater via wells or standpipes; these water sources are often heavily polluted. Sometimes the urban poor buy their water from water tankers. In Karachi, Pakistan, poor people spend up to a quarter of their incomes on water, while middle- and high-income groups have both water connections and sewerage, for which they pay proportionately much less.

Desertification and disasters such as drought have also added to the problems of water scarcity, making economic development for poor countries even more difficult.

However, many economists argue that water scarcity does not have to be an absolute barrier to economic development. They point out that the real problem is not water scarcity but poor management of water. Poor management has lead to the resource being undervalued and squandered. For them, involving private companies—usually through partnerships with government—in the provision of water supply and sanitation and the fair pricing of water resources are a more advantageous way forward.

Some economists also argue that even if a country has a scarcity of water, it can specialize in extracting those resources that it does have, then trading them with other countries for water. Economists call this theory comparative advantage. The oil-rich countries of the Middle East, for example, have still managed to move forward in terms of economic growth despite their scarcity of water.

In the first article—a document issued by the UN—the importance of access to water for a country and its people to develop sustainably is stressed. The second article, by journalist Jacob Primley, agrees that water is an important resource, but gives examples of water-poor regions that are thriving economically

FRESHWATER
United Nations Division for Sustainable Development

YES

✓ "Water is needed in all aspects of life. The general objective is to make certain that adequate supplies of water of good quality are maintained for the entire population of this planet, while preserving the hydrological, biological and chemical functions of ecosystems, adapting human activities within the capacity limits of nature and combating vectors of water-related diseases. The multi-sectoral nature of water resources development in the context of socio-economic development must be recognized, as well as the multi-interest utilization of water resources for water supply and sanitation, agriculture, industry, urban development, hydropower generation, inland fisheries, transportation, recreation, low and flat lands management and other activities" (Chapter 18, Agenda 21).

The rationale for the sustainable development and management of freshwater resources is clearly articulated in chapter 18 of Agenda 21. Today it is widely recognized that an integrated approach to freshwater management offers the best means of reconciling competing demands with supplies and a framework where effective operational actions can be taken. It is thus valuable for all countries at all stages of development.

Further recommendations to support the implementation of chapter 18 were taken by the Commission on Sustainable Development at its second (1994) and sixth (1998) sessions; by the Report of the Expert Group Meeting on Strategic Approaches to Freshwater Management in Harare 1996, the United Nations General Assembly at its nineteenth Special Session to review the implementation of Agenda 21 (1997) and reviewed by the World Summit on Sustainable Development (2002) through its Plan of Implementation.

Current global water challenges and future targets are clearly stated in the Millennium Development Declaration (2000)—which includes the access to safe drinking water as one of its Millennium Development Goals—and are strengthened and expanded in the Plan of Implementation of the World Summit on Sustainable Development. The key role

Following the Rio Earth Summit of 1992, Chapter 18 of Agenda 21 listed a number of reasons for making water scarcity a priority in sustainable development. Of the uses of water listed which do you think is the most important and why?

The goals of the UN Millennium Development Declaration included the eradication of poverty, the reduction of child mortality, the improvement of maternal health, the combating of HIV/AIDS, malaria and other diseases, and the promotion of environmental sustainability.

COMMENTARY: Water privatization

Privatization is when businesses or industries change from public to private control or ownership. Water privatization is a subject that has attracted much debate in recent years. Water has become increasingly scarce in poor regions because of increases in population, the overexploitation of resources, and the pollution of existing resources. This situation has been made worse by global warming and resulting droughts and desertification.

The case against privatization

Opponents of water privatization point out that private companies are only concerned with profits. Privatization results in water prices increasing. Many poor people in regions of Africa, for example, find themselves unable to pay for water and use water from streams instead, increasing the incidence of water-borne diseases. This is what happened in Kwa Zulu-Natal Province, South Africa, when in 2000 the government made the people of Ngwelezane pay for water that previously they had been receiving for free. As a result, more than 200 people contracted cholera.

Critics also say that water companies are reluctant to invest in poor rural communities but focus their investments on urban areas. In Sri Lanka, for example, a water privatization plan has come under criticism from environmentalists. They argue that the reasons for privatizing water—to provide an economic disincentive to wasting water by making people pay for it—ignores the fact that large amounts of water lost in agricultural irrigation projects flow back into the agricultural system. As a result of privatization, it will be the poorest farmers who will suffer.

The case for privatization

To counter this argument, many economists point to evidence showing that countries that have a privatized water system have a more efficient use of water. Private companies are able to charge more for their services and so have more money to invest in new water systems. This in turn means that more people—nearly always the poorest—are then connected to a main water system, allowing them to avoid having to buy expensive water from water tankers or having to use contaminated water from wells, streams, or rivers. For example, since the privatization of the water supply in Manila, Philippines, about 10 million people have piped water, compared to 7 million before privatization. In Argentina in 1995 the introduction of water privatization brought increased profits and productivity. As a result, the water company increased investment in the infrastructure from $25 million per year to $200 million per year, and that was reflected in better water and sewerage systems. The direct result of this was that after 1995 child deaths from diseases caused by water quality and availability declined by as much as 24 percent in the poorest areas.

of sustainable water management for poverty eradication has been one of the key outcomes of the World Summit on Sustainable Development [WSSD]. The plan of implementation outlines several central statements related to freshwater and sanitation issues:

• Halve, by the year 2015, the proportion of people without access to safe drinking water.

• Halve, by the year 2015, the proportion of people who do not have access to basic sanitation.

• Combat desertification, and mitigate the effects of drought and floods.

• Develop integrated water resources management and water efficiency plans by 2005, with support to developing countries.

• Support developing countries and countries with economies in transition in their efforts to monitor and assess the quantity and quality of water resources.

• Promote effective coordination among the various international and intergovernmental bodies and processes working on water-related issues, both within the United Nations system and between the United Nations and international financial institutions.

The emphasis on action-oriented policies and implementation has been the main focus of the World Summit for Sustainable Development. Two further initiatives have complemented the plan of implementation: Partnership initiatives (Type II outcome) and the WEHAB Initiative.

The partnership initiative aims at establishing new partnerships supporting the implementation of sustainable development issues bringing together governments, intergovernmental organizations, non-governmental organizations, scientific and research communities, local authorities, universities and business and initiating new forms of collaboration among all stakeholders. The WEHAB initiative, focusing on five key thematic areas of crucial global importance: Water, Energy, Health, Agriculture and Biodiversity (WEHAB), was proposed by the UN Secretary General Kofi Annan to bring additional impetus on action at the World Summit for Sustainable Development. The WEHAB initiative consisted of a series of all discussion rounds and interactive moderated dialogues with governments and all major stakeholders at WSSD.

In recognition of the central importance of water resources as a key to sustainable development, the United Nations General Assembly proclaimed the year 2003 as the International Year of Freshwater. The International Year of Freshwater provides the international community with an excellent opportunity to raise awareness globally, promote best practices, motivate people and mobilize resources in order to meet basic human needs and manage water in a sustainable way. The International Year activities are being coordinated, on behalf of the UN system, by UNDESA [United Nations Department of Economic and Social Affairs], UNESCO [United Nations Educational, Scientific and Cultural Organization] with the support of UNEP [United Nations Environment Programme].

The Division for Sustainable Development, through its Water, Natural Resources and SIDS [Small Island Developing States] branch, provides project execution and policy advisory services at the request of interested countries to promote and support in practice integrated water resources management at the international, national, regional, local and basin level. These services are based on a contemporary technical cooperation model that links current political discussions with the realities in the field.

According to the UN, as many as 1.2 billion people do not have access to safe drinking water, and 2.4 billion people do not have access to proper sanitation. As a result, up to 3 million people die every year from diseases caused by unsafe water. The International Year of Freshwater in 2003 was established in order to "raise awareness and galvanize action to better manage and protect" water. Go to www.water year2003.org to find out more.

THE WATER'S RISING—BUY WATER
Jacob Primley

X Everyone knows that fresh water is vital: Without it, human life becomes unsustainable in a matter of days at most. It is also a finite resource. Since 1942, consumption has quadrupled as the world's population has doubled. Scientists have estimated that the world's maximum potential production of fresh water is no more than 3,350 cubic miles (14,000 cu km) a year. Yet that is not much more than the amount already being used, and the global birth rate shows no signs of slowing down. The United Nations (UN) predicts that up to seven billion people in 60 countries could face a water shortage by 2050 when the world's population is expected to reach 9.3 billion. Meanwhile climate change is bringing desertification to previously fertile areas: Spain is suffering more droughts than ever before in recorded meteorological history as the Sahara seems to be spreading out of Africa onto the northern shore of the Mediterranean Sea.

Many scientists believe that the planet is rapidly heating up—the phenomenon known as global warming—because of increased industrial pollution.

Dying of thirst
Some day soon we are all going to die of thirst; the process has already started—the tabloid headlines can be seen long before the onset of the hallucinations associated with dehydration. Yet it is easier to write a scare story than to tell the truth, and water is an emotive subject. So a few facts may help keep the "crisis" in perspective. They may also reveal the greatest investment opportunity of the 21st century.

The global situation
Of the world's 191 nations, only nine share 65 percent of the total annual water resources. Canada, Congo, Greenland, Guyana, French Guiana, Iceland, India, and Suriname have the most, together with the U.S. state of Alaska. It is easy to identify poor countries that have little water—Egypt, for example, which receives more overseas water aid than any other nation—but to attribute their poverty exclusively to their aridity is simplistic and inaccurate: There is no cause and effect link between water and wealth. This is easy to demonstrate by looking at the cases of Kuwait and Qatar.

The author argues that there is no cause-and-effect link between water and wealth. Do you agree with this assessment? Can you think of any countries that have an abundance of water that are very poor?

206

Water towers in Kuwait. Kuwait uses its wealth from oil to invest in recycling and desalination water plants that give it an abundance of fresh water.

Dutch-born British economist David Ricardo (1772–1823) came up with the economic theory that a country gains from trade with another country when it has relatively lower costs. This became known as "comparative advantage."

Since its foundation in 1948 Israel has received considerable aid from the United States. Do you think that countries with water scarcity should be given aid by richer countries to develop their water resources?

The Gaza Strip is an area of land on the Mediterranean Sea under Israeli occupation. It is home to over one million Palestinians.

These two small states on the Persian Gulf have no rivers, and receive no more than seven inches (175mm) of rain annually; in a dry year, this figure may fall as low as one inch (25mm). Yet Kuwait has one of the highest per capita incomes on earth, and Qatar is also immensely wealthy. They get most of their fresh water by desalinating sea water and recycling waste water, processes for which they pay out of the money they earn from their only significant natural resource: Oil. There is an important economic truth here: People who cannot produce a necessary commodity themselves pay others to provide it for them. That is what David Ricardo called comparative advantage.

Israel is another example of a Middle Eastern state whose lack of fresh water has not hampered its economic development. Although the nation has a natural source in the Jordan River, it is not in itself sufficient to meet domestic requirements of a densely populated and arid region. Yet the government has rendered previously unfarmable regions fertile by diverting some of the river water, particularly into the Negev Desert, and also by desalinating sea water.

Is it solvable?

For all the tabloid prophecies of imminent doom, Gordon Young, coordinator of the U.N. World Water Assessment Program, said in 2003 that most of the world's water crises could be resolved at a cost of between $50 billion and $100 billion a year. It is not that there is insufficient fresh water, but rather that too much of it is not in the right place. What is lacking is the political will to get the water to where it is most urgently needed.

In some parts of the world, one nation or group may restrict another's access to fresh water for political reasons. That is the situation that currently obtains in the Gaza Strip, which a UN report found to have as little water as any of the 180 nations it surveyed.

Yet the main justification for the failure to act has so far been based on ecological principles. When President George W. Bush suggested in 2003 that water from Canada might be used to irrigate the American South West, Canadian Environment Minister David Anderson replied tersely that "we have a policy of not exporting water." The objections are partly historical—why do something we've never done before?—but mainly environmental: There are grave concerns about the damage that such a trade might do to the Great Lakes. They contain nearly a fifth of the world's fresh water, but in two of them, lakes Michigan and Huron, between 1998 and 1999, water levels fell by 22 inches (55 cm), the biggest and fastest drop in recorded history. The fall was caused mainly by dry weather, but water consumption is also rising, and the U.S. National Oceanic and Atmospheric Administration has predicted that levels may fall a further two feet (60 cm) by 2030.

Pricing water

The global fresh water market may be an idea that has found its time. The price of water is increasing rapidly—it is being called "the oil of the 21st century"—and wherever there is a potential market in anything there are entrepreneurs looking for ways to tap into it. One of the pioneers is McCurdy Enterprises, a Newfoundland construction firm, which is currently working on a $24 million plan to ship water every week from Canada in specially lined oil tankers to the Southern United States and other destinations it will not reveal. Bulk water currently sells for about 24¢ a gallon in the United States; McCurdy tankers have a payload of 132 million gallons; every fully laden tanker will therefore earn the shippers over $3 million. At the moment, such trafficking is illegal, but Canada's ban on bulk water shipments may soon face legal challenge from those who regard it as a violation of the North American Free Trade Agreement (NAFTA). Enron and Monsanto are watching developments with interest. In the view of Johan Bastin of the European Bank for Reconstruction and Development: "Water is the last infrastructure frontier for private investors." Smart money looks set to take the plunge.

The North American Free Trade Agreement (NAFTA) was signed in 1992 and came into effect in 1994. Under the agreement there is meant to be a gradual removal of almost all trade restrictions between the United States, Canada, and Mexico. See Volume 18, Commerce and Trade, Topic 15 Has NAFTA cost the United States jobs?

Summary

The first of the two articles starts with an extract from Chapter 18 of Agenda 21—a global program to promote sustainable development, which emerged from the Rio Earth Summit (1992). The extract outlines just how important water is in terms of its role in poverty eradication, and hence development, worldwide. The piece also contains details of the action-oriented plan that came out of the World Summit on Sustainable Development in Johannesburg some 10 years later. Among others, goals of the plan included halving the proportion of people who do not have access to safe drinking water by 2015; halving the proportion of people who do not have access to basic sanitation by 2015; combating desertification and reducing the effects of droughts and floods; and improving water resources management and water use efficiency. It is clear from the document that the UN considers access to water to be vital to sustainable development.

In the second article journalist Jacob Primley does not dispute that water is an essential resource. However, he does believe that it is not essential for economic development. He points out that "of the world's 191 nations, only nine share 65 percent of the total annual water resources." Although it is easy to identify countries that are both poor and arid, such as Egypt, he argues that it is inaccurate and oversimplistic to attribute their poverty to aridity alone. To back up his argument, he gives examples of water-poor countries that have prospered, such as Kuwait, and shows that by selling their natural resources, they can reinvest in water resources. Primley also claims that privatizing water would help solve much of the existing water problems.

FURTHER INFORMATION:

 Books:

Allan, Tony, *The Middle East Water Question: Hydropolitics and the Global Economy*. New York: I.B. Tauris, 2002.

Postel, Sandra, and Linda Starke (ed.), *Last Oasis: Facing Water Scarcity* (The Worldwatch Environmental Alert Series). New York: W.W. Norton and Company, 1997.

Ward, Diana Raines, *Water Wars: Drought, Flood, Folly and the Politics of Thirst*. New York: Riverhead Books, 2002.

 Useful websites:

www.un.org/works/sustainable/freshwater.html
UN International Year of Freshwater 2003 site.
www.un-urbanwater.net/
UN site on managing water for African cities.
freshwater.unep.net/index.cfm?issue=water_scarcity
UNEP site on water scarcity.

The following debates in the Pro/Con series may also be of interest:

In this volume:

 Part 4: Population, food, and water

 Topic 15 Have measures to improve food security been successful?

 Water: A crisis situation? pages 212–213

DOES WATER SCARCITY PREVENT ECONOMIC DEVELOPMENT?

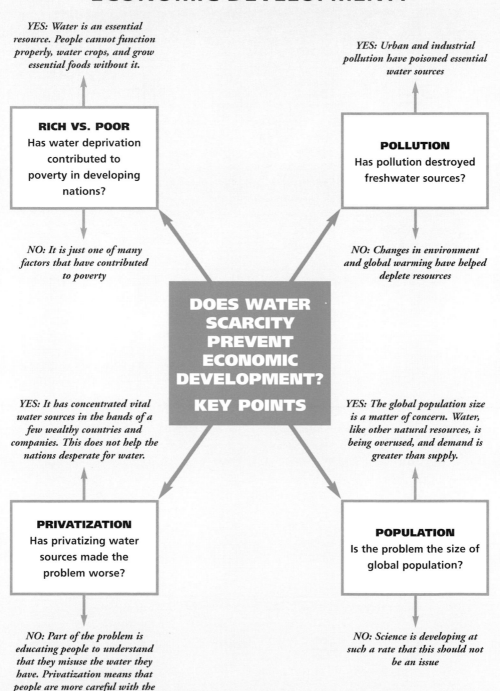

YES: Water is an essential resource. People cannot function properly, water crops, and grow essential foods without it.

YES: Urban and industrial pollution have poisoned essential water sources

RICH VS. POOR
Has water deprivation contributed to poverty in developing nations?

POLLUTION
Has pollution destroyed freshwater sources?

NO: It is just one of many factors that have contributed to poverty

NO: Changes in environment and global warming have helped deplete resources

DOES WATER SCARCITY PREVENT ECONOMIC DEVELOPMENT?

KEY POINTS

YES: It has concentrated vital water sources in the hands of a few wealthy countries and companies. This does not help the nations desperate for water.

YES: The global population size is a matter of concern. Water, like other natural resources, is being overused, and demand is greater than supply.

PRIVATIZATION
Has privatizing water sources made the problem worse?

POPULATION
Is the problem the size of global population?

NO: Part of the problem is educating people to understand that they misuse the water they have. Privatization means that people are more careful with the water they use.

NO: Science is developing at such a rate that this should not be an issue

WATER: A CRISIS SITUATION?

"Thousands have lived without love,
not one without water."
—W.H. AUDEN (1907–1973), BRITISH POET

Since time began, water has helped civilizations develop and
their economies flourish, while drought and famine have caused the decline
and fall of many others. In the 21st century the Earth faces the problem of
whether there is enough water to sustain life as we know it. Critics argue that
the supply is not the problem, but that the resource is being misused,
mismanaged, and wasted. Other commentators claim that something
radical has to be done if humankind and the Earth's other rich and
diverse range of life forms are to survive.

The "Blue Planet"

Around 70 percent of the Earth is covered with water, earning it the nickname
the "Blue Planet." But while 97.5 percent of this amount is salt water, only 2.5
percent is fresh water—the kind needed to sustain humankind—and two-thirds
of that amount is locked away in glaciers and permanent snowcover. Fresh
water is further reduced through pollution. Although water is a renewable
resource, there is a great differential in its availability to different regions around
the world. Pollution and climate change have both reduced the amount
of fresh water available, exacerbating the water problem.

• Pollution: The United Nations World Water Development Report (WWDR)
estimates that some 2 million tons of waste are disposed of in rivers, oceans,
and streams every day; this includes industrial and chemical waste, human
waste, and agricultural waste, such as fertilizers and pesticides. In developing
countries the poor are the worst affected, with some estimates claiming that
50 percent of the population use polluted water.
• Climate: Estimates in the WWDR indicate that climate change will account for
a 20 percent increase in global water scarcity. In tropical and subtropical areas
low and sporadic rainfall and hotter weather have contributed to water
shortages. Precipitation, which is the main source of water for human use and
for the ecosystem, is forecast to decrease between latitudes 30°N and 30°S.
Weather conditions in these areas are set to become more extreme and
damaging to freshwater supplies. Typhoons, flooding, droughts, and mudslides
are all expected to occur more often.

The poverty–health cycle

In developing countries water-related diseases cause most illnesses and deaths. In 2000 over two million people died due to water sanitation and hygiene-related illnesses. The majority of them were children under five, and they died from illnesses that were largely preventable. The illnesses included:

- Water-borne diseases: caused by drinking contaminated water, they are gastrointestinal illnesses, such as diarrhea.
- Water-washed diseases: when there is insufficient water for washing, bacteria and parasites can causes diseases like scabies and trachoma.
- Vector-borne diseases: caused by insects and snails that live in water ecosystems; they include malaria and schistosomiasis.

Currently 1.1 billion people lack access to adequate water supplies and 2.4 billion to adequate sanitation. If water supply and sanitation were improved, infectious diarrheas could be reduced by around 17 percent every year. Although vaccinations are not available for many water-related diseases, and parasites have developed resistance to antibiotics and other drugs, access to clean drinking water, basic food, and personal hygiene would all help reduce water-borne and water-washed diseases.

Experts agree that by promoting investment in providing clean and reliable water supplies to developing countries, expanding existing water supplies, and providing education in personal and family hygiene, the water problem would significantly improve. Changes in irrigation techniques, such as lining canals and avoiding standing and slow running water, would also make a difference to mortality rates.

Food security for a growing world

About 777 million people in developing countries are undernourished. This means that they receive less than the 2,800 calories estimated to provide adequate nourishment each day. Most food-producing agriculture depends on rainfall, but in developing countries about one-fifth of arable land is irrigated. Wastewater is an important source of irrigation water—accountable for about 10 percent of all water used to irrigate land in developing countries.

The United Nations estimates that irrigation efficiency is currently at about 38 percent around the world, but that it will rise to 42 percent by 2030, reducing the problems of vector-borne diseases.

Water as a human right

In November 2002 the Committee on Economic, Social, and Cultural Rights (CESCR) adopted a General Comment on the right to water. The 145 countries that ratified the CESCR now officially recognize that water is a limited natural resource and that access to it is a fundamental human right. Each member country must ensure that its citizens have access to safe and secure drinking water, "equally and without discrimination."

GLOSSARY

acquired immunodeficiency syndrome (AIDS) a disease that destroys the ability of the immune system to combat infections and certain cancers, exposing the victim to repeated infections that may eventually be fatal. AIDS is caused by human immunodeficiency virus (HIV).

blue planet a term used to describe the Earth, which makes reference to the fact that 75 percent of the planet's surface is covered by water.

Common Agriculture Policy (CAP) a European approach to farming established following World War II to increase productivity, create a fair standard of living for farmers, and allow regular food supplies to reach consumers at reasonable prices.

Convention on the Rights of the Child (CRC) a legally binding treaty adopted by the United Nations in 1989. It affirms the right of all children to life, survival, and personal development, as well as the right to hold or express their own opinions.

debt crisis a critical situation in which many countries have debts that they are unable to repay. In the closing decades of the 20th century, a large number of developing countries were unable to maintain repayments on development loans because several factors (a rise in world interest rates, a global recession, and low commodity prices) caused the size of their debts to increase rapidly.

developing country a poor country that is undergoing a process of economic modernization through the development of an industrial and commercial base.

discrimination the act of treating others unfairly on the basis of their race, color, gender, sexuality, nationality, religion, education, or economic status.

ethnic cleansing action intended to remove or extinguish members of a certain ethnic group from a country or region.

female genital mutilation (FGM) any procedure involving the partial or total removal of external genitalia, performed for cultural, religious, or medical reasons. Also known as female circumcision.

food security a description of a situation in which a nation's population has unhindered physical and economic access to enough safe and nutritious food to meet its dietary needs and food preferences for active and healthy life.

foreign aid financial or goods assistance given by rich nations, international humanitarian organizations, or financial institutions to countries in need.

free trade international trade that is not subject to restrictions or barriers.

gender inequality discrimination on the basis of sex, which may take economic, political, social, or cultural forms.

globalization the expansion worldwide of the culture, influence, and economic concerns of leading western nations.

gross domestic product (GDP) an economic measure of a country's wealth based on the total value of goods and services produced by a nation's residents during a specific period (usually a year).

gross national product (GNP) GDP plus the income accruing to domestic residents from investments abroad, less the income earned in the domestic market by foreigners abroad. *See also* GDP.

human rights the rights people have as human beings, irrespective of citizenship, nationality, race, ethnicity, language, sex, sexuality, or abilities. Human rights become enforceable when they are codified as conventions, covenants, or treaties.

imperialism a term used to describe one (usually rich) nation's domination— politically, economically, or culturally— of another (less powerful) nation.

import a commodity bought in from abroad.

indigenous people the original inhabitants of a particular place, usually today an ethnic minority group such as Native Americans or Australian Aboriginal people.

inequality disparity in distribution of a specific resource or item, such as income, education, employment, or health care.

International Monetary Fund (IMF) an international organization established in 1945 to promote international monetary cooperation, exchange stability, and orderly exchange arrangements.

Millennium Challenge Account (MCA) U.S. plan to reduce poverty in the poorest nations. In return for aid countries have to show measurable progress toward just government and economic freedom.

nongovernmental organization (NGO) an organization independent of government. NGOs lobby for human rights and environmental issues, and monitor governments and other organizations in areas that fall within their mandate.

patent a legal document issued by governments that grants exclusive rights to the inventor of a product or service.

population control regulation of birthrate through government policies, often adopted in developing countries to assist in the reduction of poverty and deprivation.

poverty the situation facing people whose material needs are not satisfied.

price discrimination the selling of the same good or service to different buyers for different prices.

protectionism an economic doctrine that attempts to protect domestic producers by placing tariffs and quotas on imports.

refugee a person living outside of his or her country who is unable or unwilling to return because of fears of persecution on racial, religious, political, or social grounds.

reproductive rights the right of individuals and couples to decide freely the number, spacing, and timing of their children.

sanctions coercive measures taken against a nation as a penalty for disapproved conduct and to enforce certain laws or standards. They are usually economic but can also be military.

Structural Adjustment Programs (SAPs) economic policies that countries must follow to qualify for new World Bank and International Monetary Fund (IMF) loans. SAPs emphasize export-led growth, privatization, trade liberalization, and the efficiency of the free market.

sustainable development a form of economic growth that seeks to use renewable rather than finite resources and to minimize the permanent damage done to the environment by economic activity.

tariffs taxes placed on imports. *See also* World Trade Organization.

tourism the traveling to and staying in places outside native environments for leisure, business, or other purposes. Tourism is the world's largest growth industry.

transnational corporation (TNC) an enterprise that operates in a number of different countries and that has production facilities outside its home country.

World Bank the name by which the International Bank for Reconstruction and Development (IBRD) and the International Development Association (IDA) have come to be known. Both organizations are designed to finance projects that enhance the economic development of member states; they provide low-interest loans, interest-free credit, and grants for developing countries.

World Trade Organization (WTO) an international organization founded in 1995 as a result of the final round of the General Agreement on Tariffs and Trade (GATT) negotiations. The WTO monitors national trading policies, handles trade disputes, and enforces GATT agreements designed to reduce discriminatory practice in international trade, such as tariffs.

Acknowledgments

Topic 1 Do Rich Countries Have a Duty to Give Financial Help to Their Former Colonies?

Yes: "Remembrance of Things Past" by Liz McGregor, *The Guardian*, September 7, 2001. Copyright © 2003 by Liz McGregor. Used by permission.

No: "The Irrationality of 'Colonial Guilt': A Homage to Lord Bauer." Copyright © 2003 by Michael Newland. Used by permission.

Topic 2 Is Corruption a Major Issue in Preventing Economic Growth?

Yes: From "Corruption: A Persistent Development Challenge" by J. Brian Atwood. *Economic Perspectives*, Vol. 3, No. 5. November 1998. Courtesy of the Office of International Information Programs.

No: "Dr. Hanke Presented A Market Economy Manifesto for Bulgaria," Bulgarian Economic Forum. Used by permission.

Topic 3 Is Good Governance Key to Poverty Reduction?

Yes: "Good Governance: The Key to Poverty Reduction and Prosperity in Bangladesh" by Frederick Templeton, the Joint World Bank/ERD Seminar on Loan Administration Change Initiative (LACI) & Financial Accountability, Dhaka, December 1, 1999.

No: "Good Governance: Issues for ACP-EU Political Dialogue" by Nancy Kachingwe. Presented to the 28th Session of the ACP–EU Council of Ministers, May 16, 2003. Used by permission.

Topic 4 Does Religion Hinder Development?

Yes: "Interview with Rev. Manchala Deenabandhu on the subject of casteism," *Echoes*, Issue 17, 2000. Copyright © 2000 by the World Council of Churches. Used by permission.

No: "Rethinking Buddhism and Development: The Emergence of Environmentalist Monks in Thailand" by Susan M. Darlington, *Journal of Buddhist Ethics* 7, 2000. Copyright © 2000 by *Journal of Buddhist Ethics*. Used by permission.

Topic 5 Is Tourism Consistent with Sustainable Development?

Yes: From "How Tourism Can Contribute to Environmental Conservation." Copyright © 2002 by United Nations Environment Program (UNEP). Used by permission.

No: "Tourism's Three Main Impact Areas." Copyright © 2002 by United Nations Environment Program (UNEP). Used by permission. UNEP Disclaimer: The designations employed and the presentation of the material in this publication do not imply the expression of any opinion whatsoever on the part of the United Nations Environment Program concerning the legal status of any country, territory, city, or area or of its authorities, or concerning delimitation of its frontiers or boundaries. Moreover, the views expressed do not necessarily represent the decision or the stated policy of the United Nations Environment Program, nor does citing of trade names or commercial processes constitute endorsement.

Topic 6 Should Rich Countries Donate a Set Percentage of Their GNP to Aid?

Yes: From "Boost U.S. Foreign Aid, Big-Time" by Helena Cobban, *Christian Science Monitor*, December 13, 2001. Copyright © Helena Cobban. Used by permission.

No: From "Does Aid Matter," *New Internationalist*, Issue 285. Used by permission.

Topic 7 Will the Millennium Challenge Account Foster Sustainable Develpoment?

Yes: From "The MCA Promotes Sound Economic Policies" by E. Anthony Wayne, *Economic Perspectives*, Vol. 8, No. 2. March 2003. Courtesy of the Office of International Information Programs.

No: From "The Millennium Challenge Account: Unlearning How to Make Aid Work" by Aldo Caliari, *World Hunger Notes*, August 6, 2003. Used by permission.

Topic 8 Would Increased Investment in Education Reduce Poverty in Developing Countries?

Yes: "Class Wars" by Oliver Robertson, Amina Kibria, Juanita Rosenior, Duane O'Garro, and Kierra Box, *New Internationalist*, Issue 315, August, 1999. Used by permission.

No: "Poverty Reduction in Developing Countries: The Role of Private Enterprise" by Guy Pfeffermann, *Finance and Development*, Vol. 38, No. 2, June 2001 (published by the International Monetary Fund). Copyright © 2001 by the IMF. Used by permission.

Topic 9 Have Persisting Gender Inequalities Prevented Latin American Countries from Reaching Their Full Growth Potential?

Yes: From "Latin America and Caribbean Countries Make Progress in Gender Equality But Continue to Limit Pariciplation of Women in the Labor Market," *DevNews Media Center*, News Release No: 2003/242/LAC, March 5, 2003. Copyright © 2003 by the International Bank for Reconstruction and Development/The World Bank. All rights reserved.

No: From "Wanted: A New Latin American Agenda for Economic Growth," *Hispanic News*, April 26, 2003.

Topic 10 Are Protectionist Policies Essential in Initiating Economic Growth in Developing Nations?

Yes: From "Findings in Detail: The U.S. and Chiquita at the WTO," Ross-Robinson and Associates. Used by permission.

No: "Development Decisions of the DOHA Conference" by The Holy See, The Vatican. Used by permission.

Topic 11 Have Heavy Agricultural Subsidies Damaged the Economies of Poorer Nations?

Yes: "The Disaster of International Foreign Aid Programs" by Ken Schoolland, *International Society for Individual Liberty Pamphlet Series.* Reprinted, 1998. Used by permission..

No: "EU's Vow on Caribbean Bananas Hard to Keep" by *SUNS-South–North Development Monitor.* Used by permission.

Topic 12 Do Patents Lead to Higher-Priced Drugs?

Yes: "Make AIDS Drugs Available to All" by Mathew Flynn, *New Internationalist,* Issue 346, June 2002. Used by permission.

No: "Patents and AIDS Drug Research," Letter to *Washington Post* by Alan Holmer, October 11, 2002. Used by permission.

Topic 13 Is Population Control Essential in Poor Nations?

Yes: "Population Control: Good Stewardship?" by John Guillebaud, *Triple Helix,* Winter 2000. Copyright © 1997 by Christian Medical Fellowship. Used by permission.

No: From "Don't Fund UNFPA Population Control" by Stephen Moore, Cato Institute, May 15, 1999. All rights reserved. Copyright © 2003 by CATO Institute. Used by permission of the Cato Institute.

Topic 14 Is the Protection of Indigenous People More Important than Economic Development?

Yes: "From "ANWR Environmental Issues Threaten Alaskan Natives" by Ruth Steinberger, *Lakota Journal,* 2001. Used by permission of *Lakota Journal* (editor@lakotajournal.com).

No: "Canada Cree Now Back Power Project on Native Lands" by Ben Harder, *National Geographic News,* July 2, 2002. Used by permission.

Topic 15: Have Measures to Improve Food Security Been Successful?

Yes: "Improved Food Security for the Most Vulnerable in Indonesia" by USAID. Used by permission.

No: "Global Food Security" by G. Edward Schuh (www.usinfo.state). Used by permission.

Topic 16: Does Water Scarcity Prevent Economic Development?

Yes: "Freshwater" published by United Nations Division of Sustainable Development. Copyright © United Nations. Used by permission.

No: "The Water's Rising—Buy Water" by Jacob Primley. Used by permission of the author.

The Brown Reference Group plc has made every effort to contact and acknowledge the creators and copyright holders of all extracts reproduced in this volume. We apologize for any omissions. Any person who wishes to be credited in further volumes should contact The Brown Reference Group plc in writing: The Brown Reference Group plc, 8 Chapel Place, Rivington Street, London EC2A 3DQ, U.K.

Picture credits

Cover: Corbis Saba: J. A. Giordano; **Corbis:** Owen Franken, 113, Gideon Mendel, 6/7, 156, 160/161, Kevin Schafer, 207; **Corbis Sygma:** R.P.G., 29; **Digital Vision:** 212/213; **Richard Jenkins:** 46/47; **Rex Features:** Sipa Press, 81; **Still Pictures:** Paul Harrison, 192; **Travel Ink:** Abbie Enock, 183

SET INDEX

copyright in **6**:188-89
economy
    foreign policy and **8**:33,70-71,72
    high dollar and **18**:166-77
    NAFTA and U.S. jobs **18**:190-201
    trade with countries with poor
        human rights records
        18:202-13
    see also protectionism; trade,
        U.S. flag, and the Pledge of
        Allegiance **16**:34-45
    foreign aid from **14**:74-75, 76-79,
        84
    foreign policy *see* foreign policy, U.S.
    and global warming/greenhouse
        gases **4**:10-11, 13, 15, 25, 27, 71,
        86, 89-91, 93
    history
        and the atomic bomb **13**:126-37
        the civil rights movement
            13:152-63
        the Civil War **13**:34-47
        and Columbus Day **13**:10-21
        communism in the 1950s
            13:140-51; **15**:75
        the FBI and Martin Luther King
            13:164-75
        and the League of Nations
            13:88-99
        the Nineteenth Amendment and
            women **13**:62-73
        and Pearl Harbor **13**:112-25
        the Persian Gulf War **13**:190-201
        Prohibition **13**:74-85
        Reconstruction **13**:48-59
        were the Framers racist?
            13:22-33
        see also New Deal; September 11
            attacks; Vietnam War
    and human rights **13**:164-65
        foreign relations with countries
            that abuse human rights
            15:190-201
        of indigenous people **15**:178-89
        and International Criminal Court
            jurisdiction **15**:202-13
        record **15**:166-77
    and the IMF **18**:90-91
    inequality in **1**:11, 12-19, 20
    interventionism **13**:187, 203, 213
    "melting pot" **16**:100
    minimum wage **3**:90-99, 106; **18**:135
    official language of **1**:86-97
    racial diversity **1**:23
    refugees to **15**:89
    religious freedom **1**:119, 121;
        7:114-25; **15**:171
    and science **1**:108-11, 112;
        17:108-11, 112
    and Third World debt **3**:159-60
    trade *see* trade, U.S.
    see also African Americans; Native
        Americans; United States
        government
United States government **2**:60-61
    antifamily policies **11**:38
    checks and balances **2**:131-32
    democracy **2**:8, 46-57, 124, 125
        versus capitalism **2**:35, 36-38, 44
    and the economy **3**:64-77
    federal bureaucracy too big? **2**:61,
        62-73

and the federal judiciary **2**:55, 193
and health
    and free-market approach to
        health care **10**:8-9, 22-33
    health care for the elderly **11**:161
    legalization of the abortion pill
        RU-486 **10**:9, 48-59
    mandatory testing for HIV/AIDS
        10:9, 36-47
    and medical marijuana **10**:9, 60-73
    smokers should pay for
        treatment of smoking-related
        diseases? **10**:9, 74-85
    universal health-care coverage
        10:8, 10-21
moral principles in politics
    2:176-87
more power for state governments?
    2:61, 74-85
and plutocracy **2**:38
policing the Internet? **6**:165
separation of powers **2**:53, 60,
    98-109; **7**:38, 39, 49
should subsidize the arts? **12**:34-45
two-party system **2**:61, 86-97, 168
and wartime censorship **6**:10-11
see also elections, U.S.; government;
    president(s), U.S.
United States v. Fordice (1992) **16**:191
United States v. Miller (1939)
    1:153-54, 157
Universal Declaration on the Human
    Genome and Human Rights
    1:159; **17**:159
Universal Declaration of Human Rights
    (UDHR) **2**:27; **8**:144; **9**:215; **15**:11,
    13, 23, 31, 34, 53, 62-73, 166
    and asylum **15**:93
    and interference **15**:201
    and marriage **15**:129
    and women **15**:100, 120-25
universalism **1**:113; **17**:113
universe, the, expanding **1**:11; **17**:11
universities
    "managerial" **16**:171-72, 174
    money for science research at
        1:95-96; **17**:95-96
    see also education, higher
Untouchables (Dalits) **14**:50, 52-53
Urban Institute **16**:106
Uruguay
    privatization in **3**:44
    recessions **14**:111
USAID **14**:26-27, 32, 74
    Food-for-Work programs **14**:189,
        193, 198, 199
USA PATRIOT Act (2001) **7**:191; **9**:63,
    66, 67, 179, 215; **15**:35
Usual Suspects, The (film) **1**:149;
    17:149

V

vacations **3**:26
vaccinations
    enforced **10**:87, 112-23
    polio vaccines and AIDS **5**:100-111
vandalism **9**:78
V-chips **6**:9, 22-23, 48-59
vegetarian diets, healthier? **10**:124-25,
    126-37
Venezuela, recessions **14**:111

Vernonia School District v. Acton
    (1995) **7**:179, 180-88
Versailles, Treaty of **2**:101; **13**:99
vests, bulletproof **1**:56-57; **17**:56-57
Veterans Administration **10**:10
Viacom **18**:102
Vidal, Gore **1**:147; **17**:147
Vienna Conference (1993) **15**:115, 117,
    118
    Vienna Declaration **15**:64-67, 66, 82
Vietcong **13**:177, 189
Vietminh **13**:176
Vietnamese children, adoption of **11**:82
Vietnam War **2**:110-11, 116-17, 175,
    196; **13**:188-89
    and censorship **6**:10-11
    My Lai killings **9**:9, 49, 50-58;
        13:179, 189
    postwar medical symptoms **10**:193
    was avoidable? **13**:176-87
violence
    against the fetus **15**:140, 141
    and the arts **12**:190, 204, 207, 211,
        213
    rap lyrics **12**:131
    media **6**:8, 19, 39-40, 44-45, 46, 47,
        60-71
    see also V-chips
    to attain human rights **15**:100-111
    violent protest **1**:99, 126-37; **7**:140-51
Virginia Plan **7**:11, 19
viruses, from outer space? **1**:60-71;
    17:60-71
visual aids, in presentations **12**:108-9
vitalism **10**:97, 98
Vollmer, August **9**:88
Volstead Act (1919) **13**:74
    and crime **13**:78-79
Voltaire **15**:10
voting
    prisoners and **9**:174
    "voice votes" **18**:118
    see also elections, U.S.; suffrage
Voting Rights Act (1965) **11**:25
voucher programs, school **16**:48-59,
    77, 115, 117, 157
VSA Arts **12**:158

W

wage(s)
    better education and **14**:109
    equal pay (men/women) would
        reduce poverty? **11**:163,
        188-99
    minimum **3**:63, 90-101, 106; **7**:82;
        11:53
        multinational corporations and
            18:128-39
    U.S. **3**:90-99, 106; **18**:135
Wagner, Richard **12**:177
Wagner Act (1935) **13**:105; **18**:49
Walesa, Lech **18**:55, 56
Wal-Mart Stores **18**:100, 107,
    168-69
Walsh-Healy Act (1936) **9**:194
Wanglie, Helga **10**:108
war
    cause of recessions? **18**:23, 33
    censorship **6**:10-11, 12-15, 20, 21
    do wartime laws violate civil
        liberties? **9**:60, 62-73